ANTISLAVERY AND ABOLITION IN PHILADELPHIA

ANTISLAVERY, ABOLITION, AND THE ATLANTIC WORLD

R. J. M. BLACKETT AND JAMES BREWER STEWART,

SERIES EDITORS

ANTISLAVERY AND ABOLITION IN PHILADELPHIA

EMANCIPATION AND THE LONG STRUGGLE FOR RACIAL JUSTICE IN THE CITY OF BROTHERLY LOVE

EDITED BY **RICHARD NEWMAN**
AND **JAMES MUELLER**

LOUISIANA STATE UNIVERSITY PRESS)|(BATON ROUGE

Published by Louisiana State University Press
Copyright © 2011 by Louisiana State University Press
All rights reserved
Manufactured in the United States of America
FIRST PRINTING

DESIGNER: Amanda McDonald Scallan
TYPEFACE: Whitman
PRINTER AND BINDER: McNaughton & Gunn, Inc.

Library of Congress Cataloging-in-Publication Data
Antislavery and abolition in Philadelphia : emancipation and the long struggle for racial justice in the City
of Brotherly love / edited by Richard Newman and James Mueller.
    p. cm. — (Antislavery, abolition, and the Atlantic world)
Includes index.
ISBN 978-0-8071-3991-2 (cloth : alk. paper) — ISBN 978-0-8071-3992-9 (pdf) — ISBN 978-0-8071-3993-6
(epub) — ISBN 978-0-8071-3994-3 (mobi) 1. Antislavery movements—Pennsylvania—Philadelphia—His-
tory. 2. Abolitionists—Pennsylvania—Philadelphia—History. 3. Free African Americans—Pennsylvania—
History. 4. Philadelphia (Pa.)—History—18th century. 5. Philadelphia (Pa.)—History—19th century. I.
Newman, Richard S. II. Mueller, James, 1941–
  F158.44.A67 2011
  326'.80974811—dc23

                                                                2011020450

CONTENTS

PREFACE

A Brief Note on the Preparation of the Volume

Though the essays collected here illuminate Philadelphia's complex abolition-ist past, they grew initially out of contemporary debates over the historical memory of slavery, race, and abolition at Independence Mall in Philadelphia. One of the jewels of the National Park Service (NPS) system, visited annually by millions of people from around the world, Independence Mall is home to the Liberty Bell, the Pennsylvania State House (which welcomed both the Continental Congress that drafted the Declaration of Independence and the Constitutional Convention of 1787), and the President's House (also known as the "First White House," which served as the home of Presidents Washington and Adams during Philadelphia's tenure as the nation's capital city between 1790 and 1800). A world heritage site, Independence Mall remains for many in and beyond the United States the very symbol of American liberty.

However, the discovery in recent years of African American sacred spaces within the confines of Independence Mall has prompted serious questions about the historical relationship between slavery and freedom in early Philadelphia, as documented in *Slavery and Public History: The Tough Stuff of American Memory*, edited by James Horton and Lois Horton (New York, 2006). Debate has centered on two specific sites, both of which came to light through the diligent work of NPS scholars, independent historians, academic researchers, and citizen-activists. First, renovations for a planned bus terminal at the National Constitution Center (near Fifth and Arch Streets) revealed that the area had been home to a former slave and founding member of several free black institutions named James "Orinoco" Dexter. Second, independent historian Ed Lawler discovered that George Washington once converted parts of the President's House (at Sixth and Market Streets) into slave quarters. Further research showed that the nation's inaugural president shuttled a group of nine slaves back and forth between Mount Vernon and Philadelphia to avoid complying with Pennsylvania's gradual abolition act (which provided out-of-state masters a six-month grace period). In both cases, members of the local black community were the first to demand a fuller recognition of free black leaders as well as enslaved people in the commemorative landscape of Independence Mall. NPS officials eventually joined with local historical institutions and city leaders to plan events which marked the importance of the Dexter and President House sites. While the National Constitution Center has placed a rather disappointing commemorative plaque near the Dexter site, the city of Philadelphia has planned a memorial to the enslaved people who lived with Washington at the President's House. A great collection of documents and newspapers articles on these and other issues in Philadelphia can be found at www.ushistory.org/presidentshouse/index.htm.

Against this backdrop, Jim Mueller and the NPS solicited essays from several scholars on Philadelphia antislavery movements. Many of these papers were delivered first at the 2005 Society for Historians of the Early American Republic meeting in Philadelphia. Other chapters were added in the intervening years, as the book went through various revisions, and a co-editor (Richard Newman) taken on. By publishing them together now as Antislavery and Abolition in Philadelphia, we hope that the present volume will inform and inspire some of those visitors who stop by one of the bookstores in Independence Mall to learn more about slavery and freedom in both Philadelphia and American culture.

The co-editors would like to thank several individuals who rendered invaluable aid to this project, beginning with the volume's distinguished authors (many of whom stayed on board throughout). National Park Service officials at Independence Mall—particularly Doris Fanelli and Jed Levin—offered initial and continuing support, for which we remain grateful. Phil Lapsanksy and John Van Horne of The Library Company helped smooth out rough edges of the project at key stages of its development. Robert Ulin, dean in the College of Liberal Arts at Rochester Institute of Technology, generously helped defray the cost of the volume's preparation, without which support the project might have foundered. Stan Ivester and Christine Van Horne provided expert copyediting and indexing work, respectively, in the final stages of the project, for which we remain much in their debt. And James Brewer Stewart and Richard Blackett offered sustained and richly textured commentary on every essay—a rarity on edited volumes but nothing out of the ordinary for these distinguished scholars. This volume would not have been possible without their scholarly insights and collegial support. Finally, our editor, Rand Dotson at LSU Press, has been nothing less than a saint, skillfully shepherding the manuscript through all stages of revision.

We would also like to thank Harvard University Press and Cambridge University Press for permission to partially republish versions of chapters 4 and 8, respectively.

—RN and JM

ANTISLAVERY AND ABOLITION IN PHILADELPHIA

Introduction

RICHARD NEWMAN AND JAMES MUELLER

From the colonial era through the Civil War, Philadelphia served as one of the American antislavery movement's main theaters of operation. It was, in the parlance of the day, abolition's keystone city. Even the briefest overview of abolitionist highlights shows that the City of Brotherly Love played a key role in the evolution of abolitionism and free African American life. When, for instance, the global slave trade ballooned at the end of the seventeenth century, filling colonial American ports with increasing numbers of enslaved people, Philadelphia Quakers issued the Germantown Protest of 1688. In the middle of the eighteenth century, as domestic slavery grew, Philadelphia became the North American center of abolitionist writing as generations of activists issued books and pamphlets decrying bondage as a sinful institution. In the midst of the American Revolution, Pennsylvania passed the western world's first gradual emancipation law from the then-state-capital of Philadelphia, which had recently doubled as the headquarters of the Continental Congress. A few years after that, the Pennsylvania Abolition Society (or PAS, the world's first antislavery organization) petitioned the Constitutional Convention for an end to the overseas slave trade. In the early 1830s, Philadelphia hosted the inaugural national conventions of both free black activists and the American Antislavery Society. And in the 1850s, the City of Brotherly Love was perhaps the most prominent urban crossroads of the Underground Railroad, as black and white activists helped shepherd hundreds of fugitive slaves to freedom. As one scholar has recently argued, Philadelphia's grand mix of Quakers, black reformers, and radical abolitionists made it "the country's first laboratory of abolition."[1]

Antislavery and Abolition in Philadelphia re-examines the long struggle for racial justice in Philadelphia during the eighteenth and nineteenth centuries. Comprising scholarly essays by a distinguished group of historians, the book ranges over cultural, economic, social, religious, and political landscapes. The volume's editors believe that this broad survey of themes will interest and inform citizens as well as specialists who want to learn more about one of abolitionism's central cities. Indeed, while *Antislavery and Abolition in Philadelphia* is not intended as a seamless narrative of the city's various abolitionist movements and personalities—chapters play off of one another but also reflect each author's conception of what themes, groups, and individuals stand out in Philadelphia's antislavery tradition—a central idea informs the book: that Philadelphia abolitionists (black, white, religious, secular, male, female) grappled with the broader meaning of black freedom earlier and more consistently than perhaps anyone else in American culture.

(1)

Why reconsider Philadelphia antislavery movements now? Although the broader topic of abolitionism has a rich historiographic tradition, this is a felicitous moment to return to Philadelphia's antislavery roots and development. Indeed, a number of recent anniversaries testify to the city's impressive, if complex, abolitionist past. The year 2010 marked the 250th anniversary of the birth of celebrated Philadelphia abolitionist Bishop Richard Allen. Born a slave, Allen bought his own freedom and then helped organize some of the leading institutions in African American culture, including the Free African Society in 1787 and Bethel African Methodist Episcopal Church a few years later. He was also one of the nation's earliest civil rights reformers, challenging white leaders to ban bondage and institute racial equality as a way of extending the empire of liberty beyond the color line. Beyond Allen, two recent bicentennials have celebrated other milestones in Philadelphia's (and Pennsylvania's) struggle for racial justice: 2008 marked the 200th anniversary of both slave trade abolition in the United States (which Philadelphia reformers helped secure through decades of protest) and statutory freedom for Pennsylvania slaves (who, according to the state's gradual abolition act of March 1780, would be liberated at the age of twenty-eight, or 1808). Public and scholarly commemoration of these events (in conferences, museum exhibits, and symposia) reminded people both in and beyond Philadelphia that the black freedom struggle transcended rural (read: plantation) landscapes; indeed, northern urban locales remain vital to our understanding of abolitionism, free black life, and the meaning of freedom in the pre–Civil War world.[2]

In fact, as the essays in this volume show, despite Pennsylvania's status as a relative outpost of Atlantic slave society, it would be the first colony in the British empire to spawn radical antislavery messengers and the first polity on the North American mainland to undergo a reconstruction of race relations via an abolition act.[3] This last point is particularly important, for with free people of color accounting for roughly 8 percent of its population by the close of the eighteenth century, the Quaker State would be among the first in Atlantic society to grapple with the twin issues of emancipation and integration—the fate of African Americans in civil society. In a very real sense, what the twentieth-century Swedish commentator Gunnar Myrdal labeled the "American Dilemma"—rigid racial inequality in the land of the free—had its roots in the Pennsylvania experience.[4]

For some Philadelphia abolitionists, early versions of the American Dilemma were visible at Pennsylvania's very creation. Well before Americans established "liberty and justice for all" as their national standard, Pennsylvania founder William Penn dedicated his colonial experiment to New World liberalism: the proposition that all ethnic groups, racial minorities, and religious sects could live in harmony under one government. Yet Penn himself sanctioned the slave trade as a way to build his fledgling colony. Moreover, Philadelphia soon became British North America's leading port, its merchants worrying little about their connections to the slave trade, slave-derived goods, or slave-derived profits.[5] Nevertheless, one of those early groups seeking religious asylum—the Society of Friends—made Philadelphia a worldwide center of antislavery thought and action. "There is a saying," the Germantown Protest declared, "that we shall do to all men like us as we will be done to ourselves, making no difference of what generation, descent or color they are." By the American Revolutionary era, the Society of Friends became the only religious group in American culture to ban both slave trading and slaveholding itself.[6]

Of course, African-Americans were in many ways the Atlantic world's first abolitionists. During the eighteenth century alone, there were nearly five hundred documented slave ship rebellions on British schooners, or nearly one per month. In Pennsylvania, that tradition of slave restiveness continued, as runaway slave ads in Benjamin Franklin's *Pennsylvania Gazette* illustrated. Between the 1730s and 1790s, masters from Pennsylvania, Virginia, Maryland, Delaware, New York, and New Jersey placed nearly a thousand fugitive slave notices in Poor Richard's famous paper, testifying to blacks' desire to flee bondage. And when Pennsylvania established its emancipation decree in 1780, both enslaved people and kidnapped free blacks made the Quaker

State an abolitionist Mason-Dixon line—an intra-America boundary between slavery and freedom. In no small way, Pennsylvania became the equivalent of abolitionist borderlands throughout the Atlantic world, including Spanish Florida during the colonial era and British Canada before the Civil War. Even if it did not guarantee liberty, making it to the Quaker State increased a black person's chances of gaining freedom.[7]

During the early national and antebellum periods, as a range of essayists in this volume show, free black activists made Philadelphia a center of African American reform. In the hands of Richard Allen, James Forten, Absalom Jones, Robert Purvis, Jarena Less, Sarah Mapps Douglass, and countless others, the racial hopes and failures of the American nation came into a more critical focus than ever. "This land which we have watered with our tears and our blood," Richard Allen vigorously asserted in *Freedom's Journal*, "is now our mother country." For Allen and other early black leaders, the fate of American liberty itself depended on the United States' ability to transcend racial oppression.[8] During the Civil War era, black Pennsylvanians offered the most eloquent testimony to this prophecy by providing more African American troops to the Union cause than any other state. Camp William Penn, a main training ground for black troops, was situated just beyond Philadelphia proper.[9]

Of course, Philadelphia's abolitionist story is filled with disturbing incidents and dashed hopes. Despite its virtuous service on behalf of black freedom, the PAS remained segregated for several decades. Moreover, many Philadelphia churches opposed radical antislavery measures in the years leading to the Civil War while the state of Pennsylvania actually rescinded black voting rights altogether in a new constitution of 1838. Race riots flared during the 1830s and 1840s, as many white citizens opposed a newly militant antislavery movement locally as well as nationally. Pennsylvania Hall, a magnificent Philadelphia building dedicated to abolitionist speakers, lasted only a few days before arsonists torched it in May of 1838; female abolitionists meeting inside the hall (located near Fifth and Arch, across the street from the present-day National Constitution Center) were lucky to get out alive. And during the Civil War, as African Americans answered the call for military service, streetcars remained segregated in the City of Brotherly Love. Even after the war ended, advocates of equal suffrage were harassed and physically assaulted. (Black voting rights returned to Pennsylvania only with the passage of the Fifteenth Amendment.) So strong were these undercurrents of racism that twentieth-century African American civil rights reformers derisively labeled Philadelphia "Up South."[10]

This often disheartening history notwithstanding, Philadelphia remained a guidepost in the struggle for black freedom. Already in 1807, English reformer Thomas Clarkson saluted Philadelphia Quakers as transatlantic heroes whose struggles to end both slavery and the slave trade shaped all subsequent abolitionist movements.[11] In 1855, James McCune Smith, one of the leading black intellectuals and physicians of the pre–Civil War era, encouraged all people of color to visit Richard Allen's Mother Bethel Church as a shrine of the ongoing black freedom struggle.[12] Perhaps the words of Rev. Martin Luther King Jr., who attended Crozier Theological Seminary in nearby Chester, Pennsylvania, best frame our understanding of Philadelphia racial reformers—the generations of men and women who fought for freedom even when its prospects appeared bleak. Fearing that he would never live to see true equality, King took to quoting the biblical passage in which Kind David despaired of seeing the Promised Land. "You did well that it was in your heart," King paraphrased, to mean that the dream of freedom existed within our hearts.[13] When so few American reformers envisioned racial justice as the heart of American liberty, a host of Philadelphians most certainly did.

(2)

Re-examining Philadelphia's abolitionist past resonates for still another reason: it illuminates the significance of urban locales in the history of both slavery and freedom. In the current scholarly moment, cities figure more prominently in the study of emancipation than perhaps ever before. From Lima, the capital city of Peru whose black population helped lay the foundation for a national abolition edict in 1854, to New Orleans, a multiracial city that served as a crossroads of black activists throughout the Atlantic basin, to London, whose vibrant abolitionist community helped stir antislavery imaginations in both the United States and Europe, urban locales became focal points of debates over black freedom throughout the eighteenth and nineteenth centuries.[14] As Doug Egerton powerfully asserts, for instance, though urban environments and economies could certainly stifle black aspiration, cities often facilitated African-descended people's ability to amass capital, organize, and thereby create "psychological independence" from bondage.[15] Cities also offered both free blacks and enslaved people access to a range of cultural resources that abetted the struggle for justice: abolitionist communities and organizations (which, if nothing else, often provided legal aid to endangered free people of color and fugitive slaves alike), a vibrant press (and therefore access to transatlantic information about abolitionism), and philanthropic networks that underwrote a range of racial reform activity (from abolitionist political protest to emigration and colonization schemes). Far from an outpost, cities played a key role in emancipating movements throughout the Atlantic basin.

Within the United States, Philadelphia was just one of several cities along the Atlantic seaboard whose racial landscape was altered by abolitionist movements, free black activism, and fugitive slaves. For instance, both New York and Baltimore (roughly ninety miles north and south of Philadelphia, respectively) contained potent mixtures of racial reformers whose constant activism undermined bondage during the early republic. At the close of the eighteenth century, New York City contained the largest concentrations of slaves in the North, with out of every five persons stuck in bondage (over twenty thousand slaves existed statewide). Yet between the 1790s and 1830s, abolitionist networks, free black communities, and enslaved people themselves helped make slavery anathema to New York's political culture and economy. Several anti-slavery laws were passed at the state level: the first, a gradual abolition law of 1799, functioned very much like Pennsylvania's; the last, taking effect on July 4, 1827, banned bondage forever from the Empire State. While a protracted and even problematic process (perhaps a third of New York City's enslaved population was sold south on the domestic slave trade before abolitionist laws could apply), abolitionism made New York City a free black mecca that spawned the nation's first newspaper owned and edited by African Americans (*Freedom's Journal*), an African Free School (which trained antebellum leaders ranging from Henry Highland Garnet to Alexander Crummell), and "vigilance" societies dedicated to aiding fugitive slaves.[16]

Although part of a "slave society" in the Chesapeake, with larger numbers of bondmen and bondwomen in Maryland than anywhere in the North, Baltimore underwent a rather impressive racial transformation too. Gradual abolition societies appeared during the 1780s and 1790s, bolstered by the expansion of evangelical preachers (particularly Methodists, who held their founding conference in Baltimore in 1784) roaming the Atlantic seaboard with messages of interracial brotherhood and universal freedom. Baltimore was also a print capital within the South, and for generations of people of color it became one of the only places below the Mason-Dixon Line to allow abolitionist publications to proliferate. Benjamin Banneker published his abolitionist challenge to Thomas Jefferson from Baltimore in 1792, while Daniel Coker printed his antislavery discourse, "A Dialogue Between a Virginian and an African Minister," here in 1810. Moreover, slaves themselves used Baltimore's rather expansive economic environment to enhance their prospects of attaining liberty. Hiring out practices, which initially gave new life to urban slavery (as masters with excess slave laborers could send them to Baltimore for a season and still retain their wages), inspired many African Americans to negotiate for freedom agreements with masters in and around Baltimore. Fugitive slaves seeking asylum in nearby Pennsylvania further undermined slavery's operation, as many masters found it easier to create indenture agreements with bondmen and bondwomen rather than continually chase them down. In exchange for not running away, these deals stipulated, enslaved people would work for a term of years before being liberated. All of these trends translated into the creation of a different Baltimore: by the 1830s, there were twice as many free blacks as slaves. Little wonder that Baltimore became a black capital of the upper South.[17]

Of course, recent scholarship on both New York City and Baltimore recognizes the continuing struggle people of color faced in the urban core. As a key staging ground for colonizationist movements, for example, Baltimore's racial landscape was both dynamic and tricky to maneuver. While many of the American Colonization Society's white supporters favored removing free people of color altogether from the United States, others saw colonization as a moderate brand of antislavery activism. Moreover, if the majority of free blacks along the Atlantic seaboard opposed the group, many Upper South slaves believed that colonization offered their best chance of gaining freedom.[18] In New York City, free blacks found not only freedom but consistent employment discrimination. In short, cities were far from a racial heaven for antebellum blacks. Yet in Baltimore and New York, as in Philadelphia, free black communities grew and even thrived in the decades leading to the Civil War. Abolitionist networks continued to operate in these cities, offering legal support to kidnapped free blacks and fugitive slaves. It is no mistake, for instance, that Frederick Douglass, one of the most famous abolitionists of the nineteenth century, was first stirred to freedom as a hired out slave in Baltimore, before escaping to New York City (where African American reformer David Ruggles spirited him to asylum). For the rest of his life, Douglass plied his abolitionist trade in a variety of urban locales, from New Bedford and Boston, Massachusetts (where he joined the organized antislavery movement), to London (where he fled when his first autobiography made life in the United States dangers). By the time he settled in the fast-growing city of Rochester, New York, in 1847, Douglass knew that urban society was in many ways the bedrock of modern abolition-ism. The only other place he chose to live after that was Washington, D.C.[19]

With these connections between urban landscapes and black freedom movements in mind, it is clear that Philadelphia can and must assume a more central place in transatlantic scholarship on slavery and freedom. Like other urban locales in and beyond the United States, it became a crossroads of abo-litionist activity, African American activism, and both philosophical and politi-cal meditations on the meaning of black freedom. Its own attenuated gradual emancipation process notwithstanding, Philadelphia was a key part of a black urban archipelago that stretched far north and far south. For instance, just as fugitive slaves from myriad southern locales sought freedom in the City of Brotherly Love, so too did representatives of Haiti (founded in 1804 as the first black republic in the Western Hemisphere) envision Afro-Philadelphians as a key transatlantic constituency—a potential source of free black immigrants, black economic power, and black philanthropic outreach.

Similarly, Philadelphia offered former slaves and free blacks newfound economic and cultural opportunity. Undeterred by the first Fugitive Slave Law of 1793 (a congressional act authorizing slave rendition), or discussions in Pennsylvania over limiting black migration (state legislators debated the matter several times in the early 1800s)), or even passage of a much tougher Fugitive Slave Law in 1850 (which compelled captured blacks to prove their freedom and coerced non-slaveholding whites into aiding slave catchers), Afri-can Americans continued to stream into antebellum Philadelphia. Already by the early nineteenth century, over a third of Afro-Philadelphians hailed from southern locales. In the city, black émigrés discovered that abolitionists had listings in city directories while free blacks had formed a variety of religious and benevolent institutions. There was also a broader range of employment and housing options than in the countryside. And in Philadelphia, as many of the essays in this volume illustrate, migrating blacks also found each other—that is, communal power. By the Civil War era, Philadelphia boasted the larg-est single free black population in the United States—nearly twenty thousand persons, a rather staggering number at the time. Here blacks moved, met, and to a great extent lived on their own terms. "This was the first gather-ing in one American community of a large number of former slaves," Gary Nash has noted in *Forging Freedom*, his celebrated study of the city's free black community. "Perhaps more important than their numbers, however, was the latent power of a new group self-consciousness." For, as Nash commented, "once formed," the black community "could not be obliterated, whatever the magnitude of hostility toward its members."[20]

Of course, as the essays in *the book* also show, black Philadelphians were not the only ones who found inspiration (and frustration) in the city's dynamic racial past. Although they often disagreed with one-another, abolitionists, politicians, religious reformers, and black activists in the City of Brotherly Love all recognized that Philadelphia would play a significant role in regional, national, and even international discussions of emancipation. To understand the City of Brotherly Love as a key part of American abolitionist debates is only a reiteration of a process that began in the eighteenth century and continued through the Civil War era.

(3)

The essays comprising this book are grouped into three sections. The first, "Liberating Philadelphia," features a single, overarching essay by the distinguished scholar Ira Berlin on blacks' long march toward freedom in the City of Brotherly Love. Though in many ways a stand-alone essay, Berlin's chapter touches on themes other authors examine in more detail: the significance of early challenges to bondage in the Quaker city, the often charged political and social debates accompanying abolitionism, and, perhaps most importantly, African Americans' struggle to shape a free existence in an urban society profoundly ambivalent about both black liberation and the prospect of racial equality. Berlin's essay reminds us that, in the urban North no less than in southern slave locales, labor (the struggle to work and provide for self and family) often defined African-Americans' day-to-day lives. Yet even in the midst of incredible hardship, black freedom dreams took flight in Philadelphia. Indeed, by locating the city's racial past largely in African-Americans' struggle for justice—rather than emphasizing Quaker emancipation policies and/or the efforts of white abolitionists to secure black freedom—Berlin's chapter exemplifies main trends in the study of slavery and freedom. For African-Americans themselves (as wage earners, as family members, as culture producers and bearers of African traditions, and as abolitionists and self emancipated freedom seekers) now dominate studies of race and slavery in the early Atlantic world. Similarly, Berlin concludes, one must begin any study of slavery and freedom in Philadelphia by focusing on the lives of African-descended people.

The book's second section, "Establishing Black and White Abolitionist

Movements in Philadelphia," focuses on several groups of racial reformers who came to personify the antislavery struggle in and beyond Philadelphia during the eighteenth and early nineteenth centuries. From the Society of Friends to the Pennsylvania Abolition Society to free black activists, Philadelphia was home to successive waves of abolitionists prior to the 1830s. Yet the essays in this section do not emphasize triumphalism—Philadelphians' seemingly mythical ability to overcome the hurdles of an oppressive racial past. Rather, as these chapters show, emancipating Philadelphia was constantly remaking itself in light of new abolitionist developments, from colonial concerns about the sin of slaveholding to early national African Americans' claim to equal citizenship in the early 1800s. David Waldstreicher's chapter trenchantly re-examines the earliest Quaker antislavery activists and the colonial world that shaped their then-radical view that slavery was out of step with both revealed religion and modern philosophical trends. Recapturing the significance of the deep Quaker roots of American abolitionism, as he points out, remains a significant task, for Benjamin Franklin has eclipsed his forbears as an abolitionist icon in recent years. Yet Franklin's late in life abolitionist transformation, in Waldstreicher's view, was less testament to his moral vision and more a culmination of antislavery trends dating back to Philadelphia's rise as an Atlantic port and cultural entrepôt at the beginning of the eighteenth century. Indeed, the city's rising metropolitan status meant that Quaker reformers—many of whom were internationally-minded merchants too—could envision slavery in Philadelphia as merely a smaller version of a more disturbing plantation machine that engulfed black lives in the Caribbean. Thomas Tryon, Benjamin Lay, Ralph Sandiford—Waldstreicher hails these Quaker reformers as the visionaries who launched an antislavery movement with global ramifications.

Julie Winch and Richard Newman pick up Waldstreicher's story of a constantly evolving abolitionist struggle in Philadelphia by looking at the rise of free black reformers and the Pennsylvania Abolition Society, respectively. Winch's penetrating portrait of the city's black abolitionist community points out that generations of reformers agreed on a central premise: racial equality must follow emancipation. Whether this meant political freedom (voting rights) or personal liberty (the right to protection from discrimination) mattered less to African-American reformers than the plain fact that the emancipation struggle would remain incomplete until city, state, and even national authorities recognized people of color as equal citizens. Newman analyzes the Pennsylvania Abolition Society's struggle to build a national abolitionist movement that both met the demands of people of color and yet struggled with the very idea that Winch considers essential to black abolitionism: African-American equality in the New Republic. Although the PAS heroically stood up for black rights in courts of law in and beyond Philadelphia, the group never admitted black members and registered ambivalence about African-Americans' equal place within the United States. Some PAS members even sympathized with, or joined, colonization movements. Concerned black activists looked for new allies, helping to transform abolitionism itself into a movement for racial equality as well as abolitionism. Nevertheless, as Newman shows, American antislavery movements continued to struggle with the meaning of black involvement and leadership well beyond the 1830s.

Gary Nash, one of the nation's most respected scholars, offers a more focused picture of the debate over emancipation's meaning in early national Philadelphia. Concentrating on two prominent Philadelphians, free black leader James Forten and political abolitionist-cum-colonizationist Tench Coxe, Nash wonderfully illustrates the divergent definitions given to black freedom. For Forten, black freedom was born of a revolutionary struggle that encompassed African-Americans as well as whites—indeed, Forten himself had volunteered for revolutionary duty as a teenager after hearing the Declaration of Independence read in the back of the old State House. Like other black leaders, Forten saw equal citizenship as a right, not a gift. Tench Coxe, a one-time member of the Pennsylvania Abolition Society and famous political economist, came to see Forten's vision as not only problematic but dangerous, for black liberty (he eventually believed) would undermine the development of a white man's republic. As Nash argues in tones that agree substantially with Newman and Winch, already by the 1820s Philadelphia was a community divided by the meaning of its own abolitionist past. To the extent that the city (like the nation) would eventually overcame such divisions, we can point to the continued exertions of free black activists and radical white abolitionists, who refused to acknowledge Coxe's contention that the United States was a white republic.

Section Three of *the book,* "Expanding Abolitionism In and Beyond Philadelphia," examines Philadelphia abolitionism from several interesting and ramifying vantage points: global benevolent culture, religious reformers beyond the Society of Friends, and the antebellum stage. Though these essays stretch back to the early national period, they all emphasize intensifying abolitionist debates in the City of Brotherly Love during the 1830s, 1840s, and

1850s. Caleb McDaniel's informative essay looks at Philadelphia reformers' role in shaping an "antislavery cosmopolitanism" among transatlantic abolitionists. Noting that British and Garrisonian abolitionists are often credited with cultivating a philosophical liberalism that allowed antislavery activism to transcend national borders, McDaniel nicely shows that Philadelphia reformers first articulated versions of antislavery cosmopolitanism following the revolution. By imbuing their struggle with a robust sense of globalism, in fact, members of the Pennsylvania Abolition Society and the Philadelphia Antislavery Society connected seemingly disparate wings of the antislavery struggle: one founded on Enlightenment notions of human perfectibility and rationalism, the other born of revivalism's belief in the brotherhood of human beings before God. In this way, McDaniel shows that type of radical philosophical critique undergirding early Quaker abolitionism (and described in superb detail by David Waldstreicher) became ingrained in the organized antislavery movement of the nineteenth century.

Dee Andrews revealing essay shows that Quakers were far from alone in grappling with the meaning of slavery and abolitionism. Indeed, Philadelphia's religious community as a whole struggled with the abolitionist cause between the American Revolution and Civil War. From the Anglican Church, which baptized increasing numbers of people of color in the eighteenth century, to independent black Methodist and Episcopal denominations, which dominated African-American political and social landscapes during the nineteenth century, religious Philadelphia was awash in debates over how people of faith should respond to slavery and black freedom. Following the lead of other essayists, Andrews provides a picture that is at once local and national, showing the many ways that Philadelphia congregations debated abolitionism. So heated was the atmosphere by the 1840s, Andrew shows, that even some African-American churches examined whether or not to remain figureheads of the antislavery movement. With an increase in racial mobbing occurring in certain city neighborhoods, black religious activism could threaten both black congregations and black lives. Yet other religious reformers refused to be bullied by local or national anti-abolitionist sentiment, making antebellum Philadelphia one of the more dynamic urban centers considering the connection between faith and liberty.

Moving from religious stages to the theater itself, Heather Nathan's terrific chapter illuminates the cultural side of abolitionist debate. Far from a sanctuary that allowed antebellum Philadelphians to escape heady political matters, the stage became a conduit of racial hopes and fears. By dealing with material on slave rebellion, black leaders, and the horrors of bondage, among other things, playwrights, actors and audiences all attempted to confront the reality of black freedom taking shape in the world around them. To be sure, the stage itself was often segregated—we don't get to see African-American actors or playwrights much before the Civil War. Yet, in Nathans' artful rendering, the Philadelphia theatre serves as a key barometer of Philadelphians' complex racial mindset. For on the stage, no less than in society itself, slavery, race, and emancipation remained highly sensitive and even risky topics. That denizens of the Philadelphia stage returned again and again to these themes tells us that Philadelphians remained vitally concerned with the impact of abolitionism locally as well as nationally.

In the book's concluding essay, "Beautiful Providences," award-winning scholar Elizabeth Varon provides a compelling portrait of black Philadelphian William Still's involvement in the Underground Railroad and its meaning in the city's long and complex abolitionist past. Although the Underground Railroad story often serves as a glamorized emblem of northern white abolitionist commitment (a way for people to celebrate a glorious and uncomplicated abolitionist past), Varon's portrait emphasizes a different perspective: African American leadership of fugitive slave rescues in Philadelphia. Putting himself at considerable risk, William Still shepherded hundreds of slaves through the city during the 1850s. In Varon's eyes, Still's spirit encapsulated well over a century of abolitionist activism in the City of Brotherly Love. Indeed, his reform work made Philadelphia once again a national leader in the struggle for racial justice before the Civil War.

In this sense, Still is a most fitting figure with which to end *Antislavery and Abolition in Philadelphia*. For Varon's essay returns to an issue Ira Berlin raised at the outset: could a city founded on principles of brotherly love ever overcome its deep racial divisions? Even after the Civil War, even after national emancipation, even after he had been reunited with his own brother (who arrived at Still's doorstep one day in search of a family divided by the domestic slave trade), William Still would face a segregated world. Philadelphia streetcars separated black from white and black voting rights for the city's people of color would not return until 1870. Yet Still kept pushing for change. In no small way, the publication of his famous book, *The Underground Railroad*, in

1872 looked forward as well as backward, indicating that the spirit of racial animating antebellum Philadelphia remained crucial at the end of the nineteenth century.

Like Still's work, we hope that this book of essays will spur further reflection on the meaning of Philadelphia's abolitionist past. We also hope it will remind readers that American emancipation began not in 1865 with southern abolition but much earlier and in one of the North America's leading urban locales: the City of Brotherly Love.

NOTES

1. Fergus M. Bordewich, *Bound for Canaan: The Epic Story of the Underground Railroad, America's First Civil Rights Movement* (New York, 2005), 49.

2. "An Act for the Gradual Abolition of Slavery," passed in March 1780 in the state of Pennsylvania, rpt. with an expert introduction by Sam Rosenfeld of Columbia University, in James G. Basker, ed., *Early American Abolitionists: A Collection of Anti-Slavery Writings, 1760–1820* (New York, 2005), 89. The best book on Pennsylvania emancipation, with much information on Philadelphia abolitionists, remains Gary B. Nash and Jean R. Soderlund, *Freedom by Degrees: Emancipation and Its Aftermath in Pennsylvania* (New York, 1991).

3. On the motivations of early Pennsylvania abolitionists and their transatlantic meaning, see David Brion Davis's essays in Thomas Bender, ed., *The Antislavery Debate: Capitalism and Abolitionism as a Problem in Historical Interpretation* (Berkeley, 1992). For the widest possible context on American slavery and freedom, and Pennsylvania's place in Atlantic slave systems, see Ira Berlin, *Many Thousands Gone* (Cambridge, Mass., 1998).

4. Among the best studies on race and slavery in the early republic are Mia Bay's first chapter in *The White Image in the Black Mind: African-American Ideas About White People, 1830–1925* (New York, 2000); Bruce Dain, *A Hideous Monster of the Mind: American Race Theory in the Early Republic* (Cambridge, 2002); Douglas Egerton, *He Shall Go Out Free: The Lives of Denmark Vesey* (Madison, Wis., 2000); Graham Russell Hodges, *Slavery and Freedom in the Rural North: African Americans in Monmouth County, New Jersey, 1665–1865* (Madison, Wis., 1997); Mitch Kachun, *Festivals of Freedom: Memory and Meaning in African American Emancipation Celebrations, 1808–1915* (Amherst, Mass., 2003); Elizabeth McHenry, *Forgotten Readers: Recovering the Lost History of African American Literary Societies* (Durham, N.C., 2002); Joanne Pope Melish, *Disowning Slavery: Gradual Emancipation and "Race" in New England, 1780–1860* (Ithaca, N.Y., 1998). See also James Brewer Stewart's excellent essay, "The Emergence of Racial Modernity and the Rise of the White North 1790–1840," *Journal of the Early Republic* 18 (Summer 1998): 181–217, and Richard S. Newman, "Not the Only Story in 'Amistad': The Fictional Joadson and the Real James Forten," in *Pennsylvania History* 67, no. 2 (Spring 2000), 218–39.

5. Though in large part a biography of Ben Franklin, David Waldstreicher's *Runaway America:*

Benjamin Franklin, Slavery and the American Revolution (New York, 2004) also offers a wonderful examination of Quaker antislavery currents in early America.

6. On Quaker antislavery debates, see especially Jean R. Soderlund, *Quakers and Slavery: A Divided Spirit* (1985; rpt. Princeton, N.J., 1988).

7. On Pennsylvania's antislavery borderland, see Richard S. Newman, *The Transformation of American Abolitionism: Fighting Slavery in the Early Republic* (Chapel Hill, N.C., 2002), chap. 3. See also Gabor Boritt and Scott Hancock, eds., *Slavery, Resistance, Freedom* (Oxford, 2007).

8. I treat this theme more fully in *Freedom's Prophet: Bishop Richard Allen, the AME Church, and the Black Founding Fathers* (New York, 2008).

9. On black activism and community life in Philadelphia and beyond during the early republic, see: Gary B. Nash, *The Forgotten Fifth: African-Americans in the Age of Revolution* (Cambridge, 2006) and *Forging Freedom: The Formation of Philadelphia's Black Community, 1720–1840* (Cambridge, Mass., 1988); John Saillant, *Black Puritan, Black Republican: The Life and Thought of Lemuel Haynes, 1753–1833* (New York, 2002); Richard S. Newman, *Freedom's Prophet: Richard Allen, the AME Church, and the Black Founding Fathers* (New York, 2008); and Julie Winch, *A Gentleman of Color: The Life of James Forten* (New York, 2002).

10. See Matthew Countryman, *Up South: Civil Rights and Black Power in Philadelphia* (2006; rpt. Philadelphia, 2007).

11. See Thomas Clarkson, *The History of the Rise, Progress, and Accomplishment of the Abolition of the African Slave-Trade by the British Parliament* (London, 1807).

12. *Frederick Douglass' Paper*, May 11, 1855.

13. See Taylor Branch, *At Canaan's Edge* (New York, 2006), 706.

14. On emancipation and black freedom in various urban locales in the Atlantic world between 1780 and 1880, see: Tommy L. Bogger, *Free Blacks in Norfolk, Virginia, 1790–1860: The Darker Side of Freedom* (Charlottesville, Va., 1997); Gretchen Gerzina, *Black London: Life before Emancipation* (London, 1995); Kimberly S. Hanger, *Bounded Lives, Bounded Places: Free Black Society in Colonial New Orleans, 1769–1803* (Durham, N.C., 1997); Alison Dorsey, *To Build Our Lives Together: Community Formation in Black Atlanta, 1875–1906* (Athens, Ga., 2004); Christine Hunefeldt, *Paying the Price of Freedom: Family and Labor among Lima's Slaves, 1800–1854* (Berkeley, Calif., 1994); Wilbert Jenkins, *Seizing the New Day: African Americans in Post–Civil War Charleston* (Bloomington, Ind., 1998); Michael Fitzgerald, *Urban Emancipation: Popular Politics in Reconstruction Mobile, 1860–1890* (Baton Rouge, La., 2002).

15. See Douglas R. Egerton, "Slaves to the Marketplace: Economic Liberty and Black Rebelliousness in the Atlantic World," *Journal of the Early Republic* 26, no. 4 (Winter 2006): 617–39, quotation at 622.

16. On New York City, see, among others, Shane White, *Stories of Freedom in Black New York* (Cambridge, Mass., 2002), and *Somewhat More Independent: The End of Slavery In New York City, 1770–1810* (Athens, Ga., 1991); Leslie Harris, *In the Shadow of Slavery: African Americans in New York City, 1626–1863* (Chicago, 2003); Graham Hodges, *Root and Branch; African Americans in New York City and East Jersey, 1616–1863* (Chapel Hill, N.C., 2000); Craig Wilder, *In the Company of Black Men: The African Influence on African American Culture in New York City* (New York, 2001); and David N. Gellman, *Emancipating New York* (Baton Rouge, La., 2006).

17. On Baltimore, see especially Christopher Phillips, *Freedom's Port: The African American Community of Baltimore, 1790–1860* (Urbana, Ill., 1997), 2–3., and T. Stephen Whitman, *The Price of Freedom: Slavery and Freedom in Baltimore and Early National Maryland* (Lexington, Ky., 1997).

18. On colonization's broad meaning in the Upper South, see especially Mary Tyler-McGraw, *An African Republic: Black and White Virginians in the Making of Liberia* (Chapel Hill, N.C., 2007).

19. On Douglass's escape, see especially Graham Hodges, *David Ruggles: A Radical Black Abolitionist and the Underground Railroad in New York City* (Chapel Hill, N.C., 2010).

20. Nash, *Forging Freedom*, 136 (statistic on black southerners in Philadelphia circa 1800); quotations at 7, 65.

I.

LIBERATING PHILADELPHIA

The Evolution of an Emancipation Outpost

CHAPTER 1

Slavery, Freedom, and Philadelphia's Struggle for Brotherly Love, 1685 to 1861

IRA BERLIN

Few cities have played a larger role in American history prior to the Civil War than Philadelphia, and few people played a larger role in the history of antebellum Philadelphia than those of African descent. Although neither as visible as the Quakers nor as numerous as the Scotch-Irish, Germans, and later the Irish, African Americans shaped the growth, ethos, and reputation of Philadelphians among themselves and throughout the Atlantic world. As enslaved and then free people, black men and women helped construct the city, protect it against its enemies, enhance its wealth, and make it the world-wide capital of abolition. The city's early commitment to slave emancipation established its reputation as the standard bearer for freedom and an icon of universal brotherhood. Yet the realities of black impoverishment and racial exclusion contradicted the city's boast. As slave and free, black Philadelphians faced restrictions on where they could work, live, play, travel, educate their children, and even bury their dead. The periodic explosions of racial violence only highlighted the pervasive discrimination black people faced and revealed the distance between the city's cherished ideal and its disconcerting reality. Philadelphia's struggle to make its celebrated image as the City of Brotherly Love conform to the realities of daily life framed the first two hundred years of the city's history. It placed black Philadelphians at the center of war against slavery and the contest for equality in their city and their nation.[1]

Even before William Penn planted his city between the banks of the Delaware and Schuylkill rivers, people of African descent had inhabited the Delaware Valley. Arriving in the early seventeenth century with Dutch settlers, many of them were doubtless Atlantic creoles, men and women with broad experience in the Atlantic as sailors, translators, and petty traders. But these early black arrivals—familiar with the languages, religions, and trading etiquettes of their Europeans and Native Americans counterparts—were soon outnumbered when, in 1684, the *Isabella*, a slave ship out of Bristol, delivered some 150 Africans to the city. Quickly snapped up by the European settlers, African slaves equaled about one-seventh of Philadelphia's population. In all probability, these men and women, many of whom had been captured in the interior of Africa, spoke no English and had little familiarity with either Christianity or the peculiar brand of Protestant pietism that ruled Philadelphia.[2] Their arrival transformed both the city and the city's black population, establishing a pattern whereby black life would be constantly reconstructed. The changing character of slavery in Philadelphia shaped the struggle over freedom in the city and influenced it far beyond the city's boundaries.

Just as Africans had replaced Atlantic Creoles, African Americans soon replaced Africans. No major shipment of African slaves followed the *Isabella*'s arrival until well into the eighteenth century. Rather than coming by the boatload, slaves dribbled into Philadelphia in small numbers generally from the sugar islands of the West Indies. Some of these were simply the unsalable remainders—so-called "refuse slaves"—from slavers who had disembarked their human cargos but failed to rid themselves of the old or disabled. Others, however, had been born in the West Indies, spoke English, and enjoyed some familiarity with English ways.[3]

Whatever its various sources, Philadelphia's black population grew slowly following the *Isabella*'s arrival. In 1720, the city's slave population had barely climbed above two hundred, and the proportion of the population enslaved fell to 10 percent or less.[4] In the years that followed, the number of slaves increased, although their proportion of the population fluctuated as the city's prosperity waxed and waned. Philadelphia remained a society with slaves, sometimes edging upon, but never becoming, a slave society.

Most slaves lived and worked in close proximity to whites, for—although slaveholding was widespread among white Philadelphians and nearly universal among the propertied classes—most owned only one or two or at most a half-dozen of slaves. Slave women worked in the homes of their owners—cleaning, cooking, and caring for their owner's children. Slave men had a wider range of employment, laboring around the docks, loading and unloading the ships, stocking warehouses, and driving drays. But they also could be found in the city's boatyards, cooperages, mills, ropewalks, and other small manufactories.

Although some rose to the artisanal ranks, most slave men shouldered a shovel, pushed a broom, or wielded an ax. They hauled and lifted but rarely practiced a skilled trade.

Employment patterns of black slaves did not differ radically from those of other unfree or bound workers, particularly German and Scotch-Irish indentured servants. Although white employers preferred European servants to African slaves, they viewed these diverse workers as interchangeable elements in Philadelphia's labor force. As long as white European servants remained available, slave importation remained low. But when events conspired to limit the supply of servant labor, employers quickly turned to slave workers. In 1731, following the repeal of the colony's impost on slave imports, the slave population surged, increasing to over seven hundred. A similar African influx followed in 1756 when the outbreak of war blocked the north Atlantic sea lanes. Slaves entered the city in large numbers, often directly from Africa. The character of the black population changed along with its size. The many languages of Africa once again mingled with the dominant English and German as well as Dutch, French, and Welsh on the streets of Philadelphia.[5]

The periodic re-Africanization of Philadelphia's slave population also reflected the difficulties black people had reproducing themselves. Abusive treatment, poor nourishment, cramped quarters, and the city's cold, damp climate left newly arrived black men and women susceptible to diseases to which they had little immunity. Soaring rates of slave morality were compounded by low fertility. The small units in which slaves resided, along with a sexual balance weighed heavily toward men, hindered the formation of black families. Few enslaved men and women lived to see their children grow to adulthood; hardly any achieved the status of grandparents.[6] Black people had difficulty creating a society of their own.

During the middle of the eighteenth century, a small African American population slowly emerged and joined together to create a distinct community. These native-born peoples, like the earlier Atlantic creoles, spoke English and other languages of the larger Atlantic, but their point of reference was the North American mainland rather than the larger Atlantic. With increasing confidence, they navigated Philadelphia's streets and back alleys and traded on their owners'—and their own—behalf. Some converted to Christianity, and several hundred received baptism in the city's Anglican churches by 1760. A few attended the school attached to those churches, learning to read and write, while others studied at the Quaker school for "negroes and mulattos." Many more found Christ and a bit of book learning in the evangelical awakening that convulsed the city in the middle of the eighteenth century, bringing black men and women into the growing Methodist societies. Their increasing confidence and connectedness provided the impetus to challenge slavery.[7]

Knowledge of the city, its diverse peoples, and its complex economy also gave African American slaves an appreciation of the changes that were transforming Philadelphia, which at mid-century ranked as the second largest city in the British empire. From their perspective, none was more important than the growing opposition to slavery within the city's influential Society of Friends. Although first confined to a small group of radicals, antislavery sentiment slowly grew within the larger Quaker community. Despite opposition from slaveholders within their ranks, Philadelphia's Friends began to disengage from the institution of chattel bondage. In 1758, Philadelphia's Yearly Meeting moved against slavery, and some Quakers freed their slaves. Free people of color, previously an infinitesimal part of Philadelphia's black population, grew in numbers and visibility. Their very existence challenged slavery.[8]

The city's free black population continued to increase in the 1760s—even as the slave population grew—while colonial leaders articulated their growing conflict with Britain in the language of slavery and freedom. Denunciations of British trespasses on American liberty and the enslavement of Americans to their British overlords spoke precisely to the condition of enslaved Africans and African Americans. Black people and their white abolitionist allies seized the rhetoric of slavery and freedom and turned it to their advantage.[9]

The language of equality found support from the evangelicals, whose numbers grew in the mid-century revivals. Believing that all were equal in the sight of God, they had welcomed slaves into the fold, often giving them a place of prominence in their churches. Evangelicals found the presence of black slaves—the lowest of the low—proof that they were God's chosen people. Philadelphia Methodists would number large among freedom's friends, and many black people switched their religious affiliation from the Anglican to the Methodists societies.[10]

Opportunities for freedom expanded further when America's simmering conflict with Britain exploded into open warfare, and the rebel Americans, calling themselves Patriots, justified their revolution with assertions of universal equality. The war also divided slaveholders into Loyalist and Patriot factions, permitting black people to escape bondage in large numbers by exchanging military service for freedom on one side or the other. Most slave men and women chose the British side, in large measure because British commanders offered freedom first and most persistently. When the British occupied Philadelphia, many slaves quickly joined His Majesty's "Pioneers." Other slaves, however, fought for the Patriots or were freed by Patriot masters and mistresses who embraced the notion of equality embedded in their Declaration of Independence adopted in their home city. James Forten, the future leader of Philadelphia's black community, served aboard Patriot Stephen Decatur's *Royal Louis* and when captured maintained his loyalty to the new American republic, declaring "never, NEVER, shall I prove a traitor to her interests." Still most slaves cared about neither the Loyalist nor the Patriot cause, but opportunistically took their freedom amid the tumult of war.[11]

Wartime flight struck slavery a mighty blow. During the war, fugitive slaves in Philadelphia doubled in number, even as slavery declined. As soldiers, sailors, military laborers, and camp followers, hundreds of enslaved black men and women eluded their owners and passed into free society. Even those who avoided military service found the army's presence a useful subterfuge in securing their escape. Caesar, a fugitive from nearby Chester, fled by claiming "he came last from the southern army, and that he is a freeman." When the British army left Philadelphia in 1778, residents complained a "great part of the slaves hereabouts were enticed away." Between 1775 and 1780, Philadelphia's slave population fell by a quarter.

Success, moreover, bred success. Black people who gained their freedom pressed all the harder for universal emancipation, demanding first the release of their families and friends and then all black people still in bondage. Newly freed blacks—eager to secure an end to slavery—offered to pay a special tax to compensate slaveholders for their loss of property and thereby ensure that emancipation would not cost white taxpayers a cent. Formal petitions, augmented by informal but unmistakable words and deeds, revealed that black people expected liberty would soon be theirs.[12]

The wartime erosion of slavery encouraged direct assaults against the institution itself. In 1775, as the Patriots declared their independence, some of city's leading revolutionaries joined together with Quaker radicals like Anthony Benezet to found the Society for Relief of Free Negroes Unlawfully Held in Bondage, which morphed into the Pennsylvania Abolition Society (PAS). Although the new organization excluded black members and initially included slaveholders within its ranks, black men and women staked out a parallel position of leadership against slavery that they would not relinquish until its final abolition.[13] The PAS—amid the war—helped bring the full weight of Philadelphia's republican idealism to bear on slavery. In passing the abolition law in 1780, the revolutionary government of Pennsylvania called slavery "disgraceful to any people, and more especially to those who have been contending in the great cause of liberty themselves." Like all such half-measures, the act's ringing declaration of revolutionary principles was freighted with the dead weight of compromise that contradicted those very principles. Not only did the Pennsylvania law fail to free a single slave born before its passage, but it kept the children of slaves born thereafter locked in bondage most of their productive lives. Abolitionists failed to achieve full emancipation in Pennsylvania until 1847.[14]

While gradualism confounded the process of emancipation, the greatly expanded free black population pressed for the final demise of slavery. "It is the momentous question of our lives," declared black Philadelphians in 1781. "If we are silent this day, we may be silent for ever." Free blacks, many of them just a step removed from slavery, assisted slaves—often their families and friends—in buying their way to freedom with hard cash. But it was not merely the freed people's cash that proved most subversive to slavery, but their example that a black person could be free.[15]

White Philadelphians with slaveholders in the lead countered free black activism. They urged the repeal of the abolitionist legislation. When that failed, they used the gradualist provisions of the 1780 law to delay emancipation. For example, a Pennsylvania ironmaster registered the birth of a six-month-old black girl in 1811, assuring that she would serve him for the next twenty-eight years. Gradual emancipation thus slowed the progress of freedom and kept many free black men and women under the domination of white men and women, often their former owners, even after they had been legally freed. Other slaveholders sold their slaves out of the state rather than allow them—or at least their descendants—to escape bondage at some distant day.[16]

While abolitionists and slaveholders dueled, slaves took matters into their own hands. They offered to pay their owners for an early exit from slavery. If refused, they ran away in such numbers and with such persistence—fleeing repeatedly if recaptured—that slaveholders eventually agreed to end slavery. According to one estimate, between half and three-quarters of the young slave men in Philadelphia absconded from their owners during the 1780s. If retaken they fled again and then again until recalcitrant owners recognized the futility of retaining them in bondage.[17]

To these mainland migrants were added black refugees who had been caught in the insurgency that transformed Saint Domingue into the world's first black republic. The great exodus from Hispaniola, which began in 1791, continued for more than a decade, spurred by a brutal civil war that engulfed the island. In 1793, the first mass evacuation—a flotilla of nearly two hundred ships bearing approximately four thousand white refugees, nearly two thousand slaves, and several hundred free people of color—stopped at the nearby Caribbean and mainland ports of Havana, Kingston, Charleston, Norfolk, and New Orleans. But several hundred also landed in Philadelphia as well as other northern ports. The entrance of refugees into the mainland grew as the exiles were chased away from one refuge after another by slaveholders fearful of the contagion of revolution.

Frightened by the influx of black men and women, officials did their best to bar their entry, particularly those directly touched by the revolutionary events in Saint Domingue. Pennsylvania lawmakers, supported by the mayor of Philadelphia, urged a prohibition on the entry of black people and the creation of a registration system that would require free black people to carry freedom papers. But with no place else to go, desperate refugees stayed in place and added to the city's growing black population.[18]

Still, slavery lingered in Philadelphia, and, as it did, new forms of subordination emerged. Manumitters required their slaves to agree to long-term indentures as part of the price of freedom. Often newly emancipated black people left bondage and entered servitude in the same motion. Even without prompting from their former owners, poverty forced many freed people to indenture themselves or their children to white householders. The number of black people indentured in Philadelphia shot upward, growing from five in 1780 to forty in 1785 to over three hundred annually during the mid-1790s. Although servitude, unlike slavery, was not hereditary, servants lived under the control of a master or mistress, and the rights to their labor could be sold or traded like other property. The more closely that indentured servitude became identified with black labor, the smaller the difference between the treatment of slave and servant. Moreover, by controlling slave children, slaveholders maintained a hold on their parents, even those who were free. Black people ensnared in such arrangements often found themselves living in circumstances that looked suspiciously like the old bondage.[19]

Freedom arrived slowly and imperfectly in Philadelphia; still it arrived more rapidly than it did in the surrounding countryside. With the countryside identified with the remnants of slavery, rural black men and women—fugitive and free—gravitated toward Philadelphia, propelling the city's black population upward. Refugees from the states to the south added to the influx, as one southern state after another barred the entry of free blacks and made manumission contingent upon removal. Would-be southern manumitters, prohibited from freeing slaves within their own jurisdictions, sent their former slaves northward with Philadelphia often serving as their first stop.[20]

Located on the crossroads between freedom and slavery, Philadelphia's black population grew faster than that of Pennsylvania as a whole. At century's end, almost two-fifths of the state's black population came to reside in Philadelphia. The city's black population also grew faster than its white. In 1780, less than one in twenty-five of Philadelphia's residents was black; by 1820 that proportion had grown to almost one in nine. In 1810, as Philadelphia became a freer city, it also became a blacker city.[21] As the center for black freedom in the emerging free states, Philadelphia also became the hub of antislavery.

Philadelphia's newly freed slaves defined the meaning of freedom and pressed to expand its reach. Emancipation was a signal event in Philadelphia's history, as important to black Philadelphians as the Emancipation Proclamation or the Thirteen Amendment would be to black southerners nearly a century later. The refugees from slavery who crowded into Philadelphia joined the resident population in celebrating their liberation. The men and women who had awaited that moment for more than a hundred years did not tarry in shaking off the heavy weight of domination.

Among the numerous indicators of the great post-revolutionary climacteric were the new names black people adopted with the arrival of freedom. Cato, Venus, and Sambo largely disappeared from Philadelphia's streets and back alleys, remnants of a bygone age when masters ridiculed the slaves' lowly status by tagging them with great names. Instead, black men and women took common Anglo-American names and raised the diminutive to its full form. Everywhere, Billy and Sukey became William and Susan. Since most slaves had but a single name, freedom allowed them the opportunity to adopt a surname. A few like James Dexter adopted the name of their owner, but most took names of their trade (Barber, Carpenter, or Cooper), color (Black, Brown, or occasionally White), or new status (Armistad, Freeman, or Liberty). When the opportunity arose, William and Susan became Mr. and Mrs. William Freeman. Within a decade of freedom's official arrival most black Philadelphians had surnames.[22]

In the shadow of freedom's first arrival, the reformulation of black identity did not stop with a new name. No institution was more central to the lives of black people—yet no institution was made more vulnerable by slavery—than the family. As slaves, black men and women had been dispersed across the landscape at their masters' whim, as the slave family had no legal standing. Husbands and wives generally lived apart, and parents had been regularly separated from their children. Freedom allowed former slaves to reconstruct their domestic life on a new, more secure foundation. In quick order, black Philadelphians solemnized their marriages, giving informal unions the stamp of official state and church sanction. At the same time, they began to gather children, parents, and more distant kin. Although the process was painfully slow, it paid immediate dividends, for when black people came together under one roof, they ate better and lived longer. Infant mortality rates fell as parents devoted more time to their children, without the heavy hand of slaveholder interference. During the 1790s, there were over four hundred more births than deaths among black Philadelphians, and the city's African American population grew through natural means.

Establishing independent households apart from the white slaveowners who had dominated their lives nevertheless proved a difficult task. While many departed their masters' households, poverty forced most newly freed blacks to take residence with employers, who agreed to make space for children when they hired parents. In 1800, two decades after the Pennsylvania lawmakers enacted their gradualist plan, more than half of the black population still resided in white households. Even those black families who managed to extricate themselves from white households often had to double up, with two or more families living in a single household. Numerous black families took in boarders to make ends meet. Although black families were generally smaller than white ones—reflecting a later age of marriage, a lower birth rate, and the necessity of apprenticing children—black households contained many more "extra people" under the same roof than did white households.[23]

The difficulties in establishing independent households reflected an emancipation that promised no more than legal freedom. Pennsylvania's gradualist abolition made no provision to compensate former slaves for their long years in bondage. It offered them no training for a craft or guarantee of steady work or a living wage. Slaveholders, who had freed their slaves because they believed that slavery was inconsistent with the Declaration of Independence or that all men were equal in the sight of God, saw in those beliefs no requirement that they provide their former slaves with a trade or patronize their shops or stores. Once having freed their slaves, slaveowners expressed little or no concern for their fate, and the law did not require them to provide slaves with a trade or even the smallest token for their previous service. Many newly freed slaves had difficulty finding work. But black men and women did not merely fall in occupational standing. Slave craftsmen frequently had difficulty finding work at the trades they had practiced as slaves, as white employers refused to hire free blacks for any but the most menial job.[24]

In freedom, most black men and women remained confined to the un-skilled and service sectors of the economy, laboring as before as cooks, washer-women, seamstresses, coachmen, gardeners, and valets. White Philadelphians, who had a long acquaintance with black people in the role of servants, simply exchanged enslaved servants for free ones. Thus, as free blacks replaced slaves in the population, they also replaced them in the domestic labor force, assuring employers of a steady supply of household workers. The demand for domestics grew during the post-revolutionary years, as the merchants and professionals separated home and residence and as a new mercantile elite escalated the requirements of a comfortable domestic setting. The laundress who labored within those homes became a ubiquitous black figure in Philadelphia as else-where in the North, the very symbol of black womanhood. "The women," reported the Pennsylvania Abolition Society flatly in 1795, "both married and single, wash clothes for a living."[25]

The range of economic opportunities was only slightly greater for black men who, in addition to laboring as coachmen and valets, found work as day laborers. In 1800, at least 40 percent of Philadelphia's free black heads of households were "laborers," a broad category that included almost every black man without an identifiable skill. At best, such work was hard, dirty, irregular, and unremunerative. Often it could be demeaning, as with the black laborers who cleaned streets, swept chimneys, and disposed of night soil. If all workers had difficulty finding work in the years after the revolution, black workers had more trouble than most. Some fell out of the ranks of the employed and into dependency or charity.

Unable to find work in the city, free black men took to the sea in increasing numbers. Work on merchant ships, coasting vessels, whalers, and even some men-of-war provided a broad avenue of economic opportunity for newly freed men without capital or place in society. In the years following the revolution, one-fifth of Philadelphia's maritime work force was black, and one-quarter of its adult black men (and still a larger proportion of the able-bodied) were sailors. Opportunities for sailors grew in the 1790s as the Napoleonic wars increased European demand for American goods and with it employment for merchantmen of all sorts. The large number of men who took to the sea further shifted the sexual balance of the urban black population toward women, whose limited economic opportunities and poor pay—even when compared with black men—assured impoverishment. Poverty, in turned, constrained the ability of black Philadelphians to expand freedom's terrain.

Nonetheless, some ambitious black men and women found a niche in the middle ranks of American society, entering the mechanical trades and securing small proprietorships. A handful became merchants and manufacturers. James Forten, who eventually employed about thirty workmen—white and black—in his sail-making operation, stood at the front rank of these successful businessmen. The number of black artisans and tradespeople increased slowly but steadily during the post-revolutionary decades, as did the number of professionals, most of whom were ministers and teachers.[26]

As they carved a niche for themselves in Philadelphia's economy, African Americans remade their community, establishing the institutional structure of black life in freedom and reshaping the movement against slavery and for equality. Many of these African American institutions rested upon the informal, clandestine associations black Philadelphians had created in slavery. Others drew on the experiences slaves had gained while interacting with the white members of the Pennsylvania Abolition Society who had assisted their passage from slavery. But freedom also created new problems that required new solutions. Ranking high among these was the need to bury the dead and provide for the departed's kin. As slaves, black Philadelphians had labored to gain full control of their burial rites, but even their successes rested upon the sufferance of their owners and were subject to the oversight of municipal authorities. With freedom, the responsibility was fully theirs. During the post-revolutionary years, black Philadelphians moved quickly to meet this essential human need. In 1787, the Free African Society, a quasi-religious benevolent association, attempted to lease the Strangers Burial Ground, where Philadelphia black people had been buried since the early eighteenth century. When that failed, they purchased ground of their own.

The Free African Society soon turned to the problems of the living. The society instituted regular procedures respecting marriage and established a register to record them. As its role in burying the dead and marrying the living suggests, the society was fast transforming itself into a church. In 1790, its members organized a "Union" congregation with the aim of incorporating the entire black community within a single body. The process—sped by the growing antagonism to free blacks within the established churches and the desire of black people to worship by themselves—foundered upon social as well as denominational differences within the black community. By 1794, Philadelphia's Union Society had metamorphosed into the St. Thomas's African Episcopal Church under the leadership of Absalom Jones, while Richard Allen had established an independent Methodist congregation that would eventually become Mother Bethel of the African Methodist Episcopal Church and the seed of the AME denomination.[27]

In the years following the 1780 emancipation, African churches emerged as the central organization in what Absalom Jones called the struggle to "throw off that servile fear, that habit of oppression and bondage [had] train[ed] us up in." Drawn by the promise of otherworldly salvation and the prospect of controlling their earthly destiny, black people rushed to join the new churches. By century's end, both Jones's African Episcopal Church and Allen's African Methodist Church had nearly doubled their memberships from their beginnings less than a decade earlier. The process of Christianization took on new speed as leadership passed from white to black churchmen.

The new churches served a variety of functions. Within their walls, black people educated themselves and their children, insured themselves against disaster, protected themselves against kidnappers, planned for their future, and, perhaps most important, set the standards for their deportment as a free people. Everywhere such associations turned political, issuing condemnations of slavery and racial discrimination and demanding the vote and other elements of citizenship.[28]

"African" churches, schools, and societies revealed the massive transformation of black life that accompanied the revolution involved more than an alteration of status. The Free African Society began its articles of incorporation with the words: "We, the free *Africans* and their descendants. . . ." Philadelphia's peoples of African descent were no longer Angolans, Kongoes, Mandes, or Mandingos whose forebears had first arrived on the *Isabella* in 1684. The designation "African" that adorned their places of worship, education, contemplation, and recreation revealed the transformation of people of African descent after more than a century in Philadelphia. Although some black Philadelphians spoke earnestly about returning to Africa, it was manifest that their journey would be as African Americans who hoped to transform the continent with the ideas and institutions drawn from their experience as revolutionary republicans and evangelical Christians. In the first decades of the nineteenth century, as most black Philadelphians completed their transitions from slavery to freedom, a new African American society took shape.[29]

At the fore of this new society stood a new leadership class. Fired in the furnace of a republican revolution and a Christian awakening, these men and women had come of age with freedom. Many owed their liberty to the changes unleashed with the American Revolution, and they shared the optimism that accompanied American independence. Generally wealthier, more literate, and better connected with white people than most former slaves, these upward-striving and self-consciously respectable men took the leadership of the enlarged free black population and stood in the vanguard of those advocating the liberation of black people. Pointing to the Declaration of Independence, they petitioned for a ban on the slave trade and pressed for a general emancipation. When Pennsylvania slaveholders attempted to amend the Act of 1780 and re-enslave many of those who had recently been emancipated, black petitioners successfully petitioned the state legislature not to return former slaves to "all the horrors of hateful slavery" after restoring "the common blessings they were by nature entitled to." And once black people exited slavery, they demanded equality, attacking limitations on their right to sit on juries, testify in court, and vote. By choice and of necessity, they pressed the cause for the city's ideal of universal brotherhood. They soon realized their equality could not be achieved within the city of Philadelphia as long as slavery flourished outside its limits.[30]

The Reverend Richard Allen and sailmaker James Forten stood atop the new leadership class. Born in Philadelphia in the 1760s, they had taken different routes to prominence. Allen had spent his formative years as a slave in Delaware, where he had been sold as a youth. After purchasing his freedom, he returned to his native city as a free man and an enthusiastic convert to Christianity. During the 1780s, he rode the Methodist circuit preaching the gospel between Boston and Charleston, eventually receiving an appointment as assistant minister in Philadelphia's St. George Methodist Church. When St. George's white congregants betrayed their egalitarian heritage and threatened to remove the black members to the gallery, Allen led the black members out of the church. In 1794, he officially opened Bethel African Methodist Episcopal Church, "separate," Allen emphasized, "from our white brethren." Allen's church grew rapidly. Within a year, it had over one hundred members, and within ten years it had almost five hundred. By the second decade of the nineteenth century, its membership numbered in the thousands. Mother Bethel would become the largest black church in Philadelphia, and Allen the city's preeminent black religious leader.[31]

James Forten took another route to prominence. Unlike Allen, he was born free and attended the African school sponsored by the Society of Friends. Captured by the British on the *Royal Louis*, an American privateer, he spent seven years as a prison of war. Forten returned to Philadelphia after the war and apprenticed himself to Robert Bridges, a successful white sailmaker. Forten showed none of Allen's religious zeal. He eschewed membership in Bethel for Absalom Jones's more decorous St. Thomas Episcopal Church and, instead, mastered the business of sail-making. Forten rose through the ranks in Bridges's sail loft and eventually became the shop's foreman. In 1798, when Bridges retired, he turned the enterprise over to Forten. By the beginning of the nineteenth century, Forten emerged as Philadelphia's leading black businessman.[32]

Allen and Forten were men of property and respectability. Like other self-made men, they were proud of their achievements and certain their experience provided a guide that would elevate the race and provide the basis for a universal emancipation. Their discipline, desire for improvement, and careful adherence to the rules of gentlemanly respectability reflected the values of the influential white men who led the Pennsylvania Abolition Society. Like those men, Allen and Forten did not hesitate to lecture "their people" on the importance of hard work, temperance, frugality, piety, and the allied virtues that made for respectability as a necessary precondition for emancipation and citizenship.

Much of their intended audience—enjoying neither property nor respectability—hardly heard the message of their self-appointed patrons. Eager to claim the immediate rewards of freedom, the poorer, less well-connected spent their wages on new frocks and waistcoats. While the respectables met in the quiet decorum of their sitting rooms to debate the issues of the day, the newcomers joined together in smoke-filled gaming houses and noisy midnight frolics. Their boisterous lifestyle, colorful dress, plaited hair, eelskin queues, and swaggering gait scandalized the respectables like Allen and Forten. While the respectables saw such behavior as a calumny upon the race and a special threat to their own efforts to secure full equality, the newcomers disdained the pretensions of black men and women who acted "white."[33]

While black Philadelphians wrestled with their internal divisions and the very definition of what it meant to be "of color," most white Philadelphians paid such differences small heed. To them, it mattered little whether black people were propertied or penniless, skilled or unskilled, or Anglicans or Methodists. Color—any recognizable evidence of African descent—trumped all, as white Philadelphians embraced a new racial ideology that condemned black people as congenitally improvident, lazy, and ignorant. Prior to the revolution, explaining the degraded status of black slaves had been easily done within the confines of a society that deemed hierarchy normative. It required no particular resort to racialist ideologies and served no particular purpose in a society in which subordination was ubiquitous. However, once equality became normative, the poverty, illiteracy, and degradation of most black people—particularly free ones—needed an explanation. Race provided a handy one. While members of the Pennsylvania Abolition Society clung to environmentalist notions that circumstances—previous enslavement, the lack of formal education, and the absence of remunerative employment—explained African American degradation, other ideologies emerged as Negrophobia grew rampant in Philadelphia. Charles Caldwell, who studied medicine at the University of Pennsylvania, dismissed the older environmentalism and instead maintained that black people were deficient in reason and morality by nature. Thomas Branagan, an Irish immigrant, mixed his opposition to slavery with a heady brew of racism. At first, such notions were confined to marginal men like Caldwell and Branagan. But before long they entered respectable society, gaining the support of such distinguished white Philadelphians as Tench Coxe, a former officer of the Pennsylvania Abolition Society, who would denounce black people as congenitally incompetent, and Quaker leaders who refused to admit black members to the Society of Friends.

As Philadelphians turned the calendar on the eighteenth century, other changes in the city's demography and economy eroded the egalitarian spirit of the revolution and promoted a new, harsh Negrophobia. During the nineteenth century, European immigrants—with the Irish in the lead—poured into Philadelphia. Although the black population continued to grow, the white population surged upward more rapidly. Philadelphia became whiter.[34]

As the European newcomers pressed black workers for jobs, the already marginal economic status of black Philadelphians slipped still further. Black tradesmen and artisans found their small niche in the city's service economy shrinking. "If a man of color has children, it is almost impossible for him to get a trade for them, as the journeymen and apprentices generally refuse to work with them, even if the master is willing," noted one black Philadelphian in 1831. But it was not just black artisans who felt their ambitions constrained. Immigrants—especially the Irish—ousted black people from unskilled and domestic labor, as Irish teamsters and roustabouts took control of drayage and the docks and Irish women became the domestics of choice for prominent Philadelphia families. Most importantly, the new manufactories refused to employ black workers, barring black men and women from the most dynamic sector of Philadelphia's economy.[35]

The political position of black Philadelphians followed their economic decline. In 1800, the Jeffersonian Democratic-Republican Party—with its strong southern base—gained control of the national government. Black men and women found petitions to the national Congress to abolish the slave trade, end slavery, and repeal the Fugitive Slave Act dismissed out of hand as slavery expanded across the continent and new slave states entered the Union. Some white Philadelphians concluded that there was no place for black people in their city or their country. During the early years of the nineteenth century, they began to speak of "repatriating" black people to Africa or elsewhere, as if the nativity of African Americans stood outside the bounds of the United States.

The logic of colonization encouraged state and local officials to circumscribe the rights of black people, tax them more heavily, punish them more severely, and even deny them citizenship. In 1838, a revision of Pennsylvania's constitution stripped black men of the suffrage. Thereafter there were periodic attempts to limit the physical mobility and constrain the citizenship of black people. Even when these proposals failed, the racist impetus behind them put black people at risk. With increased frequency and brazen openness, white thugs and hoodlums—often in alliance with Philadelphia's gentlemen of property—assaulted black men and women on the city's streets. White kidnappers roamed the city, seizing free blacks—especially children—and selling them south into slavery. Black Philadelphians even found themselves barred from the celebrations of the American independence that they had helped secure.[36]

Against these assaults on their liberty and their person, black Philadelphians counterattacked, reasserting their leadership of the struggle against slavery and for the egalitarian cause. Mobilizing their revolutionary heritage, they turned the universalism of the Declaration of Independence against those who would deny them a full place in American society. At every opportunity they reasserted the city's ideal of brotherly love. "This idea," Forten affirmed 1813, "embraces the Indian and the European, the Savage and the Saint, the Peruvian and the Laplander, the white Man and the African, and whatever measures are adopted subversive of this inestimable privilege, are in direct violation of the letter and spirit of our Constitution, and become subject to the animadversion of all, particularly those who are deeply interested in the measure." While hurling the founding statement of American nationality at white Philadelphians, black men and women also organized within the city and the state. With the assistance of the Pennsylvania Abolition Society, they lobbied state and city lawmakers to counter various instances of discriminatory legislation, which were proposed with increasing frequency beginning in the 1830s. Again and again, they beat back attempts to amend the Pennsylvania Constitution with measures that would deny them their citizenship. If in fact Philadelphia would be a city of brotherly love, then they would be part of it.[37]

Not content to defend against the assaults on their liberty, black Philadelphians took the offensive. Nowhere was the counterattack more evident than in their ferocious opposition to colonization. Following the American Revolution, as black Philadelphians asserted their identity as African Americans, their interest in Africa peaked. Both Allen and Forten praised their ancestry and emphasized the transatlantic connection. Forten joined with his friend Paul Cuffe, a black Massachusetts sea captain and entrepreneur, in promoting trade and commerce with Africa.[38]

But if white colonizationists hoped that the pride black Philadelphians took in their African origins would promote the removal scheme, they were most disappointed. Almost universally, black Philadelphians viewed colonization as a contradiction to the city's founding ideal. To them, it was nothing less than a slaveholder's plot to deport them and other free blacks, thereby strengthening the institution of slavery. They viewed colonization rhetoric—which emphasized the indolence, thriftlessness, and criminality of black people—as a threat to their rights and a source of violence against their persons. They abhorred the colonizationist's insinuations that they were not Americans and the United States was not their country. "This is our home, and this is our country," proclaimed black Philadelphians led by Allen and Forten. "Beneath its sod lie the bones of our fathers; for it some of them fought, bled, and died. Here we were born, and here we will die."[39]

As they turned against colonization, a new, more assertive form of opposition to slavery emerged, and again black Philadelphians were in the vanguard. Putting aside the decorous and often paternalistic emancipationism of the Pennsylvania Abolition Society, black Philadelphians reaffirmed the connection between their own liberty and the liquidation of slavery everywhere. In 1831, when William Lloyd Garrison called for immediate abolition, black Philadelphia was at his side. Almost single-handedly, James Forten bankrolled Garrison's *The Liberator,* purchasing dozens of subscriptions and encouraging others to subscribe.[40]

The turn toward immediatism marked a sharp break with the past. Black Philadelphians grew increasingly assertive. The Pennsylvania Abolition Society had never accepted black men for membership and would not until 1842 when Robert Purvis, Forten's mixed-race son-in-law, was granted membership. Black men and women demanded a full role in the new movement. They found allies in young white men and women for whom the revolution was just a memory but who embraced its principles fully. Some were Quakers, many had been touched by feminist ideology, and all desired to remake the United States according to the Founders' principles. New, more militant organizations arose. Alongside the Philadelphia-based Pennsylvania Anti-Slavery Society stood the American Moral Reform Society, the Clarkson Anti-Slavery Society, the Female Anti-Slavery Society, the Workingmen's Anti-Slavery Society, and dozen of more ephemeral organizations. Some boycotted slave-produced goods, others published antislavery newspapers and tracts, and still others operated stations on the Underground Railroad, which hustled some two thousand southern slaves to freedom. As new abolitionist organizations appeared, the leadership role of black men and women became increasing visible.[41]

As Philadelphia's abolitionists grew in number and strength during the fourth decade of the nineteenth century, the movement reflected the divisions within the black community and the increasingly complex relations of black and white. Philadelphia's black population stood at over eight thousand, not including the large numbers who resided in the outlying suburbs of Moyamensing, Spring Garden, and North Liberties, all of which would soon be annexed to the city proper. Most had gained their freedom—or were descended from people who had gained their freedom—as a result of the 1780 Emancipation Act. Others were new to the city, fugitives from the South whose freedom had been secured by the Vigilant Association, which by the early 1840s assisted more than a dozen runaways each month.[42] Whatever their origins, black men and women differed by lineage, wealth, skill, and education, as well as complexion—black and brown—and other matters of physiognomy that gained special weight in a racially based slave society.

Their connections with white abolitionists were equally complex. Like Robert Purvis, a few black abolitionists shared the lifestyle of members of the white middle class. But most black men and women did not, and the differences in wealth and education strained relations within the movement, particularly when black Philadelphians created their own network of churches, schools, and fraternal societies.

Small wonder then that antislavery Philadelphians spoke with many voices. Their differences were reflected in tactics and strategies for both assaulting slavery in the South and pressing for equality in the North. Others manifested themselves from the divisions within the larger national movement, and still others reflected local issues and personalities. Both black and white Philadelphians maintained a variety of other commitments that sometimes complemented the movement against slavery and sometimes competed with it. For some, the commitment was to their church; for others, it was to sexuality equality. These different interests were multiplied by the nearly one hundred organizations from business organizations to fraternal associations, from debating societies to sewing circles, that composed Philadelphia's civil society. While some men and women focused their attention within their families, neighborhoods, or trades, others reached outside the city, traveling throughout the North and across the Atlantic. Bridging the differences within Philadelphia's antislavery movement required enormous forbearance and deep commitment to a common goal.

This was especially true for black abolitionists. Whether advocates of education or immigration, amelioration or revolution, they could not escape the central problem of African American life, particularly as the expansion of slavery and the deepening of racial exclusion challenged their freedom during the 1850s. With the passage of the new Fugitive Slave Act, kidnappers and slave traders stalked the streets of Philadelphia. Black men and women who had escaped slavery fled the city, and many people of free origins—some of whose freedom reached back generations—considered abandoning the city and the nation as new threats hammered them. In 1857, the Supreme Court shamelessly declared that black people had no rights any white person need respect. Not since the arrival of the *Isabella* did black Philadelphians face such a dismal future. Realizing the city's ideal never seemed more distant.

Suddenly, in the spring of 1861, as the long-simmering dispute between

North and South broke out into open warfare, hope was renewed. Recalling an earlier war that had propelled their parents and grandparents to freedom, black Philadelphians saw an opportunity to transform their lives in the ways the American Revolution had altered the lives of their forebears. Black men volunteered for an opportunity to smite the slavocracy with the understanding that military service would strike a blow against racial exclusion and discrimination if not fulfill the promise of a City of Brotherly Love. At first, they were ignored and then they were rejected, with sharp reminders that the war was a white man's work and the struggle was over Union, not slavery. But on January 1, 1863, with the promulgation of the Emancipation Proclamation, the call to arms was extended to them. During the course of the war, over eight thousand black men enlisted in Pennsylvania.[43] Many of them were fugitives from the South, but others were natives of the state, and a good number of these were Philadelphians. Their efforts in the final destruction of slavery in the United States brought to a conclusion a struggle that had begun nearly two centuries earlier and breathed life into a promise that men and women of diverse origins and colors could live in accord with their city's boasted ideal.

NOTES

1. The reference to Philadelphia as the City of Brotherly Love was alive probably at the city's founding. In 1830, *The Annals of Philadelphia* declared, "The very name of Philadelphia is impressive, as importing in its original Greek sense—brotherly love: thus giving to the original place the peculiar characteristic trait of unity of interests and purposes, i.e., the "City of Brotherly Love." More eloquent words follow this. Thus, from the beginning, the first arrivals knew that the city was named by William Penn with brotherly love specifically in mind. John F. Watson, *The Annals of Philadelphia*, 2 vols. (1830; Philadelphia, 1890), vol. 1: 14. I would like to thank Gary Nash for the reference.

2. Gary B. Nash, *First City: Philadelphia and the Forging of Historical Memory* (Philadelphia, 2002), 39; Ira Berlin, "From Creole to African: Atlantic Creoles and the Origins of African-American Society in Mainland North America," *William and Mary Quarterly* 53 (1996): 252–88.

3. Nash, *First City,*142–52; Berlin, "From Creole to African: Atlantic Creoles and the Origins of African-American Society in Mainland North America," *William and Mary Quarterly* 53 (1996): 252–88. For the distinction between a society with slaves and a slave society, see Moses I. Finley, *Ancient Slavery and Modern Ideology* (New York, 1980), and Ira Berlin, *Many Thousands Gone: The First Two Centuries of Slavery in Mainland North America* (Cambridge, Mass., 1998), 7–11.

4. Gary B. Nash, "Slaves and Slaveowners in Colonial Philadelphia," *William and Mary Quarterly* 30 (1973): 249–52; Gary B. Nash, *Forging Freedom: The Formation of Philadelphia's Black Community, 1720–1840* (Cambridge, Mass., 1988), 13–16.

5. Nash, "Slaves and Slaveowners in Colonial Philadelphia," 224–40.

6. Jean R. Soderlund, "Black Importation and Migration in Southeastern Pennsylvania, 1682–1810," *Proceedings of the American Philosophical Association* 133 (1989): 146–50; Nash, *Forging Freedom*, 34.

7. Dee E. Andrews, "From Natural Rights to National Sins: Philadelphia's Churches Respond to Antislavery, 1760–1860," below; Nash, *Forging Freedom*, 17–39.

8. W. Caleb McDaniel, "Philadelphia Abolitionists and Antislavery Cosmopolitanism," below, and Christopher Densmore, "'Let Us Make Their Case Our Own': The Anti-Slavery Work of the religious Friends of Philadelphia," unpublished paper on file in the archives at Independence National Historic Park, Philadelphia.

9. Soderlund, "Black Importation and Migration in Southeastern Pennsylvania," 148, 151–52; Nash, *Forging Freedom*, chap. 2; Berlin, *Many Thousands Gone*, chap. 9.

10. Andrews, "From Natural Rights to National Sins," below; Nash, *Forging Freedom*, 18–22.

11. Nash, *Forging Freedom*, chap. 2; quotation in Nash, "Race and Citizenship in the Early Republic," below.

12. Nash, *Forging Freedom*, 46–57; Gary B. Nash and Jean R. Soderlund, *Freedom by Degrees: Emancipation in Pennsylvania and Its Aftermath* (New York, 1991), 76–77, 88–89, 138–39; Winch, "Self-Help and Self-Determination," below; quotation in Billy G. Smith and Richard Wojtowicz, eds., *Blacks Who Stole themselves: Advertisements for Runaways in the Philadelphia Gazette* (Philadelphia, 1989), 132–33.

13. Richard Newman, "The Pennsylvania Abolition Society and the Struggle for Racial Justice," below.

14. Quoted in Nash, *Forging Freedom*, 64–65; Nash and Soderlund, *Freedom by Degrees*, 102; McDaniel, "Philadelphia Abolitionists and Antislavery Cosmopolitanism," and Densmore, "Let Use Make Their Case Our Own."

15. Quoted in Nash, *Forging Freedom*, 64–65; Nash and Soderland, *Freedom by Degrees*; Berlin, *Many Thousands Gone*, 228–39.

16. Nash, *Forging Freedom*, chap. 2; Nash and Soderland, *Freedom by Degrees*. chap. 4, quotation on 101.

17. Nash and Soderland, *Freedom by Degrees*, 119–23, 139.

18. Gary B. Nash, "Reverberations of Haiti in the American North: Black Saint Dominguians in Philadelphia," *Pennsylvania History* 65 (1998): 44–73; Nash, *Forging Freedom*, 140–44, 174–76, 180–83; Nash and Soderland, *Freedom by Degrees*, 180–81.

19. Nash and Soderland, *Freedom by Degrees*, chaps. 6–7, esp. 194–95.

20. Nash, *Forging Freedom*, 138, 142–43; Soderlund, "Black Importation and Migration into Southeastern Pennsylvania," 150–52; Newman, "The Pennsylvania Abolition," below.

21. See www.census.gov/.

22. Nash, *Forging Freedom*, 77–88.

23. Ibid., 7–76, 158–170; James O. Horton and Lois E. Horton, *In Hope of Liberty: Culture, Community, and Protest among Northern Free Blacks, 1700–1860* (New York, 1997), chap. 4.

24. Berlin, *Many Thousands Gone*, 245; Litwack, *North of Slavery: The Negro in the Free States, 1790–1860* (Chicago, 1961), chap. 4.

25. Nash, *Forging Freedom*, 74–75, 152–53, quotation on 156.

26. Nash, *Forging Freedom*, 144–50, 153–54; Cathy Matson, "Adversity and Achievement: Philadelphia's Economy, 1775 to 1857," unpublished essay on file in the archives at Independence National Historic Park, Philadelphia. W. Jeffrey Bolster, *Black Jacks: African American Seamen in the Age of the Sail* (Cambridge, Mass., 1997), 2–38, 113–16, 159–65; Julie Winch, *Philadelphia's Black Elite: Activism, Accommodation, and the Struggle for Autonomy, 1787–1848* (Philadelphia, 1988), chap. 1.

27. William Douglass, *Annals of the First African Church in the United States of America, Now Styled the African Episcopal Church of St. Thomas* (Philadelphia, 1862); Andrews, "From Natural Rights to National Sins," below; Will B. Gravely, "The Rise of African Churches in America (1786–1822): Reexamining the Contexts," *Journal of Religious Thought* 14 (1984): 58–73; and William B. Gravely, "African Methodism and the Rise of Black Denominationalism," in Russell E. Richey and Kenneth E. Rowe, eds., *Rethinking Methodist History* (Nashville, Tenn., 1985), 111–24; Carol V. R. George, *Segregated Sabbaths: Richard Allen and the Emergence of Independent Black Churches, 1760–1840* (New York, 1973); Nash, *Forging Freedom*, 109–33.

28. Winch, "Self-Help and Self-Determination."

29. Berlin, *Many Thousands Gone*, 254–55; Nash, *Forging Freedom*, 97–98, 115–16, quotation on 98.

30. Quotation in Nash, *Forging Freedom*, 64–65, and 180–83; Winch, "Self-Help and Self-Determination."

31. Richard Allen, *The Life, Experience, and Gospel Labors of the Rt. Rev. Richard Allen* (1880; rpt. Nashville, 1954); George, *Segregated Sabbaths*.

32. Julie Winch, *A Gentlemen of Color: The Life of James Forten* (New York, 2002); Winch, "Self-Help and Self-Determination," and Nash, "Race and Citizenship in the Early Republic."

33. Berlin, *Many Thousands Gone*, 254–55; Winch, "Self-Help and Self-Determination," and Newman, "The Pennsylvania Abolition Society"; Nash, *Forging Freedom*, 97–98, 115–16, quotation on 98.

34. Gary Nash, "Race and Citizenship in the Early Republic"; Richard Newman, *Transformation of American Abolition: Fighting Slavery in the New Republic* (Chapel Hill, N.C., 2002); and Newman, "The Pennsylvania Abolition Society." For a full discussion of racial ideology in the post-revolutionary years, see Bruce Dain, *A Hideous Monster, American Race Theory in the Early Republic* (Cambridge, Mass., 2002). For the proportional decline in Philadelphia's black population, see the decennial federal census.

35. Cathy Matson, "Adversity and Achievement: Philadelphia's Economy, 1775 to 1857"; quotation in *The Liberator* (Boston), February 12, 1831.

36. Emma J. Lapansky, "'Since they Got Those Separate Churches': Afro-Americans and Racism in Jacksonian Philadelphia," *American Quarterly* 32 (1980): 53–78; Richard S. Newman, *The Transformation of American Abolitionism: Fighting Slavery in the Early Republic* (Chapel Hill, N.C., 2002); Winch, "Self-Help and Self-Determination"; and Carol Wilson, "Philadelphia and the Origins of the Underground Railroad," unpublished essay on file in the archives at Independence National Historic Park, Philadelphia.

37. James Forten, *Series of Letters From a Man of Colour on a Late Bill Before the Senate of Pennsylvania* (Philadelphia, 1813), 1; quotation in Nash, "Race and Citizenship in the Early Republic"; Newman, *The Transformation of American Abolitionism*, 95.

38. See Forten, *Series of Letters From a Man of Colour*; Winch, *A Gentleman of Color*, 86, 464.

39. McDaniel, "Philadelphia Abolitionists and Antislavery Cosmopolitanism" and Newman, "The Pennsylvania Abolition Society."

40. Julie Winch, *A Gentleman of Color: The Life of James Forten* (Oxford, 2002), 190–92; William Lloyd Garrison, *Thoughts on African Colonization* (Boston, 1932); quoted in Litwack, *North of Slavery*, 25.

41. Densmore, "Let Use Make Their Case Our Own"; Wilson, "Philadelphia and the Origins of the Underground Railroad."

42. Wilson, "Philadelphia and the Origins of the Underground Railroad."

43. Ira Berlin, Joseph P. Reidy, and Leslie S. Rowland, eds, *The Black Military Experience, Freedom: A Documentary History of Emancipation* (Cambridge, U.K., 1983), ser. 2, 12.

II.
BLACK AND WHITE ABOLITIONIST MOVEMENTS IN EMANCIPATING PHILADELPHIA

CHAPTER 2

The Origins of Antislavery in Pennsylvania
Early Abolitionists and Benjamin Franklin's Road Not Taken

DAVID WALDSTREICHER

The recent profusion of work on slavery and antislavery has had the laudable side effect of moving the story of abolitionism back a few decades, to the early republic. It becomes easier to challenge complacent visions of the Founders as unthinking racists who were unable to imagine that slavery was wrong. It also becomes harder to begin with William Lloyd Garrison as the first "modern" abolitionist, or to condescend to earlier antislavery writers and activists as pious exotics who influenced no one because slavery was simply common sense from time immemorial. Yet the condescension remains and perhaps even grows amid today's bold paeans to antebellum "prophets of protest." The black and white abolitionists of the 1820s to the 1850s, we are told, invented racial equality, cross-racial political alliances, feminism, democracy, cosmopolitan globe-trotting activism (and its attendant anomie and exile), and sophisticated uses of media. These conclusions depend in part on the tendency of historians of all stripes to say that hardly anyone criticized slavery before the revolution.[1] If they are not forgotten outright, earlier critics of slavery are described as tentative, gradualist, racist, ideologically handicapped, insufficiently radical, or unable to envision the mass movement that abolition eventually had to become. Revolutionary era antislavery is upraised—and contained—as foundational. The compliment preserves the aura of pious primitivism that so underrates the political savvy of an Anthony Benezet or Phillis Wheatley.

As Ira Berlin points out, too much about antislavery's origins is lost even with the renewed emphasis on the revolutionary era. This essay describes the beginnings of antislavery in colonial Pennsylvania, and the struggles with it by Benjamin Franklin, as itself simultaneously shocking in its modernity and, nevertheless, deeply shaped by seventeenth- and early eighteenth-century controversies about war, religion, and the transformation of the international economy. Recent scholarship on the origins of slavery stresses the deeply innovative extension and transformation of the Atlantic economies that came to center on the development of plantation colonies in the Caribbean. The effects were felt in areas that did not even trade in lucrative staple crops, like Massachusetts Bay and Pennsylvania, both of which took off demographically only after developing West Indies markets. Contemporaries who saw New World colonies as opportunities for reform, rather than merely profit, found themselves presented with real ideological and practical dilemmas. They realized that the new slavery of the Americas was not from time immemorial: it was a modern development in its scale, scope, reliance on distance, and racialized nature, and by the 1680s they came to engage it critically, as a local and international problem, for that very reason.[2]

The Germantown Protest, written by the learned and sophisticated German Quaker Francis Daniel Pastorius, begins with the Golden Rule, a consistent theme in early antislavery discourse and an especially important doctrine to the Quakers who settled Pennsylvania. The petition's manner of illustrating the application of the Golden Rule, and arguing against possible objections, refers continually to an international context, in an awareness of the newness of both slavery and settlement. The European immigrants addressed by the protest are people who have been at sea and who are intimately aware of the contest of empires and religions. "How fearful and faint-hearted are many on sea when they see a strange vessel—being afraid it should be a Turk, and they should be taken, and sold for slaves into Turkey. Now what is this better done, as Turks doe?" To ask the question is to place the reader in the position of becoming a slave her or himself, which, as Linda Colley reminds us, was a very real possibility at this time. It is worse, though, because the Africans have been "for the most part" stolen: they had not voluntarily undertaken a voyage and risked capture. Neither property rights, Christian identity, nor the accepted risks of Atlantic seafaring justifies slaveholders. Instead, all three of these norms are marshaled against the trade.[3]

The Protest proceeds to take on directly the question of race, stating that "tho they [the Africans] are black," slavery remains theft. The modern reader would like to hear more, of course, but the seventeenth-century reader had other concerns, ones that center less on color, or even on who is enslaved, than on who enslaves, how, and where. "Here is liberty of conscience," insists Pastorius, referring to Pennsylvania as a special place of refuge, w[hi]ch is right and reasonable; here ought to be likewise liberty of ye body, except of evil-doers, w[hi]ch is an other case. But to bring men hither, or to rob and sell them against their will, we stand against. In Europe there are many oppressed for conscience sake; and here there are those oppressed who are of a black colour. And we who know that men must not commit adultery—some do commit adultery, in others, separating wives from their husbands and giving them to others; and some sell the children of these poor creatures to other men. Ah! doe consider well this thing, you who doe it, if you would be done at this manner? and if it is done according to Christianity? You surpass Holland and Germany in this thing. This makes an ill report in all those countries of Europe, where they hear off, that ye Quakers doe here handel men as they handle there ye cattle. And for that reason some have no mind or inclination to come hither.

In this tightly woven argument, the Germantown petitioners hit their fellow Pennsylvanians literally where they live. Racial prejudice is no different from religious oppression.[4] Slavery is compared to the repression of religious freedom in Europe: not only would a slaveholding Pennsylvania be as oppressive as the Old World left behind, but such actions might actually prevent newcomers from venturing across the ocean—returning to that all too lively image of the fearful passenger, and raising the possibility that bad publicity could jeopardize the entire project of the new colony as an asylum. Reiterating the comparison of slavery to theft and adultery, Pastorius goes so far as to assert that Pennsylvania "hath now a bad one for this sake in other countries. . . . Europeans are desirous to know in what manner ye Quakers doe rule in their province—and most of them doe look upon us with an envious eye."

Slavery threatens every Christian individually with sin and collectively, as a community, with a bad international reputation. But there is more. Pastorius knew his audience—the monthly and yearly Quaker meetings—and saved for the end an even more provocative accusation, one especially difficult for Quakers to refute. It concerned the inherently violent tendencies of slavery and the likelihood that slave resistance—cast as nearly inevitable—will end in war.

If once these slaves (w[hi]ch they say are so wicked and stubborn men) should joint themselves—fight for their freedom,—and handel their masters and mastrisses as they did handel them before; will these masters and mastrisses take the sword at hand and warr against these poor slaves, licke, we are able to believe, some will not refuse to doe; or have these negers not as much right to fight for their freedom, as you have to keep them slaves?

Quakers could not ethically condemn slave rebels' violence. As a result, in a Quaker community, slavery would not only implode, but could implicate everyone in sin. The petitioners end by asking their co-religionists to "consider well" the likelihood that slavery is nothing but theft and leads inevitably to war, humbly suggesting that they "never" have been informed, by fellow Quakers at least, "that Christians have such a liberty to do so." If so informed, they reiterate, they will immediately pass on the information to their friends in Europe, to whom "it is a terror, or fairful thing that men should be handled so in Pennsylvania."[5]

The pose of humility, as in most early modern petitions to authority, covers a multitude of politics. Pastorius and his fellow Germantowners had cast themselves as Atlantic cosmopolitans—as a direct line to an international communications network that would determine the future of the colony. They cast New World slaveholding as more of an innovation than their sect or colonization itself and one of the sort that Quakerism and Pennsylvania were meant to combat. Their petition takes a nearly global perspective while still maintaining the primacy of sin in the context of real, everyday household relations.

Every time the Germantown Petition gets rediscovered, most recently in a 2007 exhibit at the National Constitution Center, its original ineffectiveness and "lost" status is emphasized (the original document remained buried in Quaker archives until 1844). But perhaps we have it wrong: perhaps it was all too effective. In less than five months the protest was considered by the three administrative bodies above the Germantown Friends (a quick administrative response in any century). None of them actually refuted its arguments. The Dublin Monthly Meeting called it "weighty" enough to "think it not expedient for us to meddle with it here," and passed it immediately to the Philadelphia Quarterly Meeting, which likewise considered it "of too great a weight for this meeting to determine." The Burlington Yearly Meeting said a bit more. It was "not proper for this Meeting to give a Positive Judgment in this Case, It *having so General a Relation to many other Parts*."[6] This was no dismissal: it was a concession. The problem of slavery was not that it was accepted by everyone. As an institution it was related to everything else: immigration, the economy, the household (the family), religion, diplomacy, and war.

Antebellum Americans did not discover that slavery was a weighty question that implicated gender relations, international politics, and people's souls. It is entirely possible that, in some parts of North America, American slavery's particular nature, along with the analyses offered as early as the 1680s, was forgotten before it was rediscovered in all its moral and political complexity. Perhaps it was also a question of experience. Not raised with the institution, as subsequent colonists would be, some of the immigrants to the New World experienced precisely the kind of shock upon confronting slavery that James L. Huston calls the "experiential basis" of abolitionism among traveling white northerners in the antebellum period.[7] A combination of factors, in other words, made the Germantown protest particularly powerful in its arguments; this very effectiveness led to it being buried, rather than refuted, by fellow Quakers.

If the document itself did not have legs, however, the arguments did—because they were being voiced elsewhere in the 1680s. Contemporaries in England—Quakers and their fellow travelers—developed a similarly cosmopolitan, Christian, and antiwar version of antislavery that can be traced from the popular health writer Thomas Tryon through Benjamin Lay to Anthony Benezet, John Woolman, and the end of slavery among Quakers. It can also be seen, *in the act of being refused,* by Pennsylvania's greatest revolutionary, Benjamin Franklin. Franklin gives us many hitherto neglected clues about the persuasiveness and persistence of late colonial antislavery. Following this version of antislavery through the Quaker dissidents and Franklin enables us to reconsider the Founders' ambivalence about antislavery, and to reconsider Pennsylvania-style antislavery's stunning achievements and limits. What was at stake, as we see with Franklin, was nothing less than competing perspectives on America itself. Both a cosmopolitan, pious antiwar narrative and the secularizing, imperial narratives of American development and American slavery were born of colonial experience. One, however, began to make the reform of slavery a priority, while the other denied and deferred it, with tragic, violent results.

The transforming moment in Benjamin Franklin's early life occurred when he decided to offer his brother, the printer James Franklin, a deal no master could refuse. He'd feed himself for half of what James was paying for his board. The regimen earned the young apprentice money for books and time to read them. It is the first of the self-actuating decisions he made that eventually led him to sneak out from under James's beatings by running to freedom. Recalling these events more than fifty years later, Franklin left no doubt where he got the idea. He had read about the practical benefits of simple eating in the work of the only writer mentioned twice in the *Autobiography*: the man Franklin later calls "my master," Thomas Tryon.[8]

Who was Thomas Tryon? Franklin probably knew as much or more about him as we can. Tryon's own memoir has been rediscovered as a classic of the seventeenth-century reading revolution in England. He began life like Franklin, as the son of a man with too many children. Like Franklin, he was put out to service early, in his case spinning and carding. After persuading his father to buy him a small flock of sheep, Tryon used his work time to teach himself to read. At eighteen, he sold his sheep and moved to London, apprenticing himself to a hatter. There he continued his practice of working hard and eating simply to gain extra funds, and time, for books and tutors.[9]

Although Franklin scholars have never followed up on the hint, it appears that both the autobiography and the life of Franklin were deeply shaped by Tryon's example. Therefore it is all the more striking and important that Tryon developed into the first popular writer to criticize slavery.[10] To understand why, we have to pay close attention to Tryon's subsequent development, before he (again, exactly like Franklin) retired at the age of forty-eight to pursue a literary career.

Two events shaped Tryon's experience and outlook: the religious radicalism of the Commonwealth period, and the simultaneous development of England's Caribbean colonies. As an apprentice in London he converted to Anabaptism, the most socially radical of the dissenting faiths.[11] A few years later, he moved to Barbados to make fur hats, doing well enough for himself that he returned there after a year in Newfoundland and stayed until 1669. Much like the Quakers (and like Franklin's dissenting forebears who found the woolen trades crowded in England), he sought opportunity and perhaps religious freedom in the colonies. Unlike the Franklins, Tryon returned, this time to the suburbs of London, to parlay his capital and connections into a stable business, and eventually a new career.

Tryon's horror at what he witnessed in the Caribbean is apparent in his later writings; it shaped his reformist outlook generally. And when he chose to publish, the British were more than ready to hear criticisms of the West Indies and of slavery.[12] Tryon fashioned a thoroughgoing analysis and creed that made him simultaneously, beginning in 1683, one of the first important vegetarian and health how-to-book writers *and* an influential critic of slavery. Too often, though, his writings on slavery have been considered apart from his theories on diet. Like many mid-seventeenth century dissenters, he "used diet to criticize the established social order." What was different about Tryon's application of the Golden Rule to the politics of food was that he took a truly Atlantic perspective on the question of who ate what and the consequences.[13]

Tryon launched into print with *A Dialogue Between an East-Indian Brackmanny or Heathen-Philosopher, and a French Gentleman Concerning the Present Affairs of Europe*. Externalizing contemporary debates somewhat allowed for a more objective analysis of Europe's century of wars justified by empire and religion. "If men considered the weight and cares of *Empire*," comments Tryon's Brahmin, "those that are without it would rather *fly from* than *fight for it*." The other justifications of war—glory, and most of all, faith—are equally illogical and counterproductive. Wars destroy life, and thus work against God's plan; true religion preaches, and must practice, peace. Religious wars, the Frenchman retorts, allow soldiers to become "great and Honourable." The Indian replies by comparing the "butchers of men" to low-caste butchers of animals, suggesting that both tend to be gluttons when not plying their craft. Laws that oppress people—especially those that restrict liberty of conscience—lead to rebellion and more violence, as the case of the Huguenots illustrates. Tryon completes the dialogue by having the Brahmin cite Pythagoras, who visited India, as a source of vegetarian pacifism. (Tryon would later use Pythagoras as a pseudonym, and came to be considered a Pythagorean by contemporaries.).[14]

In his defining work, *The Way to Wealth, Long Life and Happiness*, published later the same year, Tryon brought his critique westward, across the Atlantic. He again compared soldiers to butchers and drew out a parallel to the "unclean devourers"—pigs, lions, wolves—who "kill and feast upon their fellow creatures." Peace and temperance, argued Tryon, were inseparable, as he raised for the first time the implications of feasts and complex recipes "enricht with East and West Indies ingredients, of themselves more than sufficient for a sober and temperate meal." Habit takes over men as well as animals, and "a man becomes a *Tyrant to himself*, and a perfect *Slave to Gluttony*" (later he calls such people "Belly-slaves"). Having established these contrasts and their results, Tryon develops a hierarchy of the clean and peaceful versus the dirty and violent, insisting that "Flesh and Fish cannot be eaten without violence, and doing that which a man would not be done unto, and making destruction of God's Creatures, which are generally more profitable living than dead (as Cows and Sheep, which are the Creatures most eaten.)"[15]

After this lengthy chapter on flesh, Tryon included not only recipes but impromptu speeches by cows, sheep, birds, and horses against their treatment by their masters—men. He incorporated the idea of those called "brute beasts" talking back in the next year's sequel, *The Country-men's Companion,* and had clearly been thinking all along about how to intervene more directly in current debates about the colonies—and not only the sugar islands. Tryon's *Friendly Advice to the Gentleman Planters of the East and West Indies* broke new ground with its lengthy "Negro's Complaint" and dialogue between an Ethiopian slave and a Christian master.

Tryon also included in *Country-man's Companion,* and published separately, a specifically tailored *Planter's Speech to His Neighbours and Countrymen of Pennsylvania, East and West Jersey.* Especially striking in the Pennsylvania essay is Tryon's remarkable ability to dissect the British colonies' military-plantation-trade complex, extending his critique of sugar, tobacco, and slavery to hides and Native-white relations. He apparently realized that the direct critique of master-slave relations was insufficient to capture the enormity and depth of North American complicity in slavery. Guns, furs, and rum constituted an international commodity chain that enveloped natives in perpetual war with each other as well as with Europeans; slaves too became commodities, an incentive to make war in America and Africa. For Tryon, Europeans had spread their social and moral diseases rather than learning from native ways while teaching them Christianity. As he had the birds of America put it, men with guns acted like swine. They violated others' natural rights, and even to the point of feeding on their own. Colonists mocked Indian, American, and African heathen, but their practices added up to cannibalism.[16]

What about the newest colony, Pennsylvania? Tryon still held out hope that the middle colonies could be about "righteousness" and peace, as the first settlers intended, if they took care to ban guns and alcohol, and refused to wear clothing not made from locally grown produce. It appears that Tryon's books were especially popular in the colonies. A surprising number of copies survive in Philadelphia-area archives. From the beginning, Quakers especially seem to have appreciated Tryon's emphasis on simple living, practical religion, enlightened child-rearing, and (in other works) dream interpretation, and he cultivated them in return. He shared publishers such as Andrew Sowle with important Quaker writers like William Penn. English Quakers gathered his manuscript *Memoirs* and published them after his death in 1703.[17]

Apparently Franklin was far from alone in finding Tryon compelling, as an example and as an inspiration. In 1715, New Jersey Quaker John Hepburn directly applied Tryon's experiments with literary form in trying to convince fellow Quakers, through a dialogue between an "American Negro Master" and a "Turk" on the justifications for slaveholding. Hepburn also put a Negro master in afterlife conversation with a "Christian," who pointed out that the same sects who seemed to approve of religious wars also endorsed slaveholding. Such Christians acted like "dogs wolves and bears." If it was shocking that Quaker slaveholding was on the increase, it was no more so than the agreement of some American Quaker colonists to pay the wages of the troops who had marched on Canada in 1711. William Penn and Robert Barclay, insists Hepburn's Christian, had thought differently: their "innocent" refusal to arm had actually spread the light. At a time when nearly half of the Quakers lived in the new world, such comparisons had tremendous implications. The slave master's response is telling: "What have we to do with such far-fetch't Proofs? Or what was in *Barclay's* day? I love to keep at home, and the Practice of our *American Christians*." Slaving is local, provincial. Antislavery is pious, historical, and cosmopolitan.[18]

Hepburn, according to David Brion Davis, was influenced by Samuel Sewall, and pointed explicitly to Cotton Mather. Both Bostonians were concerned that the reputation of the New England experiment, before God and man, might be at stake in the treatment of Africans. During these same years, growing up in Boston, Franklin knew both men and their writings intimately. As I have argued elsewhere, though, young Franklin first encountered these ideas not as a fellow planter but as a servant and a dissenter in *their* established church. The critiques of slavery launched by members of the Puritan intelligentsia, and to some extent Tryon himself (as far as familial relations were concerned), were in an important sense reformist. They were about godliness and holy, patriarchal families—not freedom and self-invention in the marketplace.[19] Franklin's problem with early antislavery criticisms was probably that, after his initial identification with the victims and his empowerment through Tryon's regimen, he could not identify himself, as a teenager (and later fugitive), in those critiques—especially after the new freedoms he began to seize depended both on the market and on others' servitude.

Tryon appears again in the *Autobiography* when Franklin identifies his first Philadelphia boss as a pious hypocrite. Samuel Keimer was a former French Prophet (Camisard) who affected Quaker habits and had proposed to open a school for slaves soon after his arrival in Philadelphia. They at first "liv'd on a pretty good familiar Footing and agreed tolerably well." Franklin and Keimer

took mutual pleasure in arguing about anything and everything; Keimer developed so high an opinion of Franklin's skills that he proposed they extend
their employment relation from printing to prophesying—to start a new sect
in which Keimer would "preach the Doctrines" and Franklin "confound all
Opponents." Franklin agreed to his doctrines (including not shaving and keeping the Sabbath) only on the condition that the printer follow a vegetarian
regimen. Franklin again displays and cites his Tryonism by creating a two-man
vegetarian cooperative with his boss, but this time as farce. He stops the narrative to tell us that, *before* setting up his vegetarian scheme with Keimer, he
had actually given up the practice, on his return voyage to Philadelphia after a
visit home. In this famous passage he tells us why:

> I believe I have omitted mentioning that in my first Voyage from Bos-
> ton, being becalm'd off Block Island, our People set about catching Cod
> and hawl'd up a great many. Hitherto I had stuck to my Resolution of
> not eating animal Food; and on this Occasion, I consider'd with my
> Master Tryon, the taking every Fish as a kind of unprovok'd Murder,
> since none of them had or ever could do us any Injury that might justify
> the Slaughter. All this seem'd very reasonable. But I had formerly been
> a great Lover of Fish, and when this came hot out of the Frying Pan,
> it smelt admirably well. I balanc'd some time between Principle and
> Inclination: till I recollected, that when the Fish were opened, I saw
> smaller Fish taken out of their Stomachs: Then thought I, if you eat one
> another, I don't see why we mayn't eat you. So I din'd upon cod very
> heartily and continu'd to eat with other People, returning only now and
> then occasionally to a vegetable Diet. So convenient a thing it is to be
> a *reasonable Creature,* since it enables one to find or make a Reason for
> every thing one has a mind to do.

What were the implications of such a change of heart—or mind? Franklin does
not say that Tryon was *wrong,* only that it was useful to rationalize his way out
of his Tryon-inspired regimen. Giving up on Tryon's regimen enables him to
"eat with other People," a direct contrast to the solitary freedoms he had seized,
with Tryon's aid, as his brother's servant. With regard to Keimer, it meant
that he could treat his employer as another fish in a predatory sea, a solitary
gobbler. And indeed, Franklin soon tells us that Keimer himself failed to keep
his part of the bargain. His boss invited Franklin and two female friends to a

break-the-fast of roast pig, and "ate it all up before we came."[20] A would-be follower of Mosaic laws, someone who imagined himself as a prophet, Keimer is exposed by Franklin as a swine who gobbled swine—a demon straight out of Tryon.

Franklin could relish Tryon's accusation that West Indian planters' invocations of Christianity, like those of Keimer and Boston's authorities, served as a mask for their power, without necessarily having to face up to any incendiary call for revolt. Nevertheless, his insistence that he had already given up on Tryon's regimen suggests that Franklin had already moved on, or domesticated Tryon, much as he would domesticate God himself into a "powerful Goodness" to be relied upon and thanked like a good friend, or permissive father.

Franklin describes this period, from 1723 into the early 1730s, as a time when he set in place the personal habits and the interpersonal "Interests" which would make him a successful printer. After a stint in London he weathered a rivalry with Keimer, conducted through printed attacks on each others' piety, and by 1729 he owned Keimer's newspaper. He expanded his market activities in order to pay off his debt. He also acquired his first African American slaves and servants, as part of a household truly his own. And he found that his perspective on things sacred had to be tuned very, very carefully. In pluralist, Quaker-dominated Pennsylvania, religion was not an easy commodity in which to speculate, and yet most public matters had ecclesiastical, if not theological, implications. In April 1730, for example, his "Letter of a Drum" ridiculed ministers who believed in witchcraft and spirit possession; he followed it up in the next issue of the *Gazette* with an equally anonymous defense of the satire, of true religion, and of the printer, whose willingness to print this reply showed his true receptiveness to religiosity. In July, when Franklin printed several essays on the origins of Christianity from a London newspaper, he heard that several divines were outraged and invited them to please reply at the same length as the original essays. The next spring, after he printed an ad from a sea captain who forbade his ship to "black gowns" and other pests, he had to defend his press as not anti-clergy but rather open to all. His first, landmark defense of freedom of the press, and his market rationale for understanding its workings, was, in other words, a plea that, notwithstanding persistent rumors, he was not irreligious. For Franklin at twenty-four, this was more of the same. His inability to break with his brother and still remain in Boston had been shaped by his "indiscreet Disputations [about] Religion" which "ma[d]e me pointed at with Horror by good People, as an Infidel or Atheist."[21]

No strong adherent to a sect, and no atheist, could have made the *Pennsyl-vania Gazette* please its various constituencies; unlike the established Quaker printer William Bradford, he had to remain open, and liberal, to provide a space for religious controversy without taking it, or its awe-inspiring implica-tions, too seriously. He understandably remained extremely sensitive to ac-cusations of imbalance or partisanship on the topic of religion—so much so that when a new Presbyterian preacher, Samuel Hemphill—the first minister to keep Franklin in a pew for successive Sundays—came under attack in 1735 for insufficient orthodoxy, Franklin, uncharacteristically enough, identified strongly with the charismatic young preacher and mistook a parish war among Presbyterians for a full-scale assault on liberty. In his second pamphlet on the subject, Franklin pulled out all the stops and accused the clergy of being en-emies of "truth and Liberty." He contrasted true "Christian liberty," a "Privilege common to Mankind," to a clergy "too fond of Power," who seemed most inter-ested in "enslaving people's minds." "Nothing, in all Probability, can prevent our being a flourishing and happy People, but our suffering the Clergy to get upon our Backs, and ride us, as they do their Horses, where they please."[22] For Franklin in 1735, religious establishments and religious doctrines endanger personal freedom and public liberty. Clerics threaten to *enslave* those who obey them. Cooler heads should prevail, and when they do, colonists join the mainstream of human and British liberty. In Franklin's emerging vision of a pluralist colony, guided by the tolerance of its Quaker business and political leaders, there is no place for moral absolutes or condemnations. It is bad for business and bad for him.

Franklin deserves credit for his consistency. He did not merely become the Quakers' pet printer: he actually kept his press open to the Quaker dissidents who were the first major antislavery writers. In March 1729, at a time when Franklin was mocking Keimer in the pages of Bradford's *Weekly Mercury,* a Quaker merchant named Ralph Sandiford came to him with an antislavery manuscript. A cautious Franklin agreed to publish it for the author, though without the printer's name on the title page; Sandiford would have to purchase and give away most of the copies.

Like Thomas Tryon, Sandiford had seen slavery at first hand in the Baha-mas and in South Carolina. He had moved to Philadelphia to find an alterna-tive but found slavery on his doorstep, in the form of an increased number of sales occurring literally down the street from his shop, especially after the assembly lowered the duty on slaves imported from ten pounds to twenty shillings. Sandiford echoed Tryon in describing the immorality of oppressing any beasts of burden. He even identified and updated a particularly North American version of Tryon's slavery-militarism-colonialism complex: when South Carolinians sold captured Indians into slavery, they encouraged Indians, and the Spanish, to do the same, provoking new colonial wars during the decades after Tryon wrote. The entire skin trade, and the exploitation of the Indians, appeared to Sandiford as part and parcel of the same colonial reliance on exploitation: "we go to the very Indies for fans and Umbrella's, which are for the same Service to us; for which the very Indians upbraid us, for Robbing the Creatures of their natural Covering, and yet cover ourselves with borrowed Hair, which is unnatural, which shews the great Degeneracy & Fall of Man from his first Creation." Such travesties of the Golden Rule could be visited back upon Englishmen by "Indians, or Turks, or Spaniards." Sandiford defined Africans as a captured nation who had not "forfeited their Country and Liberty," and whose captivity was not being redeemed in any way, as the oft-cited biblical precedents for slavery clearly required.[23]

Although Sandiford begged his readers not to mind that his sentiments had not been approved by the Quaker yearly meeting, he was banished from the sect for publishing without the meeting's approval. He died a broken man at the age of forty, in 1733. By that time, he had been befriended by another refugee Quaker merchant, Benjamin Lay, who bought copies of Sandiford's book from Franklin and continued to distribute them gratis.[24]

Lay defined himself as a direct disciple of Tryon, to the point of carrying a copy of Tryon around regularly, as both a contemporary painting and a print based on it demonstrate. A sailor who had settled in Barbados as a merchant, he earned the hostility of his fellow white islanders for attempts to ameliorate slavery. Emigrating to Pennsylvania in 1731, he hoped to find a more sympathetic audience but discovered instead that slaveholding was on the rise among Quakers, as in the colony as a whole. He took Tryon's injunctions so seriously as to embrace vegetarianism, refuse to eat with slaveholders, and refrain from wearing any products of slave labor. During the 1730s he sought a mutually supportive relationship with the animal world, raising vegetables and flax, keeping bees, building a house out of a cave, and engaging in at least one very public fast. He received admiring visitors, including Franklin and the governor of Pennsylvania, and for more than a decade sought new ways to demonstrate the ways in which slavery was "the Mother of all Sins."[25]

Lay might be called the first modern abolitionist not only because of his religiously based conviction that slavery was a sin but also because of the way he insisted that slavery leached evil throughout the entire community. Believing so, he testified regularly in Quaker meetings and churches, and was sometimes forcibly removed from them. During the 1730s and 1740s he developed more and more dramatic ways of making his point that slavery exemplified and combined all the deadly sins. On one occasion he publicly destroyed his wife's china, as a symbol of the violence wrought by sugary treats. In the most famous episode, he stood up in the Burlington, New Jersey, regional yearly meeting of 1738 to denounce slaveholding among Quakers as not only a violation of the golden rule but as the ultimate warlike act. Friends might as well renounce their pacifism and put on armor, he exclaimed, opening his overcoat to reveal his military garb below. He then took out a sword and stated that slaveowners committed a sin as grievous as murder—and thrust his weapon into a Bible which hid a bladder of red pokeberry juice, spattering himself and those who shared his bench with the ersatz blood.[26]

This most famous act of Lay's, and the one that most deeply disturbed contemporaries, reveals just how central the link of slavery to violence and war had become to Quaker antislavery. Lay excerpted Samuel Sewell's argument that "an Unlawful war cannot make Lawful Captives. And by receiving them we are in danger to promote, and participate in their Barbarous Cruelties." Franklin remembered Lay asking him to order his disordered manuscript collection of testimonies, quotations, and reflections, *All Slave-keepers That Keep the Innocent in Bondage* (1737), in any way he saw fit, but neither author nor printer failed to foreground William Burling's 1718 observation that Quaker slaveholders "Preach against fighting yet receive the plunder." Lay proceeded to observe that his predecessor Burling had been inspired during the 1680s, when "there was much Discourse about the English and Dutch People, being taken into *Turky*, or by the *Turks* into Slavery." Lay uses these facts to introduce himself as a cosmopolitan traveler. He had once sailed to Turkey and spent eighteen months aboard ship with four men who had been slaves there for seventeen years, "and I never did understand by them, they were so badly used as the poor Negroes are by some called Christians."[27]

It is clear that Franklin and Lay had an interesting relationship. Franklin printed Lay's book (though again without his own name on the title page as printer) and reported Lay's more spectacular doings in the pages of the *Pennsylvania Gazette*. Lay seems to have visited Franklin's shop regularly when he ventured from his country home in Abingdon to purchase paper, ink, legal forms, and books to give away. He also subscribed to the newspaper. Twenty years later, around the time of Lay's death, Deborah Franklin admired him enough to acquire and mount a portrait of the man her husband had called "the Pythagorean-Cynical-Christian Philosopher"—the print in which Lay conspicuously displays a copy of "Trion on Happiness." But that was when Franklin was away in London: he would later write to ask Debbie where she got the portrait. When Lay walked all the way to Philadelphia from Abingdon during his famous fast, Franklin found his breath "so acrid as to make his eyes tear and pain." There is no better image of Franklin's engagement with and distance from the dangers of antislavery than Lay's presumption and the printer's real physical discomfort in the presence of his words.[28]

Sandiford and Lay, like Franklin, attacked vanity, inhumane waste, and the pretensions of ministers. Franklin's early appreciation of Tryon, his own battles with religious authorities, and his appreciation for Quaker sobriety and egalitarianism made him receptive to these radicals' religiously based criticisms of the entire social order. They probably knew what they were doing when they approached the young printer for help. As the Hemphill affair shows, Franklin could get genuinely excited about the contemporary indictment of religious authority as a form of "slavery." He may have sympathized with Lay's attacks on religious hypocrites who sought moral authority in the community but were just as guilty of holding slaves.

And yet during these same years Franklin, as owner of the *Pennsylvania Gazette* and a general store, began to profit from slavery and the trade in slaves in multiple ways, and he began to own slaves for the first time. Precisely because of his predisposition to agree with critiques of slavery, he needed a rationale for his keeping a sympathetic distance. He found it, first, in religious pluralism, his commitment to freedom of the press which suited his desire to expand his market beyond any one denomination. This pluralism, which took God seriously but withheld the powers of divine judgment and church discipline, ignored one crucial aspect of the emerging antislavery argument from faith. Slaves, in the vision of Mather, Sewall, Tryon, Sandiford, and Lay, were not only members of the human family, but also members of a society of families whose government was subject to church as well as state.

That government, in Pennsylvania, was moderated if not completely controlled by Quakers themselves; it made sense for Quaker antislavery writers and activists to work through the meeting structure, precisely because they insisted on slavery's connection to everything else, public and private. Franklin stood on the other side of a great historical divide that people like the Quakers helped open up by insisting upon religious freedom. The private—including slavery defined as a domestic institution—was cordoned off as much as possible from political and religious disputation. Such distinctions became Franklin's bread and butter, even as he adopted a Tryonist and Quaker practice, in his newspaper and almanac, of advising individuals on how to improve themselves through hard work and non-consumption.

A further breach between Franklin and the Tryonists occurred around 1740, soon after Franklin printed Lay's book. During the 1730s, the Philadelphia meeting began to take a clear stand against slave importation. When the first of a series of invasions and imperial wars threatened the colony, Franklin emerged as a champion of armed defense, on the frontier and the seas, as a mode of equal Britishness. Quakers, by contrast, were deeply troubled by the wars of the 1740s. That stance led directly to the crisis in Pennsylvania politics that split the Quakers deeply during the Seven Years' War and the American Revolution.

Controversies over war also created the opening that enabled more Friends to hear the criticisms of John Woolman and Anthony Benezet, the next generation's Quaker antislavery travelers. Like Tryon and those he inspired earlier, they insisted on both the deeply personal and spiritual implications of one's stance toward slavery, while arguing that specifically recent developments had led colonists away from the path of peace. They adopted the Tryonist stress on sinless produce and clothing, "loosely link[ing] war, slavery, and excessive consumption." When Benezet jumped on complaints about native scalping and selling of colonial captives in 1760 and compared it to the Anglo-American production of African wars for captives, he showed that radical internationalism was still an option. He demanded a reckoning with the larger imperial context within which slavery had to be attacked if it could ever be effectively reformed. Benezet himself gambled on the American revolutionaries in the next imperial war, while other Quakers made different choices. Benezet won the battle in Pennsylvania, which enacted gradual emancipation in 1780. But he lost the larger struggle, in which the other colonies, now states, found themselves free, religiously and politically, to define sin as they saw fit.[29]

When it came to slavery, Benjamin Franklin had all the answers at a very young age. The problem was that he was listening to other voices, and finding his own, elsewhere. During his years as a statesman, after 1748, he tried to have it both ways. He listened to the prophetic voices he knew so well and agreed with them in private correspondence, promising that in the long run he was on their side. In public venues, he remained silent, fudged, or compromised, mitigating his antislavery instincts with practical politics, and, strikingly by the late 1740s, with a newly explicit racism. The rest of his career followed. He showed respect for Woolman and Benezet, and privately offered to "act in concert" on the matter of slavery in 1773, but did he ever publicly side with them?[30]

Not really. By the late 1760s he knew that the slavery issue was being used against the Americans; Quakers and their antislavery were political hot potatoes, already being used by critics of the American resistance movement in England. At the same time the French intelligentsia praised these Americans, of whom they liked to think Franklin was one, for opposing the fruits of imperialism, which they associated with their absolutist state and decadent nobility. Franklin beat a careful path between the British and the French, as well as his various North American constituencies as a colonial agent. He blamed slavery on the British and minimized its significance in the North and America in general. As the new nation's representative in France, Franklin posed as a Quaker not just by wearing a brown suit but by pretending to be more antislavery than he had ever been publicly.[31] He never held up his end of the bargain with Benezet until after the Constitutional Convention, when he had retired politically and when his home state had already abolished slavery. His presidency of the Pennsylvania Abolition Society in 1787–90 was largely ceremonial, not an active abolitionist stance.[32]

We know what was gained by Franklin's choice: a revolutionary war, and American independence. What was lost when Franklin embraced the marketplace and neutralized religion and antiwar as analytical tools and as motivating forces? Quite a bit. The earlier version of antislavery that Franklin knew as well as anyone was neither narrow nor tamely reformist; it was cosmopolitan, materialist, and theologically rigorous. The real conversion was Franklin's rejection of the "many other Parts" that Pastorius and others associated with antislavery, including antiwar, vegetarianism, and paternalism. Shades of those ideas do reappear in Franklin's writings and politics in a variety of contexts. He can be quoted amply as an advocate of dietary restraint, peace, religious freedom, and humility. That is very different, however, from being an abolitionist, or making the connections between who we exploit, what we eat, and who we are that Tryon and his Quaker followers made so clear.

And what of us and our memory? The best that can be said about our tendency to remember Franklin as a quasi-Quaker abolitionist is that we follow in the footsteps of Lay and Benezet, trying to inspire, manipulate, and wish a printer and politician into being a moral leader and activist.[33] We repeat the polemics of Garrisonian abolitionists, who claimed Franklin as their own. We ratify the Quakers' historical victory, in a sense. But we falsify the history itself, in which they, not Franklin, deserve the lion's share of the credit for the beginning of the end of slavery in Pennsylvania, and beyond.

NOTES

1. Compare Gordon S. Wood, *The Radicalism of the American Revolution* (New York, 1991), 186, with Paul Finkelman, "The Significance and Persistence of Proslavery Thought," in Steven Mintz and John Stauffer eds., *The Problem of Evil: Slavery, Freedom, and the Ambiguities of American Reform* (Amherst, Mass., 2007), 95.

2. The modernity of American slavery and its imperial and colonial nature is most effectively developed in Eric Williams, *Capitalism and Slavery* (Chapel Hill, N.C., 1944), and Robin Blackburn, *The Making of New World Slavery: From the Baroque to the Modern, 1492–1800* (New York, 1999).

3. "Germantown Protest (1688)" in J. William Frost, ed., *The Quaker Origins of Antislavery* (Norwood, Pa., 1980), 69, also at www.yale.edu/glc/aces/germantown.htm; Linda Colley, *Captives* (New York, 2002).

4. As my colleague Ralph F. Young observes in his introduction to the document in *Dissent in America: The Voices That Shaped a Nation* (New York, 2006), 31–32.

5. For useful brief discussions of the protest, see David Brion Davis, *The Problem of Slavery in Western Culture* (1966; New York, 1988), 308–9; Ira V. Brown, "Pennsylvania's Antislavery Pioneers, 1688–1776," *Pennsylvania History* 55 (1988): 62–63; and Patrick M. Erben, "'Honey-Combs' and Paper-Hives': Positioning Francis Daniel Pastorius's Manuscript Writings in Early Pennsylvania," *Early American Literature* 37 (2002): 170–71. The best recent study is Katharine Gerbner, "'We Are Against the Traffick of Men-Body': The Germantown Quaker Protest of 1688 and the Origins of American Abolitionism," *Pennsylvania History* 74 (2007): 149–72, though it exaggerates what was "unique to Germantown."

6. The three meetings' responses are included in most reprintings of the document, including Roger A. Bruns, ed., *Am I Not a Man and a Brother? The Antislavery Crusade of Revolutionary America* (1977; rpt. New York, 1980), 3–5; Alfred F. Young and Terry J. Fife, eds., with Mary E. Janzen, *We the People, Voices and Images of the New Nation* (Philadelphia: Temple University Press, 1993), 31–32.

7. James L. Huston, "The Experiential Basis of the Northern Antislavery Impulse," *Journal of Southern History* 56 (1990): 609–40.

8. *The Autobiography of Benjamin Franklin*, ed. Leonard W. Labaree et al. (New Haven, Conn., 1964), 63, 87.

9. Thomas Tryon, *Some Memoirs of the Life of Mr. Thomas Tryon* (London, 1705); Virginia Smith, "Tryon, Thomas (1634–1703)," *Oxford Dictionary of National Biography* (Oxford, 2004),

also shelob.ocis.temple.edu:2172/view/article/27783, accessed 23 July 2007; Michael V. DePorte, "Introduction" to Thomas Tryon, *A Treatise of Dreams and Visions . . . [and] a Discourse of the Causes, Nature and Cure of Phrensie, Madness or Distraction* [1689], Augustan Reprint Society vol. 160 (Los Angeles, 1973), i–ii. For Tryon and the reading revolution, see for example Kenneth Charlton and Margaret Spufford, "Literacy, Society, and Education," *The Cambridge History of Early Modern English Literature,* ed. David Lowenstein and Janel Mueller (Cambridge, U.K., 2003), 27–31; David Cressy, *Literacy and the Social Order* (New York, 1980), 7, 39; Gillian Suther land, "Education" in F. M. L. Thompson, ed., *The Cambridge Social History of Britain, 1750–1950, Vol. III, Social Agencies and Institutions* (London, 1992), 120.

10. For Tryon's importance in early antislavery, see Davis, *The Problem of Slavery in Western Culture,* 371–74; Wylie Sypher, *Guinea's Captive Kings: British Antislavery Literature of the Eighteenth Century* (Chapel Hill, N.C., 1942), 67–68; Alden T. Vaughan, *Roots of American Racism: Essays on the Colonial Experience* (New York, 1995), 74–76; Dickson D. Bruce Jr., *The Origins of African American Literature, 1680–1815* (Charlottesville, Va., 2001), 22–25, 73, 100; Philippe Rosenberg, "Thomas Tryon and the Seventeenth-Century Dimensions of Antislavery," *William and Mary Quarterly* 61 (2004): 609–42. For the lack of interest in Tryon within Franklin scholarship, see for example J. A. Leo LeMay, *The Life of Benjamin Franklin, Volume One: Journalist, 1706–1730* (Philadelphia, 2006), 215. LeMay devotes more than a chapter to influences on the young Franklin and is the leading expert on Franklin's reading.

11. Rosenberg, "Thomas Tryon and the Seventeenth-Century Dimensions of Antislavery," 640. The Germantown protesters of 1688 also had an "Anabaptist background." Frost, "Introduction," *Quaker Origins of Antislavery,* 29n1. For the Quaker debt to Anabaptists generally, see Arthur T. Worrall, *Quakers in the Colonial Northeast* (Hanover, N.H., 1980), 97; for Anabaptist radicalism, see Peter Linebaugh and Marcus Rediker, *The Many-Headed Hydra: Sailors, Slaves, Commoners, and the Hidden History of the Revolutionary Atlantic* (Boston, 2000), 64–66.

12. For the increased interest in and disillusionment with the (southern) colonies evident in British writing during the 1670s and 1680s, see Matthew Mason, "Slavery, Servitude, and British Representations of Colonial North America," *Southern Quarterly* 43 (Summer 2006): 109; Gary Taylor, *Buying Whiteness: Race, Culture, and Identity from Columbus to Hip Hop* (New York, 2005), 310; Susan Scott Parrish, *American Curiosity: Cultures of Natural History in the Colonial British Atlantic World* (Chapel Hill, N.C., 2006), 19.

13. Steven Shapin, "Vegetable Love," *The New Yorker* 82, no. 46 (Jan. 22, 2007); Anita Guerini, "A Diet for the Sensitive Soul: Vegetarianism in Eighteenth-Century Britain," *Eighteenth-Century Life* 23 (1999): 34; Tristram Stuart, *The Bloodless Revolution: A Cultural History of Vegetarianism from 1600 to Modern Times* (New York, 2007), 60–77. Keith Thomas sees Tryon as having "carried on the authentic radical tradition of the Interregnum" in *Man and the Natural World: A History of the Modern Sensibility* (New York, 1983), 291. For an especially penetrating analysis that brings Tryon's agendas together, see Kim F. Hall, "'Extravagant Viciousness': Slavery and Gluttony in the Works of Thomas Tryon," in Philip D. Beidler and Gary Taylor, eds., *Writing Race Across the Atlantic World* (New York, 2005), 93–112. In the most thorough treatment to date, Philippe Rosenberg also calls for a less sectarian reading of Tryon, while also critiquing the tendency of historians of antislavery to see Tryon's thinking as a crude or primitive anticipation of later trends ("Thomas Tryon and the Seventeenth-Century Dimensions of Antislavery").

14. *A Dialogue Between an East-Indian Brackmanny or Heathen-Philosopher, and a French Gentleman Concerning the Present Affairs of Europe* (London, 1683), 2–3, 5–7, 11–12, 18–21.

15. Tryon, *The Way to Health, Long Life and Happiness* (London, 1683), 27, 31, 36, 241.

16. Tryon, *Friendly Advice to the Gentlemen-Planters of the East and West Indies. In Three Parts* (London, 1684), 75–222; Tryon, *The Country-man's Companion* (London, 1684), 143–63; Tryon, *The Planter's Speech to His Neighbours and Countrymen of Pennsylvania, East and West Jersey* (London, 1684). Contemporary scholarship suggests that Tryon's analysis of developments in the last half of the seventeenth century was absolutely correct. Edmund Morgan, *American Slavery, American Freedom: The Ordeal of Colonial Virginia* (New York, 1975); John Thornton, *Africa and Africans in the Making of the Atlantic World, 1480–1800* (2nd ed., New York, 2000); Alan Gallay, *The Indian Slave Trade: The Rise of the English Empire in the American South, 1670–1717* (New Haven, Conn., 2002) ; Fred Anderson and Andrew R. L. Cayton, *The Dominion of War: Empire and Liberty in North America, 1500–2000* (New York, 2004); Stephanie Smallwood, *Saltwater Slavery: A Middle Passage from Africa to American Diaspora* (Cambridge, Mass., 2007).

17. Tryon, "The Planter's Speech" in *Country-man's Companion*, 104; Tryon, *A New Method of Educating Children* (London, 1695); Rosenberg, "Thomas Tryon and the Seventeenth-Century Dimensions of Antislavery," 617–18. Carla Gerona calls Tryon a "fellow traveler" of Quakers and considers his treatise on dreams a codification of Quaker dream theory. Carla Gerona, *Night Journeys: The Power of Dreams in Transatlantic Quaker Culture* (Charlottesville, Va., 2004), 101.

18. John Hepburn, *The American defence of the Christian golden rule, or An essay to prove the unlawfulness of making slaves of men* (n.p., 1715), preface, 8–9, 12–13, 15–16; Davis, *The Problem of Slavery in Western Culture,* 318.

19. Davis, *The Problem of Slavery in Western Culture,* 346; David Waldstreicher, *Runaway America: Benjamin Franklin, Slavery, and the American Revolution* (New York, 2004), chaps. 2–3.

20. Franklin, *Autobiography,* 87–89.

21. Bills from E. E. [H. S.] Warner and Charles Moore, Volume 66, Folios 46a and 71a, Benjamin Franklin Papers, American Philosophical Society; J. A. Leo LeMay, ed., *Franklin: Writings* (New York, 1987), 145–51; LeMay, *The Canon of Benjamin Franklin* (Newark, Del., 1987), 42–46; *Pennsylvania Gazette,* July 30, 1730, in Leonard W. Labaree et al., eds., *The Papers of Benjamin Franklin* (New Haven, Conn., 1959–), vol. 1: 187 (hereafter *PBF*); "Apology for Printers," *Pennsylvania Gazette,* June 10, 1731 in *PBF* 1: 194–99; see also Franklin, "With Trial at Mount Holly," *Pennsylvania Gazette,* Oct, 22, 1730, in *PBF* 1: 182–3, and *Autobiography,* 71.

22. Franklin, "Dialogue Between Two Presbyterians," *Pennsylvania Gazette,* April 10, 1735; Franklin, *Some Observations on the Proceedings Against the Rev. Mr. Hemphill; with a Vindication of his Sermons* (Philadelphia, 1735); Franklin, *A Letter to a Friend in the Country* (Philadelphia, 1735), all in *PBF* 2: 27, 37–65, 66–67, 71, 84.

23. Ralph Sandiford, *A Brief Examination of the Practice of the Times* (Philadelphia, 1729), 17–20, 22, 24–25, 38, 41; *Pennsylvania Gazette,* Dec. 22, Jan. 26, 1731; Roberts Vaux, *Memoirs of the Lives of Benjamin Lay and Ralph Sandiford* (Philadelphia, 1815), 59–73; Thomas E. Drake, *Quakers and Slavery in America* (New Haven, Conn., 1950), 39–42.

24. Benjamin Lay, *All Slave-keepers That Keep the Innocent in Bondage* (Philadelphia, 1737), 19–21.

25. Ibid., 32–33, 77, 106, 271; Vaux, *Memoirs of the Lives of Benjamin Lay and Ralph Sandiford,* 17, 20, 24, 32; Drake, *Quakers and Slavery in America,* 43–44; Andreas Miekle, "An Inquiry Concerning Benjamin and Sarah Lay, Abolitionists," *Quaker History* 86 (1997): 22–44. According to

Benjamin Rush in 1798, this print was "seen in many homes in Philadelphia," and Lay actually did "frequently" carry Tryon's book. Rush, *Essays, Literary, Moral and Philosophical* (1798; 2nd ed. Philadelphia, 1806), 299, cited in Wilford S. P. Cole, "Henry Dawkins and the Quaker Comet," *Winterthur Portfolio* 4 (1968): 43.

26. Vaux, *Memoirs of the Lives of Benjamin Lay and Ralph Sandiford*, 28, 32; Davis, *The Problem of Slavery in Western Culture*, 321–24; Drake, *Quakers and Slavery in America*, 43–46; Jean R. Soderlund, *Quakers and Slavery: A Divided Spirit* (Princeton, N J , 1985), 16.

27. Lay, *All Slave-keepers That Keep the Innocent in Bondage*, 10–11, 16, 272.

28. Ledger A & B, 174, Ledger D, 89, Benjamin Franklin Papers, American Philosophical Society; *Pennsylvania Gazette*, Aug. 10, Nov. 2, 1738; *Pennsylvania Gazette*, March 25, 1742, in *PBF* 2: 357; Franklin to Deborah Franklin, June 10, 1758, *PBF* 8: 92; Vaux, *Memoirs of the Lives of Benjamin Lay and Ralph Sandiford*, 37, 48. Lay urged his readers to go to Franklin's shop to find Robert Barclay's *Apology for the True Christian Divinity.* Lay, *All Slave-keepers That Keep the Innocent in Bondage*, 170.

29. Francis Jennings, *Benjamin Franklin, Politician: The Mask and the Man* (New York, 1996), 48, 64–64; Richard Bauman, *For the Reputation of Truth: Politics, Religion, and Conflict Among the Pennsylvania Quakers* (Baltimore, 1971), 93, 193–94; Davis, *The Problem of Slavery in Western Culture*, 330; Jack Marietta, *The Reformation of American Quakerism* (Philadelphia, 1984), 111–28; Soderlund, *Quakers and Slavery*, 26–31; Maurice Jackson, "The Social and Intellectual Origins of Anthony Benezet's Antislavery Radicalism," *Pennsylvania History* 66, Supplement (1999): 89; Gerona, *Night Journeys*, 155 (quoted), 179; Michael Meranze, "Materializing Conscience: Embodiment, Speech, and the Experience of Sympathetic Identification," *Early American Literature* 37 (2002): 101–18; Anthony Benezet, *Observations on the Inslaving, Importing, and Purchasing of Negroes* (Germantown, Pa., 1760), 3, 5; Phillips P. Moulton ed., *The Journal and Major Essays of John Woolman* (New York, 1971), 61–62, 232–33.

30. Franklin to Anthony Benezet, Feb. 10, 1773, *PBF* 20: 40–41; Anthony Benezet to Granville Sharp, April 1773, in Roberts Vaux, *Memoirs of the Life of Anthony Benezet* (York, U.K., 1817), 47; Gary B. Nash, "Franklin and Slavery," *Proceedings of the American Philosophical Society* 150 (Dec. 2006): 618–35. Nash concludes that Franklin had undergone "an important change," 631. For an interpretation closer to my own, see Emma Lapsansky-Werner, "At the End, an Abolitionist?" in Page Talbott, ed., *Benjamin Franklin: In Search of a Better World* (New Haven, Conn., 2005), 273–97.

31. Franklin's skill at depicting the British as war-mongers and enslavers during these years suggests, rather, a selective appropriation of the Tryonist-Quaker legacy for American nationalist purposes.

32. See Waldstreicher, *Runaway America*, chaps. 8–9.

33. Early nineteenth-century abolitionists did better, though, with their own forebears, publishing biographies of Lay by Roberts Vaux and Lydia Maria Child, for example. John Greenleaf Whittier wrote a poem about Pastorius and the Germantown Protest.

CHAPTER 3

Self-Help and Self-Determination

Black Philadelphians and the Dimensions of Freedom

JULIE WINCH

At the state convention of "colored citizens" that met in Harrisburg in December 1848, the seven-man organizing committee issued a bold statement outlining their agenda. "Our fathers sought personal freedom . . . but now we contend for political freedom."[1] On the face of it they seemed to be declaring that one phase of the struggle people of African descent in Pennsylvania had been engaged in for decades was over. Now the heirs of the "fathers" (and not a few of the mothers) who had prevailed in the contest for "personal freedom" were vowing to fight on for something more, for "political freedom."

Did their talk of one struggle having been brought to a successful conclusion and another about to begin mean the delegates believed slavery had been dealt its death blow? Hardly. It was true that in 1847 Pennsylvania lawmakers had voted to end slavery once and for all, almost seventy years after the passage of the state's landmark Gradual Abolition Act.[2] But slavery was not a dead issue for the "colored citizens" of Pennsylvania, as convention delegates were painfully aware. All seven of the men who penned the statement about "political freedom" and seemingly juxtaposed it to "personal freedom" understood only too well that the contest was far from over. All seven—five of them from Philadelphia, home to the largest concentration of African Americans in Pennsylvania, and one of the largest in the Union—had risked their own freedom time and time again to shelter runaway slaves who made it across the Mason-Dixon Line.[3] And when Congress approved a far more stringent Fugitive Slave Law in 1850, they would go on doing so. None was apathetic about slavery. One of their number, Robert Purvis, was a charter member of the American Anti-Slavery Society. Several more were active in abolitionist organizations at the state and national levels.[4] All understood the impact that slavery had in innumerable ways on the daily lives of black people across Pennsylvania.

Slavery as an institution was dead in their home state, but not throughout the nation. And even in Philadelphia, even in the City of Brotherly Love, a beacon of hope to thousands of fugitives from the "peculiar institution," slavery's legacy was visible everywhere. One need only spend a day or two in the city to understand that black people experienced economic marginalization, that they were frequently the targets of racial violence, and that, in terms of the rights they enjoyed, they were essentially non-citizens. When the duly accredited delegates from Philadelphia—Purvis, his old friend William Whipper, long-time activists Samuel Van Brackle and James J. G. Bias, together with Mifflin Wistar Gibbs, a representative of the "rising generation"—boarded the train for Harrisburg on their way to the convention, they were not preparing to turn their backs on the war against slavery to focus exclusively on "political freedom." They were readying themselves to fight for an end to all that slavery had stood for and continued to stand for. "Personal freedom" and "political freedom" were inextricably linked. As long as slavery existed anywhere in the Union, the struggle was far from ended. In a little over a decade after the Harrisburg convention, Purvis and his colleagues would mobilize their community for war—not an ideological war, but a war in the bloodiest and most literal sense—to achieve both "personal" and "political freedom." They understood, as did so many of the women and men in their community, that they were engaged in an ongoing struggle that had its roots in the colonial era, when slavery in Philadelphia was an ever-present reality, and had continued ever since, broadening in scope to encompass the end of chattel slavery and the eradication of slavery's bitter legacy of discrimination.

(1)

For those black Philadelphians who came of age in the period from 1775 to 1800, the unifying experience was enslavement. An individual like James Forten, who would emerge as a leading opponent of slavery and one of the most successful of the city's black entrepreneurs, was a rarity. Freeborn, the child of free parents, he had never known what it was to be someone's property. He and the other 150 or so free people of color in the Philadelphia of the early 1770s lived a strange existence—not slaves, but not entitled by law or custom to the rights and privileges their white neighbors enjoyed.[5]

On the eve of the revolution, slaves were everywhere in Philadelphia, not just in the homes of elite whites. Plenty of the "middling sort" considered a slave or two a good investment. The enslaved served in a wide range of capacities—in private homes, in workshops, on the wharves and in the ship-yards, rope-walks and sail-lofts that lined the Delaware. And while it is an overstatement to say the city could not have functioned without slave labor, it certainly could not have functioned *as well.*[6]

For all of the city's long-standing commitment to the institution of slavery, though, the number of slaves actually declined as the colonial era drew to a close. One estimate is that there were 1,400 slaves in Philadelphia in 1767, but fewer than 700 by the time the War for Independence began. Only a small part of that decline can be attributed to a changing moral climate. The root cause was demographic. Simply put, more slaves were dying than were being born or imported.[7]

Some whites did experience moral and religious qualms about holding their fellow human beings in bondage, but most found it easy to dismiss the likes of abolitionists Benjamin Lay, John Woolman, and Anthony Benezet as meddlesome and misguided. By 1775, however, the pressure they and a hand-ful of their sympathizers had been exerting, combined with the slow rate of natural increase among the slave population and changing economic realities for some slaveholders in Philadelphia, had begun to have an impact. A few people liberated their slaves outright or bequeathed them their freedom. Oth-ers entered into negotiations with their slaves, accepting a pledge of faithful service for a term of years in return for eventual freedom. A fortunate few bondmen and bondwomen even managed to accumulate enough money to buy themselves. But prevailing on the white community as a whole to outlaw slavery was a tough sell. Even the Society of Friends, which in 1775, after years of internal dissension, condemned outright the practice of slaveholding, suf-fered defections, with some Quakers preferring to abandon their faith rather than give up their slaves.[8]

The members of Philadelphia's enslaved population were not prepared to wait patiently until the law changed or a slaveholder had an attack of guilt. If not as rebellious collectively as their counterparts in New York City, the slaves of Philadelphia proved they could be troublesome in a multitude of ways.[9] There were plenty of complaints from masters about recalcitrant slaves who refused to obey orders, stubbornly resisted attempts to teach them new skills, ignored curfews, laughed at threats of physical punishment, and above all absconded.

Some made good their escape. Others were recaptured, only to flee again when an opportunity presented itself. And then an opportunity arose that was greater and more alluring than any that had come their way before. War broke out between the colonies and Britain. Faced with the threat of persecution, and possibly imprisonment, Loyalist masters fled the city that had become the seat of the new revolutionary government. When Philadelphia Tories hurriedly gathered their families and their prized possessions in preparation for a move to a friendlier setting, some of those "possessions" made sure they were nowhere to be found. The slaves of Patriot owners got *their* chance towards the end of 1777, when British troops marched in and took over the city, prompting significant numbers of "rebel" masters to beat a hasty retreat—in some cases a retreat so hasty that they left their slaves behind.

The belief that the British represented freedom was already firmly entrenched among Philadelphia's slaves, as it was among slaves in many other communities, thanks to the actions of Lord Dunmore, the royal governor in Virginia. His appeal to the slaves of masters disloyal to the king to rally to his standard gained him hundreds of recruits, and sent shock waves far beyond Virginia. Masters condemned him, but slaves were heartened. The rumor going the rounds in Philadelphia that slaves were openly defying whites and telling them to wait until "[L]ord Dumore and his black regiment come" might have been nothing more than a rumor, but there were plenty of slaves in the city who looked on the British as liberators. And during the British occupation General Howe did indeed authorize the recruiting of a company of "black pioneers" to keep the streets clean and perform other essential tasks. Fed, clothed, and paid by the British, most of the "black pioneers" left with the British when they pulled out. Others simply did not wait around for the return of their Patriot masters.[10]

In 1780, in the midst of the war, white lawmakers did what the opponents of slavery had been urging them to do for so long. They enacted a gradual abolition law. On the surface that law seemed benevolent. Its framers stated in the preamble that they were grateful that "it is in our power to extend a portion of that freedom to others, which hath been extended to us."[11] It is important to remember, however, how "gradual" abolition was to be. In theory, not a single slave alive on the day the law was passed would ever be freed. To qualify for freedom you had to be born in Pennsylvania to an enslaved mother on or after March 1, 1780. Until age twenty-eight you would be bound to your mother's owner. Years of your productive working life would be spent toiling for that person's benefit. Even with all the restrictions the law imposed, so many slaveholders sought to circumvent it that further measures were needed to prevent abuses.[12]

But "freedom," even many years in the future, was still freedom. The changes wrought by the law, the uncertainty of being able to control one's slaves, economic instability, and, in some cases, serious reflections about the morality of slavery, induced substantial numbers of slaveowners to act. Philadelphia did not become a haven of black freedom overnight, but by the time the Founding Fathers gathered in the city to draft the Constitution it was home to several thousand people of color, some free, others enslaved, and still others in a twilight zone between slavery and freedom.

As the architects of the Constitution set about their work, a dozen or so black Founding Fathers were engaged in their own institution-building. The Free African Society came into being in 1787, ostensibly as a mutual benefit society, but from the start it was much more. Its officers, most of whom had been enslaved, set themselves up as the arbiters of moral behavior for the entire African American community. Black people were urged to "lay aside . . . gaming and feasting," and remember the many thousands still "starving under cruel bondage." Any lapses on their part would be seized upon by the defenders of slavery to make the case that black people were "not fit for freedom."[13]

Richard Allen, the eloquent Methodist preacher who helped establish the Free African Society (FAS), explained in his autobiography how and why its formation had preceded the creation of separate black churches. Not only was there a shortage of funds, but he admitted there had also been an initial reluctance on the part of many black Philadelphians to take what they saw as a radical step.[14] Those churches did come into being, though, as whites reacted with hostility to the idea of worshiping alongside free blacks, and as people of color became convinced of the need to take control of their own spiritual lives.

By 1793 two separate African American congregations were being formed in the city. One, which would emerge the following year as St. Thomas's African Episcopal Church, had considerable white support. It was headed by a long-time friend of Allen's, Absalom Jones. Like Allen, Jones had been a slave, and, like Allen, he had managed to buy his way out of bondage. Allen, a fiercely independent man, would not abandon Methodism, even though many of Philadelphia's white Methodists had refused to receive him as a brother. His congregation, which would eventually become Mother Bethel, grew more slowly than Jones's at first, but in time it would be the nucleus for a separate black denomination, the African Methodist Episcopal Church.[15]

Founded by men who knew only too well what slavery was, the two churches offered spiritual solace and practical aid to people grappling with the challenges of freedom. St. Thomas's first baptismal register, for instance, can be read as a profoundly antislavery document. Black parents were asserting their ownership of their children in a way they had not been able to do while they had been enslaved. They were also laying claim to themselves. Presenting themselves for adult baptism, the members of that first generation were seeking new identities. Those who had been baptized in their masters' churches were insisting on a second, more meaningful baptism in a place and from a minister of their own choosing.[16]

St. Thomas's and Mother Bethel had grown out of the non-denominational Free African Society and would quickly take over its major functions. Most obviously they would exercise moral oversight, but they would also give birth to a network of mutual aid societies. FAS members had made regular contributions to a fund each member in good standing could draw upon in times of need. The churches followed up on that initiative. In 1795 the men at St. Thomas's organized the African Friendly Society. The following year the church's women members established the Female Benevolent Society. Thereafter, the number of such societies grew steadily. As other black congregations appeared, more societies sprang up. Most churches had at least two, one for men and another for women. Occupations spawned their own societies. African American coachmen had one, as did porters. By 1831 the community had forty-four. By 1838 there were over eighty. Some were short-lived, while others survived for decades.[17]

Mutual benefit societies met a multiplicity of needs. Few black city-dwellers could feel financially secure. Illness, the death of a breadwinner, or simply a falling-out with an employer could leave a family destitute. White charity was uncertain, and freedom to starve was, as the defenders of slavery were quick to point out, a very dubious freedom indeed. As for promoting abolition, the very existence of the societies challenged notions that African Americans were incapable of managing their own lives.

Economic necessity, coupled with the stereotype of black people as criminally inclined, lay at the heart of the crisis that beset the community in 1793. Before the autumn frosts killed off the swarms of disease-bearing mosquitoes, some five thousand Philadelphians succumbed to yellow fever, the first outbreak of the deadly affliction in a generation. Scores of black citizens joined in the relief effort, helping with everything from tending to the sick to burying the dead. In his account of the tragedy, publisher Mathew Carey praised some of the black nurses but took aim at others for allegedly plundering the homes of those they had ostensibly come to help. Incensed by the aspersions cast upon their community, Richard Allen and Absalom Jones rushed into print with their *Narrative of the Proceedings of the Black People During the Late Awful Calamity*. What was on one level simply a refutation of Carey's slanders was also a carefully crafted plea for a shift in racial attitudes. The message to white Philadelphians was that they should see their African American neighbors as they were—judge them by what they saw and knew of them, and not by what they heard from their detractors. The ministers also hammered home their message by appending to the *Narrative* an antislavery discourse they entitled "A Short Address to Those Who Keep Slaves and Uphold the Practice."[18]

Yellow fever returned again and again through the 1790s, claiming thousands more victims. Each outbreak provided a vehicle for black Philadelphians to reiterate by their conduct the message Jones and Allen had endeavored to send to whites in 1793, namely that they were a people worthy of freedom and full citizenship. In 1798, for instance, St. Thomas's joined various white churches in petitioning the authorities for strict enforcement of laws against "vice and immorality" in hopes of averting divine wrath and warding off yet another visit from what had become almost an annual scourge. Black Philadelphians, or at least those who worshipped at St. Thomas's, publicly aligned themselves with "that part of the community . . . which best deserves encouragement and protection" on account of their devotion to religion and sound morality.[19]

Clearly, some white Philadelphians were prepared to concede that there were those in the African American community who merited "encouragement and protection," and some, at least, were willing to reach out to their black neighbors. It is not easy to gauge the extent of black-white interaction in this early period. There were no black-owned newspapers, nor were there any explicitly antislavery journals that might have reported on interracial initiatives of one kind or another. Nevertheless, by looking closely at the material that *is* available—letters, diaries, stray mentions in the mainstream press, and the minutes of a range of institutions—one gets glimpses into a past that was not wholly segregated by race.

For instance, although forbidden from doing so by their own Lodge, a handful of white Freemasons took to visiting the African Lodge after its formation in 1797. From time to time the Lodges marched together. In 1797, diarist

Elizabeth Drinker remarked on a parade that featured both black and white Masons, and in 1800 the officers of the African Lodge expressed their pleasure at receiving an invitation to join in observances for their late brother Mason, George Washington.[20] The African Lodge, with its relatively high membership fees and its emphasis on ritual, was unlikely to appeal to the majority of black men, and of course women had no part in its activities, so did it help to advance the cause of black freedom? In a sense it did, for Freemasons belonged to a brotherhood that (in theory) knew no lines of race. And a Freemason was by definition "free."

Some white Masons might extend the fraternal hand, some white church members might welcome black people to worship with them or collaborate with them in reforming the less godly part of society, and there were probably more friendships across the lines of race than we are aware of. But if there was one group more than any other that could be expected to be sensitive to the concerns of the African American community it was the men who made up the membership of the Pennsylvania Abolition Society.

Because it is often referred to by its abbreviated title, it is easy to forget how broad the scope of the PAS actually was. When it was first organized in 1775 it was dedicated to "the Relief of Free Negroes Unlawfully Held in Bondage," in other words, the rescuing of those who legally entitled to their liberty. Upon its re-establishment in 1784 it incorporated into its title "the Abolition of Slavery" and "Improving the Condition of the Colored Race."[21]

Although the PAS did not admit its first African American member until the 1840s, it reached out to the growing black population in many ways. It investigated abuses of the Gradual Abolition Law, often after having been alerted to those abuses by concerned members of the African American community. The PAS helped black churches operate schools. It brokered freedom contracts and found suitable placements for black "apprentices"—those individuals who were to be liberated at age twenty-eight under the Abolition Law. It also took note of the small but energetic black business class. Absalom Jones, Richard Allen, James Forten, and others in a position to offer employment and job-training were approached by the PAS and asked to hire apprentices.[22]

Occasionally the PAS sent one of its officers to a black church or benevolent society to deliver a lecture on the need for adherence to strict moral standards. To our ears today these lectures have a patronizing ring, but it is worth remembering that the community was accustomed to hearing such lectures from its own leaders. Moreover, many PAS members also belonged to organizations that targeted the white poor, and they preached to them essentially the same message of thrift, piety, and the value of honest labor. And certainly black audiences responded in a manner that encouraged the PAS to persist in its efforts. In 1801, for example, the Friendly Society of St. Thomas expressed the members' thanks "for the unceasing anxiety . . . you manifest for the temporal and eternal happiness of the African race."[23] Well aware that they had relatively few white well-wishers, free people of color and those still working their way towards freedom were in no position to criticize paternalism, even if they had been inclined to do so.

Throughout this first period of activism, and far beyond, the African American community and the PAS campaigned to end slavery once and for all. Apart from pursuing through the courts violators of the Gradual Abolition Law, the PAS made regular representations to the state and national governments, as did free people of color. How far they coordinated their efforts is a matter of conjecture. Certainly some of the most forceful defenders of slavery voiced the opinion that black people were incapable of independent action. That was abundantly clear in the response to the petition some seventy men of color from Philadelphia submitted to Congress in December 1799. "The Petition of the People of Colour, Freemen within the City and Suburbs of Philadelphia," came before the House early in the New Year. It was couched in highly respectful terms. "We do not wish," the petitioners wrote, "for the immediate emancipation of all, knowing that the degraded state of many . . . would greatly disqualify for such a change; but humbly desire you may exert every means in your power to . . . prepare the way for the oppressed to go free."[24] Lawmakers reacted with a mix of rage and derision. On the one hand, they insisted the petitioners were too ignorant to have thought of such an approach: they must be the tools of their meddling white friends in the PAS. On the other hand, they maintained the petition proved black people had become dangerously infected by the "new-fangled French philosophy of liberty and equality." The illogic of this did not seem to strike most of the congressmen. The petitioners could not be at one and the same time ignorant dupes and wily and articulate "philosophers" intent on bringing the bloody excesses of the French Revolution to America's shores. That they only wanted exactly what they asked for—a pledge from the nation's government "to prepare the way for the oppressed to go free"—was something lawmakers could not comprehend.[25]

Rebuffed by the national government, black Philadelphians turned to the state government, offering to pay a special tax to secure immediate freedom for all those who remained in bondage in Pennsylvania. That initiative went nowhere.[26] But with or without legislative action, there was reason for guarded optimism. Chattel slavery was ceasing to be a viable institution in Philadelphia. In 1790 there were 387 slaves out of a total black population of 2,489. By 1800 that number had dwindled to 85 out of 6,880.[27] The battle for "personal freedom" was not over, even in Philadelphia, but the members of that first generation could look back on significant victories.

(2)

By 1810 over 9,500 people of color called Philadelphia and its adjoining districts home. Plenty of white Philadelphians grumbled that that figure failed to take into account several thousand runaways from the South who assiduously avoided the census takers. A decade later the official tally was over 12,000.[28] The city's growing African American population evoked a wide range of responses from white residents, and those responses in turn prompted black community leaders to direct their energies in certain specific ways. The issues confronting the men and women who came of age in the period from 1800 to 1830 would be the consolidation of what the earlier generation had won in terms of "personal freedom," leading them to devise new strategies to enhance their status as full-fledged members of the larger community.

There *were* reasons to be hopeful. The action of the federal government in outlawing the overseas slave trade induced many of Philadelphia's abolitionists, black and white, to believe this might be the first step towards total emancipation. The planning of suitable observances to mark the day the ban was to come into effect, January 1, 1808, began in the summer of 1807. On New Year's Day, hundreds of black Philadelphians marched in solemn procession to St. Thomas's Church to hear Absalom Jones deliver a sermon.[29] The tradition continued, and the annual Thanksgiving addresses showcased the talents of the community's preachers. By 1830, however, it had become painfully obvious that the ending of the slave trade did not mean abolition was at hand. The ban on importations had actually led to a thriving domestic market for slaves. Free people discovered that they had to be on their guard. Each year, dozens of black Philadelphians were spirited away to the South, never to be heard of again. Organized kidnapping gangs and opportunistic individuals preyed on the unwary, eager to supply the needs of southern planters who could no longer secure new supplies of slaves from Africa.[30]

While some white Philadelphians victimized their African American neighbors by breaking the law, others turned to the law to accomplish essentially
the same thing. They had a litany of complaints. There were too many blacks
in the city. They were responsible for a wide range of criminal acts. They could
not support themselves and often made no effort to do so. Again and again
during the first decade of the new century, whites petitioned lawmakers in
Harrisburg for curbs on black migration into the state, the harsh punishment
of black vagrants, and lengthy prison terms for black lawbreakers.[31]

The African American community tried in many different ways to prove
that most of its members were hard working and law abiding. Numerous
self-help organizations sprang up. More churches came into being. More
benevolent societies were formed. Schools were opened across the city, some
operated by churches and some by private citizens, black and white. Not until
1822, however, would the city itself begin educating the children of its black
residents.[32]

Despite the best efforts of the African American community and its friends,
disgruntled whites kept up the pressure for restrictive legislation. In 1813, in
the midst of a second war with Britain, that pressure resulted in a bill that
stood a good chance of passing the Pennsylvania Senate. Among other things,
the new law would require black people to register within twenty-four hours
of entering the state. It would also empower judges to bind out black (but not
white) felons for a term of years to compensate their victims. The responses
were sadly predictable. The PAS and "sundry free people of colour" begged
lawmakers to reconsider, while various groups of whites urged the inclusion
of even more stringent provisions.[33]

The bill did not pass, but it would not be the last of its kind debated in Harrisburg. In the short term, though, Philadelphians had more on their minds
than legal restrictions. The war was going very badly, and by the summer of
1814 it seemed a conquering British army, fresh from its destruction of Washington, D.C., had its sights set on Philadelphia. Every able-bodied man was
summoned to labor on a huge defensive earthwork. African Americans came
out in droves. On one level this was a response to a common crisis, but on a
deeper level it was a demonstration to white people that their black neighbors
were worthy of respect, not fear, resentment, and second-class status.[34]

Ultimately the city's defenses were never put to the test, although the community of color was not shy about keeping its wartime contribution fresh in
the public mind. Black orators spoke of it so often that it became "a matter

of public notoriety."[35] They had good reason to do so because the years ahead would witness a concerted effort to deny black people any place in the life of Philadelphia, or indeed of the nation as a whole.

From its infancy, the American Colonization Society was beset by contradictions. The influential white men who gathered in Washington, D.C., in December 1816 to organize it ran the gamut from steadfast foes of human bondage to zealous defenders of the slave system. While a discussion of the origins of the ACS is beyond the scope to this essay, it is important to note that its title alluded to the colonization of free people of color "with their consent." How precisely that consent was to be secured depended on which of the ACS's promoters was describing its goals. Some looked to a general emancipation in the not-too-distant future, followed by the removal of the ex-slaves to West Africa, where they could establish a self-governing republic. Others had in mind the deportation—to Africa or any other suitably remote location—of those who were already free, lest they infect the slave population with unsettling notions of liberty.[36]

News of the proceedings in Washington reached Philadelphia early in 1817 and led to the calling of a mass meeting at Mother Bethel. It was a meeting at which unanimity did not prevail, for there were those, among them Absalom Jones, Richard Allen, and James Forten, who had been contemplating for some time the notion of a refuge in Africa for at least some black people if it could be coupled with the ending of slavery. They envisaged thousands of newly liberated slaves venturing across the Atlantic to make homes for themselves on a distant shore, just as waves of Europeans were making the journey across the same ocean for a fresh start in America. If the ACS was committed to just such an agenda, they considered it worthy of their support.[37] For many black Philadelphians, however, the ACS's agenda was deeply troubling. Its founders might talk of "consent," but *they* heard "coercion." They also rejected the ACS's claim to be antislavery. For them to emigrate, they insisted, would be to forsake those still held in bondage. "They are our brethren by the ties of consanguinity, of suffering, and of wrongs; and we feel that there is more virtue in suffering privations with them, than fancied advantages for a season."[38]

Over the ensuing months black leaders came around to the point of view of their constituents. Meanwhile, among white abolitionists, including those in the Pennsylvania Abolition Society, the question of colonization generated intense debate. Outside the ranks of the abolitionists there were many other whites who cared nothing about slavery and the slave trade: they embraced the scheme because it seemed best calculated to rid them of free people of color as a class.[39]

The popularity of the ACS with white Philadelphians forced African Americans to confront an unpalatable truth. Freedom had not brought acceptance. They redoubled their efforts to plant themselves in the heart of the city and make good on their claims to inclusion and equality. They re-emphasized the need for education. They collaborated with city officials to root out lawlessness. They agitated and argued. They took on their detractors, wherever they were to be found, and they maintained their pressure on the slave system, convinced their situation would never truly improve as long as the notion endured that black people were property rather than persons.[40]

(3)

By 1830 Philadelphia's African American community defied easy categorization. Women and men whose families had called the city home for a century or more lived side by side with newcomers and the children of newcomers. West Indians rubbed shoulders with New Englanders. New Yorkers worked and worshipped alongside people from the Lower South. Fugitive slaves tried to lie low and avoid anyone who might be hunting for them. Free people sent scurrying north in the wake of slave rebellions endeavored to adjust to life in a new setting. It was a sad fact that every rebellion of the enslaved produced free black refugees. That was true in 1822, after Denmark Vesey's abortive uprising in South Carolina. It was equally true in 1831, as the shock waves from Nat Turner's bloody rampage in Virginia reverberated through the South. Unwilling to look to the slave system for the root cause, vengeful whites invariably turned on the supposed instigators of servile rebellion, the free people of color. Many were forced to leave their southern homes under threat of harsh new legal restrictions on their daily lives, or the all too real possibility of violent reprisals. Philadelphia was the first safe haven for these free black victims of the slave system, just as it was for the fugitive slaves.[41]

The 1830 census recorded the presence of over 14,500 people of color in Philadelphia—the city itself and districts such as Moyamensing that did not become jurisdictionally part of the city until the Consolidation Act of 1854. By 1840 the total was almost 20,000. As for population distribution, no ward or district was without at least a few black inhabitants, but some had far more than others. In 1830, one in four residents of New Market Ward was black. The figure for Locust Ward was almost the same. In Cedar Ward, on Philadelphia's southern fringe, 19 percent of the population was black, but just a few blocks away the composition of the population was strikingly different, with African Americans making up only 5.6 percent of the population in Chestnut Ward and 4.3 percent in High Street Ward.[42]

Being concentrated in certain sections of the city was a mixed blessing. Rioters searching for black targets knew where to find them. At the same time, though, a neighborhood like the South Street corridor (roughly between Pine on the north, Shippen or Bainbridge on the south, Eleventh on the west, and the Delaware on the east) was a vibrant hub of community life. Black churches, lodges, schools, and businesses abounded, making this an attractive neighborhood for African American families to live in.[43]

White social commentator John Fanning Watson looked at the African American community in 1830 and did not like what he saw. In "the good old days" black people "knew their place." How things had changed! "Once they submitted to the appellation of servants, blacks, or negroes, but now they require to be called coloured people."[44] Joseph Willson, an affluent and well-educated man of color from Georgia, could only lament the tendency of whites in his adopted city to see black people "as one consolidated mass, all huddled together, without any particular or general distinctions, social or otherwise."[45]

The community had moved a long way from what it had been in 1780, when lawmakers had wrestled with the question of abolition, and bondmen and bondwomen had endeavored to free themselves from the shackles of slavery in the midst of the Revolutionary War. It was far larger, far more diverse, and had an identifiable class structure—identifiable at least to black Philadelphians and to those whites who cared to look. At its apex were those Watson resented and Edward Clay lampooned in his "Life in Philadelphia" cartoon series. These were the men and women who constituted what Joseph Willson termed "the higher classes of colored society." At its base were many hundreds "in the lowest depths of human degradation, misery, and want." In between were thousands more, "sober, honest, industrious and respectable—claiming neither 'poverty nor riches.'"[46] A few individuals used their wealth and their ties to prominent whites to separate themselves from the rest of the African American population. Sheer wretchedness prevented others from taking an active role in community affairs, but indifference, whether the result of wealth or want, was not the attitude of most black Philadelphians. They attended church, belonged to moral improvement and mutual aid societies, aspired to educate themselves and their children, and generally worked for their own betterment and that of their neighbors.

There was a cultural richness in the African American community that outsiders often failed to appreciate. By the early 1830s a black Philadelphian in search of intellectual stimulation and congenial company could choose from a number of literary and debating societies. The choice was greater for men than for women, and would have been greater still had people of color not found themselves excluded from the plethora of organizations that purported to welcome all but that were in practice "whites only." On the positive side, the African American societies had an educational function: people who had not had the benefit of much formal schooling could learn in a supportive atmosphere from those who had.[47]

Black literary and debating societies had a purpose far beyond the educational one—or at least beyond the educational purpose of similar societies in the white community. Their very existence furthered the twin causes of antislavery and civil rights by demonstrating to doubting whites the intellectual capacity and aspirations of people of color. They also served as training-grounds for antislavery orators, and in the period after 1830 Philadelphia produced its share of black lecturers who took the antislavery message far beyond the city. In a few cases they carried that message across the ocean. Robert Purvis and Jesse Ewing Glasgow Jr., both graduates of literary and debating societies, spent time in Britain, the one to see the world and settle his white father's business affairs, the other in pursuit of a university education. Much in demand for their speaking abilities, they joined dozens of African American women and men in speaking out about the twin evils of American slavery and American prejudice, and helping to turn public sentiment in Britain against the South and its "peculiar institution."[48]

As the labors of Purvis, Glasgow, and countless other black Philadelphians whose names are not as well known make abundantly clear, central to community endeavors in the period after 1830 was the same cause that had been at the heart of those efforts for decades—the fight against slavery and for equality. For the first generation, and for significant numbers of people in the second generation, the common experience had been enslavement. For the third generation, that was not the case, although there were still plenty of women and men in the city who had known enslavement in the South or who had kinfolk still in bondage.

For the prosperous and largely freeborn minority within a minority who constituted Philadelphia's "higher classes of colored society" in the 1830s and beyond, "abolition" was the social cement that linked them to people like themselves in other northern cities. They wrote antislavery verse, attended antislavery conventions, exchanged antislavery news, made new friends, and even found marriage partners as a result of their devotion to the antislavery struggle.[49] That is not to suggest they were in any way lacking in commitment. It was rather that abolition had become such an integral part of their lives that it provided the focus for many of their activities.

How difficult it is to distinguish between the social and the activist components of an individual's life becomes obvious when one looks at the role of many of the women in the "higher" and even the "middling" classes of "colored society." A typical meeting of the Philadelphia Female Literary Association, for instance, might see the members forgoing the delicacies that graced refreshment tables at such meetings in the white community and contenting themselves with bread and water. The money that would have gone to tea and cakes went instead to feed and shelter the scores of runaway slaves hiding out in the city. These same women kept their hands busy knitting and sewing to provide clothing for their less fortunate neighbors while their minds were occupied with literary matters. As they worked, the secretary would read aloud the writings each had placed anonymously in the box left discreetly on her table for that purpose. They would critique one another's efforts—anonymity shielding each author from embarrassing praise or wounded pride—and decide which pieces were worthy of being sent to *The Liberator* or one of the other antislavery newspapers. Add to that the fact that some of these women belonged to the Female Anti-Slavery Society, and a handful attended women's antislavery conventions, where the slavery of sex was discussed along with the slavery of race, and it is obvious that "abolition" dominated many aspects of their lives.[50]

Far removed from the genteel world of the literary circles were the black mariners who sailed out of Philadelphia to points south. Virtually every vessel clearing the port of Philadelphia had at least one or two African American crew members. Less polished as orators than the likes of Robert Purvis or Jesse Glasgow, less talented as writers than the women and men in the literary societies (and in some cases totally illiterate), they were nevertheless eloquent antislavery lecturers in their own way, carrying to southern ports the message that slavery was not the natural condition of black people. It was the awareness of the threat they posed that prompted southern lawmakers to order free black sailors from Philadelphia and other northern ports held in jail until their ships were ready to depart. They had no wish to see such men mix with their slaves, inform them that there was a world beyond the painfully limited one they knew, and perhaps even spirit them away to the North on board of their vessels.[51]

The growing perception of southern slaveholders that Philadelphia was a hub of antislavery activity and every black resident an abolitionist was not far off the mark. Practical abolition took many forms. It might involve lecturing or writing, but it might just as easily entail reaching out to a man or woman one suspected of being a runaway. A tip about where to find shelter, or a lie told on a newcomer's behalf when the constables came asking, just as effectively struck a blow for abolition.

Over the decades countless black Philadelphians, and not a few whites, had offered a helping hand to fugitives. In 1837 that informal aid became more organized with the creation of the Vigilance Committee.[52] However, the committee could not function without a support system. Black women were particularly active in advancing its work, raising funds to help cover operating expenses and setting up sewing circles to provide the fugitives with clothing. Runaways often arrived in tattered or all-too-easily identifiable garments. By clothing and in essence disguising them, these women were furthering the antislavery cause. The Dorcas Society and other sewing groups also contributed to the welfare of the free community, clothing the children of parents too poor to outfit them for school.[53]

Organized antislavery activities took many forms for the members of this third generation. There *was* an African American abolition society, established by the minister and congregation of the Second Colored Presbyterian Church, but it was short-lived.[54] Most black Philadelphians who opted to join an antislavery society joined one that claimed to welcome all like-minded people without regard to race. It is not easy to gauge how concerned most of the city's African American abolitionists were about the division of abolition into "gradualist" and "immediatist" camps. Robert Purvis, for instance, was a founding member of the American Anti-Slavery Society, but he happily accepted membership in the PAS once it was offered. When local "Garrisonian" affiliates of the AASS sprang up, he and other men of color joined them and took as active a part as they were permitted to do.[55] Ironically, it was the women in the community who enjoyed more real influence. The interracial Philadelphia Female

Anti-Slavery Society needed to draw on the talents of all of its members. Few women, irrespective of race, had any formal administrative experience in an era when home and church were expected to consume all their energies. Women of color helped found the Female Anti-Slavery Society and remained active and involved through the entire period of its existence.[56]

Of the six black national conventions that met between 1830 and 1835, five took place in Philadelphia. In a sense, of course, they could not be truly national. Men from the slave states (and it was only men who were allowed to serve as delegates) attended at their peril. The southernmost state to be represented was Maryland, and that was before Nat Turner's rebellion. Still, community leaders from across the North journeyed to Philadelphia each summer to discuss everything from the founding of a black manual labor college to the duty of God-fearing people of color to observe the Sabbath. These meetings were not antislavery in that they had not been convened for the sole purpose of condemning slavery, but hardly any debate took place that did not castigate slaveholders and those who approved of slaveholding.[57]

When the convention movement was taken over in the mid-1830s by the American Moral Reform Society, the Philadelphians, or at least a group of them, remained in control. The wrangling with prominent men of color from other cities, and eventually within the Philadelphia community, pulled the AMRS apart by 1841, but in some respects that wrangling testified to the vitality of Philadelphia's African American leadership. Not all were of one mind on every issue. The community was diverse enough that there was not and could not be unanimity. Was this a sign of weakness? Yes, but in a sense it was also a sign of strength. People reflected on the issues and argued about them. Philadelphia's African American population was politicized, conscious, reflective, and, above all, very much alive to its own interests. The differences that existed arose over what those interests were and how best to advance them.[58]

Few of the city's black residents had any illusions about the forces ranged against them. In their quest for economic self-sufficiency, for instance, they knew they could expect precious little encouragement. Job opportunities were declining, and such employment as was available was invariably in the most menial of occupations. If one were fortunate enough to have a good trade, there was no guarantee of employment. The *Register of the Trades of the Colored People of the City of Philadelphia*, compiled in 1838 by the PAS, made it abundantly clear that there were plenty of talented African American craftsmen and craftswomen who had no opportunity to use their hard-won skills.[59]

Philadelphia in the 1830s and 1840s was a city under pressure. Waves of immigrants flooded in, looking for work and a place to live. There was labor strife and economic uncertainty. Epidemic diseases—not yellow fever this time but typhoid and cholera—struck with appalling virulence. City services were overwhelmed. Long-simmering tensions frequently boiled over into violence.[60] Black people were not the only victims of the enraged mobs that were a regular feature of the urban scene in Philadelphia during this period, but they were handy targets, since it was well known that the authorities were unlikely to protect them.

Sadly, there was nothing new about racial violence in Philadelphia. What *was* unprecedented in the 1830s and 1840s was the scale of destruction. Anything, it seemed, could provoke a race riot—a dispute over access to a carousel (1834), an assault by a black man who was demonstrably insane (1835), the opening of a meeting place for abolitionists (1838), or a black temperance parade (1842). Overall, the incitement seemed to be the existence of a cohesive African American community with deep roots and every intention of staying put. When he received death threats during the riot of 1834, James Forten, now his community's elder statesman, was told that he had brought the trouble on himself by speaking out against the American Colonization Society and "prevent[ing] others from leaving the country."[61]

Demands for restrictive measures along the lines of those that mooted in 1813 prompted a bill in the Pennsylvania legislature in 1831 that was truly draconian. Black people would be required to register in their home county and would be forbidden to move about at will. Newcomers must post a five-hundred-dollar bond within twenty days of entering Pennsylvania or face arrest. A special census of African Americans would be taken so the law could be enforced. Appalled when they learned that this bill was under consideration in Harrisburg, black Philadelphians and their white allies petitioned, held meetings, and made personal appeals. Ultimately, House Bill No. 446 did not become law, but the fact that it had received strong support in the legislature and that many whites had submitted petitions favoring its passage boded ill for the future.[62]

The loss of the franchise in 1838 was another reminder that "abolition" was about much more than the ending of chattel slavery. Plenty of white Pennsylvanians, and not just those who served in the so-called Reform Convention tasked with revising the state's constitution, insisted that the "freeman" entitled to vote by the 1790 constitution under various property and residency requirements was not simply any man who was legally free. They maintained that only white men could be "freemen." Admittedly, few black Philadelphians had ever cast a ballot. Many lacked the taxable property needed to make them eligible, and prejudice and the threat of violence kept from the polls those who did qualify. With the change in the constitution, though, a clear message had been sent. In the words of the men of color who drew up a desperate appeal begging white voters to reject the new constitution, ratification would mean that black people would lose "their check on oppression, their wherewith to buy friends." Within weeks of the publication of their appeal, the constitution was approved by an overwhelming majority. A British visitor reported hearing a story that might have been apocryphal but which certainly summed up the mood in the city. "I was told that a white boy was observed seizing the marbles of a coloured boy in one of the streets, with the words, 'You have no rights now.'"[63]

By the 1840s and 1850s frustration was mounting. The tendency of some white abolitionists to ignore the plight of African Americans in the nominally free states prompted criticism of even such antislavery stalwarts as William Lloyd Garrison. There were other signs of a break with the past. With Liberia, the ACS's West African colony, becoming an independent republic, at least in name, in 1847, and with the United States toughening its policies with regard to slavery and black citizenship, some started wondering aloud if the time for an exodus had arrived. The passage of a far more stringent Fugitive Slave Law, and the Supreme Court's declaration in the *Dred Scott* case that black people had never been citizens, and by implication never could be, prompted a long, hard look at what had been anathema just a couple of decades earlier.[64]

But for every man or woman of color in Philadelphia who questioned whether slavery would ever die and whether they themselves would ever move from the margins of society to enjoy the rights of citizenship in the country of their birth, there were many more who insisted that change was coming. Rather than abandon the United States, they believed more fervently than ever that they must stay. Conflict was inevitable, and they must be ready to do their part to see that the forces of freedom prevailed. To those who scoffed that a war between North and South would not be fought over issues of freedom and slavery but over politics and economics, they responded that they must *make* it a war to end slavery and racial proscription. When war finally came, black

Philadelphians were as eager as any people in the nation to embrace the Union cause as their own. The "new birth of freedom" President Lincoln would hail as the goal of the Civil War after more than two bloody years of fighting was the goal black Philadelphians had committed themselves to achieving from the very beginning.

NOTES

1. *Minutes of the State Convention of the Colored Citizens of Pennsylvania, Convened at Harrisburg, December 13th and 14th, 1848*, in Philip S. Foner and George E. Walker, eds., *Proceedings of the Black State Conventions, 1840–1865* (Philadelphia: Temple University Press, 1978), vol. 1: 126.

2. Carol Wilson, *Freedom at Risk: The Kidnapping of Free Blacks in America, 1780–1865* (Lexington: University Press of Kentucky, 1994), 71–73.

3. For the list of committee members, see *Minutes of the State Convention of the Colored Citizens of Pennsylvania*, 132–33.

4. On the antislavery work of several of these men, see Julie Winch, ed., *"The Elite of Our People": Joseph Willson's Sketches of Black Upper-Class Life in Antebellum Philadelphia* (University Park: Penn State University Press, 2000), 127n14, 145–46n59, 164–67n113.

5. On Forten's remarkable life and achievements, see Julie Winch, *A Gentleman of Color: The Life of James Forten* (New York: Oxford University Press, 2002). The laws relating to the status of free blacks are discussed in Gary B. Nash and Jean Soderlund, *Freedom by Degrees: Emancipation in Pennsylvania and Its Aftermath* (New York: Oxford University Press, 1991), 12–13.

6. See Ira Berlin's illuminating discussion of the importance of slave labor in colonial Philadelphia in "Slavery, Freedom, and Philadelphia's Struggle for Brotherly Love, 1685 to 1861," below.

7. Berlin, "Slavery, Freedom, and Philadelphia's Struggle," below, and Gary B. Nash, *Forging Freedom: The Formation of Philadelphia's Black Community, 1720–1840* (Cambridge, Mass.: Harvard University Press, 1988), 14, 33.

8. Nash and Soderlund, *Freedom by Degrees*, chaps. 2–3.

9. On the slaves of colonial New York, see Jill Lepore, "The Tightening Vise: Slavery and Freedom in British New York," in Ira Berlin and Leslie M. Harris, eds., *Slavery in New York* (New York: New Press, 2005), 57–89.

10. Winch, *A Gentleman of Color*, 30–35; Peter H. Wood, "'Liberty is Sweet': African-American Freedom Struggles in the Years Before White Independence," in Alfred F. Young, ed., *Beyond the American Revolution* (DeKalb: Northern Illinois University Press, 1993), 170.

11. For the full text of the gradual abolition law see Roger Bruns, ed., *Am I Not a Man and a Brother: The Antislavery Crusade of Revolutionary America, 1688–1788* (New York: Chelsea House, 1977), 446–50.

12. On the debates surrounding the law, and the attempts by masters to flout it, see Arthur Zilversmit, *The First Emancipation: The Abolition of Slavery in the North* (Chicago: University of Chicago Press, 1967), 124–27, and Nash and Soderlund, *Freedom by Degrees*, chap. 4.

13. William Douglass, *Annals of the First African Church in the United States of America, Now Styled the African Episcopal Church of St. Thomas* (Philadelphia: King & Baird, 1862), 31–32.

14. Richard Allen, *Life Experience and Gospel Labors of the Rt. Rev. Richard Allen* (Nashville: Abingdon Press, 1954), 24–25.

15. On the formation of the churches, see Nash, *Forging Freedom*, chap. 4, and Julie Winch, *Philadelphia's Black Elite: Activism, Accommodation, and the Struggle for Autonomy, 1787–1848* (Philadelphia: Temple University Press, 1988), 9–15.

16. Baptismal Register, St. Thomas's African Episcopal Church. (I am grateful to the minister, vestry, and members of St. Thomas's for giving me access to this remarkable document.)

17. Douglass, *Annals of St. Thomas*, 15–47; *Hazard's Register*, March 12, 1831; "Notes on Beneficial Societies, 1828–1838," Pennsylvania Abolition Society Manuscripts, Historical Society of Pennsylvania (HSP); Charters of Incorporation, 1812–75, Records of the Secretary of State, Pennsylvania State Archives.

18. Mathew Carey, *A Short Account of the Malignant Fever, Lately Prevalent in Philadelphia* (2nd ed., Philadelphia: The Author, 1793), 77–87; Absalom Jones and Richard Allen, *A Narrative of the Proceedings of the Black People, During the Late Awful Calamity in Philadelphia* (Philadelphia: William W. Woodward, 1794).

19. *Pennsylvania Gazette*, February 21, 1798.

20. Elizabeth Forman Crane, ed., *The Diary of Elizabeth Drinker* (Boston: Northeastern University Press, 1991), vol. 2: 935. Minutes of the African Grand Lodge, Philadelphia, 1797–1800 (microfilm), Library of the Grand Lodge of Massachusetts, A.F. and A.M., Boston.

21. Jeffrey N. Bumbrey, ed., *A Guide to the Microfilm Publications of the Papers of the Pennsylvania Abolition Society* (Philadelphia: Pennsylvania Abolition Society and the Historical Society of Pennsylvania, 1976), 7, 9, 17, 22.

22. For a sense of the scope of the PAS's activities, see its General Meeting and Acting Committee Minutes (PAS Manuscripts, HSP).

23. PAS, General Meeting Minutes, 1800–1824, p. 6.

24. For the text of the petition, see John Parrish, *Remarks on the Slavery of the Black People, Addressed to the Citizens of the United States* (Philadelphia: Kimber, Conrad & Co., 1806), 49–51.

25. Peter M. Bergman and Jean McCarroll, comps., *The Negro in the Congressional Record, 1789–1801* (New York: Bergman, 1969), 241–44.

26. *Journal of the Pennsylvania House* 10 (1799–1800): 172.

27. Edward R. Turner, *The Negro in Pennsylvania: Slavery—Servitude—Freedom, 1639–1861* (Washington, D.C. American Historical Association, 1912), 253.

28. Nash, *Forging Freedom*, 137, 143.

29. *Relf's Gazette*, December 30, 1807; *Poulson's American Daily Advertiser*, January 1, 1808; Absalom Jones, *A Thanksgiving Sermon, Preached January 1, 1808, in St. Thomas's, or the African Episcopal Church* (Philadelphia: Fry and Kammerer, 1808).

30. On the operations of one kidnapping gang, see Julie Winch, "Philadelphia and the Other Underground Railroad," *Pennsylvania Magazine of History and Biography* 111 (January 1987): 3–35.

31. *Journal of the Pennsylvania House* 15 (1804): 114. For the kind of press coverage such initiatives received, see *Freemen's Journal*, July 7 and July 9, 1804.

32. Douglass, *Annals of St. Thomas*, 113–14; Leonard P. Curry, *The Free Black in Urban America, 1800–1850: The Shadow of the Dream* (Chicago: University of Chicago Press, 1981), 152–53.

33. *Journal of the Pennsylvania House* 23 (1813–14), 216, 388–89, 417, 481; PAS, General Meeting Minutes, 1800–1824, p. 181.

34. Winch, *A Gentleman of Color*, 174–76.

35. PAS, Acting Committee Minutes, 1822–42, p. 207.

36. On the origins and goals of the ACS, see P. J. Staudenraus, *The African Colonization Movement, 1816–1865* (New York: Columbia University Press, 1961).

37. Winch, *A Gentleman of Color*, 177–95.

38. *Resolutions and Remonstrances of the People of Colour Against Colonization on the Coast of Africa* (Philadelphia, 1818), 3.

39. Winch, *A Gentleman of Color*, 196–206.

40. On some of these initiatives see *Poulson's American Daily Advertiser*, July 9–10, 14, 16, 21, 23, 1818; March 3, 1822.

41. For a brief overview of the African American community in the 1830s see Winch, ed., *"The Elite of Our People,"* 9–11.

42. Emma J. Lapsansky, "'Since They Got Those Separate Churches': Afro-Americans and Racism in Jacksonian Philadelphia," *American Quarterly* 32 (Spring 1980): 57. For the breakdown of the census, see *Hazard's Register* (March 1831): 172–73.

43. Lapsansky, "'Since They Got Those Separate Churches,'" 54–78.

44. John Fanning Watson, *Annals of Philadelphia* (Philadelphia, 1830), quoted in Lapsansky, "'Since They Got Those Separate Churches,'" 62.

45. Winch, ed., *"The Elite of Our People,"* 82.

46. Ibid., 83.

47. On the various societies and Willson's observations about them, see *"The Elite of Our People,"* 87–88, 115–16, 149n71, 157n91.

48. On Purvis's activities in Britain see Winch, *A Gentleman of Color*, 260-64. On Glasgow's see *The Scotsman* (Edinburgh), January 3, 1860, and Jesse Ewing Glasgow Jr., *The Harper's Ferry Insurrection* (Edinburgh: McPhail, 1860).

49. See, for example, Winch, ed., *A Gentleman of Color*, chap. 11.

50. Julie Winch, "'You Have Talents—Only Cultivate Them': Philadelphia's Black Female Literary Societies and the Abolitionist Crusade," in Jean Fagan Yellin and John C. Van Horne, eds., *The Abolitionist Sisterhood: Women's Political Culture in Antebellum America* (Ithaca: Cornell University Press, 1994), 101–18.

51. W. Jeffrey Bolster, *Black Jacks: African-American Seamen in the Age of Sail* (Cambridge, Mass.: Harvard University Press, 1997), 199–210.

52. Minute–Book of the Philadelphia Vigilance Committee, Leon Gardiner Collection, HSP.

53. *National Enquirer*, September 7, 1837. *Pennsylvania Freeman*, July 5, 1838; March 12, 1840; November 5, 1840. *National Anti–Slavery Standard*, May 4, 1843.

54. *National Enquirer*, June 17 and June 24, 1837.

55. The records of the Philadelphia City Anti-Slavery Society and the Philadelphia Young Men's Anti-Slavery Society are included in the PAS Manuscripts (HSP). On the statewide "immediatist" organization, see *Proceedings of the Pennsylvania Convention, Assembled to Organize a*

State Anti-Slavery Society, at Harrisburg, on the 31st of January and 1st, 2nd and 3rd of February, 1837 (Philadelphia: Merrihew and Gunn, 1837).

56. Philadelphia Female Anti–Slavery Society, minute-books and correspondence, in PAS Manuscripts, HSP.

57. Howard H. Bell, comp., *Minutes of the Proceedings of the National Negro Conventions, 1830–1864* (New York: Arno, 1969); Winch, *Philadelphia's Black Elite,* chap. 5.

58. On the AMRS see Winch, *Philadelphia's Black Elite,* chap. 6.

59. PAS, *Register of the Trades of the Colored People in the City of Philadelphia and Districts* (Philadelphia: Merrihew and Gunn, 1838).

60. For an overview of conditions in the city, see Elizabeth Geffen, "Violence in Philadelphia in the 1840s and 1850s," *Pennsylvania History* 36 (October 1969): 388–410.

61. Nash, *Forging Freedom,* chap. 8; Winch, *Philadelphia's Black Elite,* 142–51; Lapsansky, "'Since They Got Those Separate Churches,'" 54–78; Edward S. Abdy, *Journal of a Residence and Tour in the United States of America* (1835; rpt. New York: Negro Universities Press, 1969), vol. 3: 324.

62. Winch, *A Gentleman of Color,* 284–87.

63. Robert Purvis et al., *Appeal of Forty Thousand Citizens, Threatened with Disfranchisement* (Philadelphia: Merrihew and Gunn, 1838), 4; John Joseph Gurney, *A Visit to North America* (Norwich, U.K.: Joseph Fletcher, 1841), 102.

64. Winch, *Philadelphia's Black Elite,* 48, 89–90, 161.

CHAPTER 4

Race and Citizenship in the Early Republic

GARY NASH

George Washington's death in 1799 triggered an outpouring of adulation for the "father of his country" and soon brought the remarkable news that in his will he provided for the freedom of his 146 slaves. The dower slaves his wife brought into the marriage were legally beyond his reach, but freeing the slaves over which he had control offered an example that powerful political leaders such as Jefferson and Madison might have emulated as an opportunity to return to the purity of the founding documents. But nearly the opposite occurred. The year 1800 brought Jefferson's presidential victory over John Adams, ushering in a four-decade era when Jeffersonians dominated the executive and legislative branches of government. Though regarded as the party of the common people, dedicated to including a broadening of the franchise, relaxing the restrictions on immigrants seeking naturalization, and restoring a state-centered republic, the Democratic-Republicans also "extended the domain of white supremacy."[1] "The Virginia [Democratic-]Republican dynasty," Rogers Smith tells us, redefined citizenship laws that eroded the rights of African Americans and, in the first quarter of the nineteenth century, even denied that free people of color were citizens at all. After 1800, "citizenship laws increasingly reflected Jeffersonian views of American nationality," leaving the Federalists (who have become in the historical literature the party of the elite) as the main defenders of black citizenship rights.[2] Thus, a state-centered republic rendered itself largely incapable of solving what was not a *state* problem but a *national* problem. The stage was being set for the creation of killing fields through which Americans of all regions, all colors, and all dispositions would walk two generations later.

The political and ideological journeys of two Philadelphians, one black, the other white—both young men of the revolutionary era and longtime residents of the city known as the capital of American benevolence and Enlightenment idealism—neatly represent the argument in the first quarter of the nineteenth century that reverberated throughout the nation on the matter of race and citizenship in the early republic. The African American was James Forten, Philadelphia's most successful black businessman up to his death in 1842. His five published letters to the public in 1813 and other subsequent writings tell us much about how black northerners were thinking about citizenship in the critical period leading up to the Missouri Compromise of 1820, Denmark Vesey's plot in 1822, and the publication of David Walker's *Appeal to the Coloured Citizens of the World* in 1829. The white Philadelphian was Tench Coxe, at first a shrewd Federalist merchant and then a longtime Jeffersonian officeholder and leading political economist. While living only a few blocks from Forten, he published two sets of essays, one in 1809, the other in the winter of 1820–21. In these essays, Coxe provided a road map that most white Americans followed in redefining citizenship and national identity in this period where the groundwork for an irreparable national fissure was laid.

(1)

James Forten thought of himself as thoroughly American from an early age. Only as he matured and became successful did he think of himself as African American. In time, he wondered whether being African American would allow those of dark skin to be American at all. Born in 1766, the grandson of an African who was one of the first enslaved Pennsylvanians to gain his freedom, Forten learned to read and write at the Quakers' African School, and he was influenced as well by Anthony Benezet, Philadelphia's Quaker reformer who devoted himself to teaching the children of the poor. Forten's father died when the boy was seven. He was eleven when the British-officered regiment of Black Guides and Pioneers, composed of escaped Virginia slaves who responded to Dunmore's Proclamation, occupied Philadelphia in the winter of 1777–78. Forten and his mother no doubt knew what the German Lutheran minister Henry Muhlenberg reported: that Pennsylvania's slaves "secretly wished that the British army might win, for then all Negro slaves will gain their freedom."[3] The flight of many of the city's slaves to the British, along with a number of free blacks, could hardly have gone unnoticed by the adolescent Forten.

But the young Forten sought a different path. Perhaps gaining his optimistic outlook from his free parents, and perhaps convinced from Benezet's lessons that Africans were no different from whites in their potential, James—

at age fifteen—signed on as a powder boy on Stephen Decatur's twenty-gun *Royal Louis*. Thus began a heroic career. For years, Philadelphians told of how he was the only survivor at his gun station when Decatur's ship dueled with a British warship in 1781; how he was captured on the next voyage and spurned an offer from a British captain to take him to England, as his son's companion, where he could pursue a satisfactory career; how he told the British Captain "No, No! I am here a prisoner for the liberties of my country; I never, NEVER, shall prove a traitor to her interests"; how he was clapped into a rotting British prison ship in New York harbor and gave up a chance to be smuggled out in a trunk of clothes to a young white sailor with whom he had become friends; how he walked barefooted from New York to Philadelphia in 1783 after the British released their American prisoners; and how, after the war, he became a valued sailmaker in the employ of Robert Bridges. When the white sailmaker retired in 1798, he handed over his sail loft to Forten.[4]

Forten imagined that the revolutionary generation's rhetoric of natural rights would usher in a biracial democracy in Pennsylvania and create a nation where color-blind national identity flowed from an allegiance to the nation and state. And why not? He had fought bravely in the American Revolution; was a pillar of St. Thomas African Episcopal church, one of two black churches founded in Philadelphia in 1793; succeeded as an artisan and businessman who employed an interracial crew of thirty sailmakers; owned a home where some of his neighbors were eminent Philadelphians; counted white merchants among his friends; and was a confidant of Paul Cuffe, the New Bedford Afro-Indian shipbuilder, merchant, and ship captain who sailed the deep blue seas all the way to Africa. Moreover, Forten held before him the preamble of the Pennsylvania Constitution of 1776, assuring him that the doctrine of human equality would be the future if the revolutionary generation remained true to its words. "All men," it read, "are born equally free and independent, and have certain natural, inherent, and inalienable rights." The preamble of Pennsylvania's gradual abolition act of 1780 also affirmed the unitary nature of humankind, what the legislators called a "universal civilization."[5] Forten believed in what a modern scholar of citizenship has claimed was the general presumption of the post-revolutionary period: "that membership [in civil society] was acquired automatically by all those born under the Republic."[6]

But Forten's faith that white Pennsylvanians would honor these commitments was wearing thin by the early years of Jefferson's presidency. Like black and some white Philadelphians, Forten took satisfaction in the slave rebellion in Saint Domingue (to become Haiti) that began in 1791, ultimately overthrowing the brutal French slave regime and establishing the first black republic in the Americas. But he also had to take the measure of much white northern fear, and that of almost all white southerners, that this revolt would spread black rebellion all over America.[7] Forten knew how refugees from slavery in the South, filtering into Philadelphia, caused white resentment and how Irish immigrants in the 1790s competed uneasily with free black people for bottom-rung jobs. Forten watched uneasily as Congress rejected petitions from black Philadelphians and the Pennsylvania Abolition Society to rescind the hated Fugitive Slave Act of 1793 and abolish the slave trade, which was still flourishing.[8]

If the rise of racial hostility in the City of Brotherly Love shook Forten's belief in one American peoplehood, he was more distressed by an outbreak of racial rancor on July 4 in about 1804 that struck at the notion of free black birthright citizenship. For years, Philadelphians of all classes and colors had gathered in the square facing Independence Hall, where the nation's birth certificate had been signed, to listen to speeches about the blessings of liberty and the prospects for national greatness. But this time, sullen whites drove free black citizens from the festivities with a torrent of curses. At this moment James Forten's political awakening occurred, perhaps also spurred by Congress's failure in 1804 to pass a bill that would free male slaves by their twenty-second birthday and female slaves by their nineteenth, a measure supported by many northern Jeffersonians.[9] The worsening situation on the ground in Philadelphia sickened Forten. Black Philadelphians, he wrote, "dare not be seen after twelve o'clock in the day, upon the field to enjoy the times" without fearing assault from whites "like the destroying Hyena or the avaricious Wolf."[10] In allowing white toughs to control public spaces in the city and to drive black Philadelphians from the celebration of nationhood, white political leaders and municipal authorities implicitly renounced the idea that citizenship was the entitlement of all free people regardless of color. "Is it not wonderful," Forten exclaimed sarcastically, "that the day set apart for the festival of liberty, should be abused by the advocates of freedom, in endeavoring to sully what they profess to adore?"[11]

Forten's alarm increased as Pennsylvania's legislature began considering bills in 1804 to seal the state off from incoming black migrants, to fasten a special tax on black householders for the support of the poor of their color, to require all free black adults to carry freedom certificates, to sentence without jury trial those failing to produce a certificate to seven years imprisonment, and to sell into slavery any black person convicted of a property crime in order to compensate the victim. Each of these provisions directly assaulted the principle that citizenship conferred fundamental privileges and immunities without distinction of color. For nine years such bills failed in the legislature, but in 1813, when the mayor and city councilmen of Philadelphia supported such bills, Forten took up his pen. "Search the legends of tyranny and find no precedent," he thundered in five published letters. "It has been left for Pennsylvania to raise her ponderous arm against the liberties of the black, whose greatest boast has been that he resided in a state where civil liberty and sacred justice were administered alike to all."[12]

What had happened to the revolutionary vision of unalienable rights? When the founding fathers and the writers of Pennsylvania's constitution said "all men are created equal," did they mean only white men (as many historians have said ever since)? Forten denied this emphatically. "This idea [of natural rights]," he affirmed, "embraces the Indian and the European, the Savage and the Saint, the Peruvian and the Laplander, the white Man and the African, and whatever measures are adopted subversive of this inestimable privilege, are in direct violation of the letter and spirit of our Constitution, and become subject to the animadversion of all, particularly those who are deeply interested in the measure."[13] The legislative bills, Forten cried, would convert the center of American benevolence into a center of repression. "The story will fly from the north to the south, and the advocates of slavery, the traders in human blood, will smile contemptuously at the once boasted moderation and humanity of Pennsylvania!" And where, asked Forten, would slaves emancipated in the South go? "Shut every state against him, and, like Pharaoh's kine, drive him into the sea.—Is there no spot on earth that will protect him? Against their inclination, his ancestors were forced from their homes by traders in human flesh, and even under such circumstances the wretched offspring are denied the protection you afford to brutes."[14]

Forten's incandescent rhetoric about universal rights and his attempt to keep at bay the rising tide of race-based legislation in the early nineteenth century made him the most important free black voice in the nation as the War of 1812 unfolded. More than black clergymen, who at this time were the principal spokesmen for their communities and nearly the only men who could put the printed word before the public, Forten challenged white power with a sharp wit and clarity of expression. "Has the GOD who made the white man and the black," he asked, "left any record declaring us a different species? Are we not sustained by the same power, supported by the same food, hurt by the same wounds, wounded by the same wrongs, pleased with the same delights, and propagated by the same means. And should we not then enjoy the same liberty, and be protected by the same laws." Forten knew many of the authors of Pennsylvania's constitution, and he now reminded the white legisla tors that these revolutionary architects "felt that they had no more authority to enslave us, than England had to tyrannize over them. . . . Actuated by these sentiments they adopted the glorious fabrick of our liberties, and, declaring 'all men' free, they did not particularize white and black, because they never supposed it would be made a question whether *we were men or not*."[15]

Forten's letters to the public—meant to appeal to the conscience of the state's legislators—may have carried weight. In any case, the legislature in 1813 drew back from patently discriminatory laws aimed at free black Pennsylvanians and all former southern slaves seeking a new life in Pennsylvania. It was an important victory. But it could not stop the juggernaut of white racial hostility bearing down on free black communities and threatening to pulverize the concept of color-blind citizenship.[16]

At first, Tench Coxe, Forten's neighbor, was not part of that juggernaut, but in a few years he began providing a rationale for it. Coxe commanded much respect as one of the most distinguished writers of his generation on American manufacturing, commerce, and political economy. After it reorganized in 1787, the Pennsylvania Abolition Society (PAS) was pleased to convince Coxe to become its secretary, for this gave the organization new breadth and respect. In 1790, Coxe joined two PAS Quaker leaders to draft the society's first petition to Congress to halt the slave trade.[17] By 1796, Coxe moved from the Federalist Party to the Jeffersonian camp; thereafter he became a Jeffersonian political lieutenant and officeholder. All the while, he thought deeply about how the American character came to be distinctive and how the new republic should define citizenship.

Coxe's first public comments on these issues appeared in a series of essays penned in 1809 on "The New World: An Enquiry into the National Character of the People of the United States of America." Here, he spun out a thesis about American uniqueness—one that James Forten might well have endorsed. Lacing his essays with references to freedom and oppression, Coxe pictured the Americans as a band of Robinson Crusoes who had banished tyranny and ushered in a heroic age of liberty. Greatly to their credit, the Americans had molded "a perfect civil uniformity, unknown and impracticable in any other maritime empire and highly influential upon the uniformity of the national character." Consistent with his earlier support for the Pennsylvania Abolition Society, where he served as secretary during the time the state's constitution was written and ratified, Coxe continued that "the white and free black inhabitants are all included in this observation; for it is a truth, that the free blacks regularly adopt and display the institutions, apparel, furniture, and habits of the whites. They are generally Episcopalians, Calvinists, and Methodists in those places where all the Christian sects are within their free observation."[18] Now he nailed down his belief in a single human race: "*Man* is justly contemplated, by our laws and by our political science, as an intelligent creation of the divine power. It is known that the highest intellect of the red and black races of men is sensibly better than that of the feeblest of the whites." From this fundamental belief flowed the notion of an unracialized citizenship. "As we cannot discriminate *as to rights* among the whites by the principle of intellect," wrote Coxe, "the same rule presses itself upon our regard with respect to the free people of the red and black races. Divine providence has ordained the existence of the coloured races of men, and we believe and know, that the same supreme authority has imperiously ordained humanity and justice among his intelligent and responsible creatures. Our institutions, therefore, consider all men alike."[19] Here was a liberal position that veered from the Jeffersonian drift toward "a racially coded system of citizenship and half-citizenship."[20]

If Forten was pleased in 1809 with Coxe's treatise on the universality of humankind and his insistence that the nation's civil institutions applied equally to free blacks as well as whites, the black sailmaker had much to be concerned about in what was issuing from other quarters in Philadelphia. Men of science also began discussing American character, race, and citizenship and were reaching foreboding conclusions. In a full-scale attack on the environmentalist theory that since the revolution had dominated thinking about racial differences, mid-Atlantic scientific thinkers now began avowing that irreparable deficiencies in moral and religious reasoning rendered large numbers of Americans useless as part of the nation's citizenry. Leading the way was Charles Caldwell, who had studied medicine at the University of Pennsylvania under Benjamin Rush, Philadelphia's leading white supporter of African American progress. In two long essays Caldwell tried to dismantle the environmentalist explanation that black deficiencies were the result of lifetimes under brutalizing slavery.[21] Foreshadowing the rise of the racist antebellum school of anthropology in the United States, Caldwell published his "Essay on the Causes of the Variety of Complexion and Figure in the Human Species" in 1811 and in 1814 followed with a similar essay arguing that differences between races were innate and thus completely resistant to environmental modification.[22] Caldwell's assertions of the inherent inferiority of Africans and their descendants, a descent into what a recent historian calls "irrationalism and narcissistic raptures over whiteness," nearly coincided with Rush's death in 1813, as if to punctuate the fact that one chapter of race relations in Philadelphia was ending and another beginning.[23] This was the vanguard *polygenesis* theory developed fully in the 1830s by Samuel George Morton, another Philadelphian. The environmentalist line of argument that supported the notion of the indivisibility of the human species—expressed so passionately by James Forten in his 1813 *Letters of a Man of Colour*—was now on the defensive.[24]

Sociology had also entered the argument through the side door, also on the side of nationality and citizenship defined as strictly a white man's affair. Impinging on arguments about the origins of the human species—whether many or one—and on related arguments about a fused citizenry or a fissured civil society was a growing fear among white northerners in the early nineteenth century about the effects of emancipation on racial intermixture.

As Winthrop Jordan has argued, the belief was "nearly universal" among white Americans that the emancipation of slaves after the revolution would "inevitably lead to racial intermixture" and that such intermingling would sadly prove "that civilized man had turned beast in the forest."[25] There were a few exceptions to be sure. Most notable was Princeton's president in the 1790s, Samuel Stanhope Smith, who hoped that emancipated slaves would be settled on western lands where they would intermarry with whites. This, he reasoned, would "bring the two races nearer together, and, in a course of time, . . . obliterate those wide distinctions which are now created by diversity of complexion" and magnified "by prejudice."[26] Also in the 1790s, Patrick Henry advocated Indian-white marriage and pushed Virginia to offer bounties for such mingling of blood. But Smith and Henry were distinctly minority voices, drowned out in the early nineteenth century by the belief that intermixture with blacks or Indians would stain white blood and that the purity of the nation itself would be fatally compromised. Thomas Jefferson's view, that the emancipated slave must "be removed beyond the reach of mixture" so that the black American would not corrupt "the blood of his master" was certainly the majority view among whites. In fact, it was one of the propelling sentiments behind all colonization schemes of the early republic.[27] "Manifestly," writes Jordan, "America's destiny was white"—at least in the view of most whites.[28]

In the Philadelphia of Forten and Coxe, virulent opposition to interracial marriage surfaced well before the black sailmaker wrote his *Letters from a Man of Colour.* Reverend Nicholas Collin, the rector of Gloria Dei Church, where many black men and women had taken vows, refused to marry a black man and the white widow of a sea captain who came to him in the winter of 1794. For the next few years, Collin wrote disapprovingly in his marriage register of similar requests, remarking that he was "not willing to have blame from public opinion" for sanctioning mixed marriages. Six years later he fretted that "a particoloured race will soon make a great portion of the population in Philadelphia" in spite of "public opinion disapproving such wedlocks."[29] Joseph Drinker, a Quaker leader, opposed granting full admission into the Society of Friends to Hannah Burrows, a light-skinned woman who attended meetings "as a preacher or teacher." If she gained membership, he reasoned, "the privilege of intermarriage with the whites," which he called "objectionable," "could not be withheld."[30]

Inherent in all such anxiety over interracial marriage was the notion that black blood would corrupt white blood. Such simmering fears came to a boil in 1806 in Philadelphia in the writings of Thomas Branagan, an avowed enemy of slavery. Of Irish Catholic background, Branagan had gone to sea at age thirteen, sailed on slave ships, supervised a slave plantation in Antigua, and landed on the shores of the Delaware River in 1799. By this time, he was thoroughly disgusted with slavery and began preaching in his self-learned manner to "the poor and needy, the halt, the maimed, and the blind."[31] In his *Preliminary Essay on the Oppression of the Exiled Sons of Africa* (1804), Branagan spoke as vigorously against the inhumanity of slavery as the most erstwhile Quaker. But a year later, in *Serious Remonstrances Addressed to the Citizens of the Northern States* (1805), Branagan combined antislavery rhetoric with a heady brew of racism. He proposed to end "the contamination of the land which is sacred to liberty" by creating a black state in the newly acquired Louisiana Territory where the "poisonous fruit" of the tree of slavery should be shipped. Then, in dripping language revealing an obsession with interracial sex, Branagan painted a picture of black males swarming over "white women of easy virtue," hell-bent on obtaining white wives and producing "mungrels and mulattoes" so rapidly that "in the course of a few years . . . half the inhabitants of the city will be people of Colour."[32] Equally ominous, Branagan, while promoting a federally established state for free black people, argued that they should not gain citizenship but should instead live out their lives as wards of the state. Coming just a year after he had defended black people as "sensible, ingenious, hospitable, and generous as any people, placed in such circumstances, and laboring under such disadvantages," Branagan's turnabout was stunning.[33]

The rising Negrophobia among ordinary white Philadelphians and the strident writing of men such as Caldwell on the innate inferiority of Africans required Forten and other black leaders to reevaluate their situation and rethink their future. As in other northern cities, some free black Philadelphians began to think of themselves as a nation within a nation. If so, it made sense to create alternative celebrations of freedom, especially after their exclusion from white festivities on the Fourth of July. In Philadelphia (as in Boston), this began in 1808. January 1—marking the end of the slave trade and Haiti's independence day since 1804—became an African American day of commemoration,[34] "the Day of Our Political Jubilee," as one black minister called it.[35] Now, black Philadelphians paraded and celebrated in their own way and on their own day. But they paraded as citizens, even though their entitlement to full citizenship was under attack.[36]

Historians have detected strains of black nationalism, or separatism, in the African American celebrations, yet the urban parades were generally "freedom festivals" meant to nurture an African American identity among people generally pursuing assimilationist ends in spite of spiraling racial antipathy.[37] This desire to be fully American was apparent in Philadelphia during the War of 1812, when James Forten chaired a black Committee of Defense and led more than a thousand black men in 1814 out of the city to strengthen the Delaware River fortifications protecting Philadelphia from British naval attacks. If not permitted to shoulder guns, black men stepped forward eagerly with shovels to prove their patriotism and discharge their civic responsibility. Two years later, Philadelphia's Russell Parrott dwelt on how the black soldier had earned the rights of citizenship by fighting in the American Revolution and the War of 1812 "with noble daring, mingling his blood in the ungrateful soil that refused him everything but a grave."[38]

But the interclass and interracial harmony that prevailed in September 1814 when black and white shovel brigades stood shoulder to shoulder did not last. A year later, white Philadelphians, claiming to be bothered by the noise of emotional religious services, destroyed a black house of worship in

the Northern Liberties. By this time, James Forten was reluctantly concluding that black Americans could achieve peoplehood and nationality only by
becoming something other than Americans. That something would have to be
outside the United States.

This, of course, was the position of the American Colonization Society,
founded soon after Forten published his *Letters from a Man of Colour.* A peculiar mixture of southerners and northerners, of proslavery and antislavery
advocates, of conservatives and liberals, the ACS proposed to purify the nation
through the removal of dark-skinned residents, in effect announcing that America was a white man's republic.[39] Black Philadelphians such as James Forten
and Richard Allen at first believed that emigrationism would be voluntary and
occur on black terms, not white.[40] They would shortly change their minds.

For black Philadelphians, the question of national identity came to a head
on a cold night in January 1817. Believing themselves a part of a biracial republic, not yet equal but progressing toward full citizenship, they flocked to a
clamorous meeting in the city's main black sanctuary, Richard Allen's African
Methodist Episcopal Church. Squeezing his way forward to the pulpit, Forten
marveled at three thousand men packing the main floor, overflowing the
U-shaped balcony, and spilling into the street. Nearly three-quarters of the
city's black men had gathered to speak their minds on citizenship and national
identity. Forten had been pondering the meeting of white political leaders
who three weeks before in Washington had founded the ACS and issued state-
ments that repatriating free black Americans to Africa was the only solution
to the nation's growing racial problem. Forten thought of his Rhode Island
friend Paul Cuffe, the Afro-Indian ship captain who for more than a decade
had been promoting resettlement in Africa, believing that black Americans
had no future in the United States.[41]

So Forten, chairing the meeting, rose to address a sea of dark faces. The
man who had staked his identity as an American and had prospered in the city
of his birth called on Philadelphia's three notable black ministers—Richard
Allen, Absalom Jones, and John Gloucester. All spelled out the advantages of
returning to ancestral homelands. Then Forten endorsed the idea, reluctantly
admitting that black Americans "will never become a people until they come
out from amongst the white people."[42] Now came time for a straw vote. Forten
called first for the "ayes," those favoring a return to Africa. Not a voice was
heard nor a hand lifted. Then he called for those opposed to this. One tremendous "no" arose, Forten later wrote, "as if it would bring down the walls of the
building. . . . There was not a soul that was in favor of going to Africa."[43]

The emotional meeting at Richard Allen's church in 1817, repeated through-out the nation over the next few years, had an annealing effect among black Americans. The black masses instinctively understood what some of their lead-ers did not—that while some white ACS leaders were sincere about helping black Americans and others were zealous to send black Christian missionaries to convert all Africans to Christianity, the colonization scheme was mostly the instrument of southerners whose main interest was a massive deportation of free blacks while providing cover for slavery's expansion.

Forten, Allen, and other black leaders in Philadelphia would dabble in colonization schemes in Canada and Haiti in the future, but never again would they speak on behalf of repatriation to Africa. The unanimously endorsed reso-lution presented after the vote taken at Richard Allen's church expressed a new commitment to abolitionism and racial equality. "Whereas our ancestors (not of choice) were the first successful cultivators of the wilds of America," the resolution affirmed, "we their descendants feel ourselves entitled to participate in the blessings of her luxuriant soil which their blood and sweat manured." Again referring to the founding documents on which common citizenship was based, black Philadelphians avowed "that any measure . . . having the tendency to banish us from her bosom, would not only be cruel, but in direct violation of those principles which have been the boast of the republic."[44]

Local supporters of the American Colonization Society still retained hope to win black northerners over to the idea of returning to Africa and in this way render moot the entire matter of black citizenship rights. In mid-1818, a Philadelphia newspaper printed a *faux* debate between William Penn (dead for almost a century), the recently deceased Absalom Jones, founder and minister of Philadelphia's St. Thomas African Episcopal Church, and Paul Cuffe, James Forten's friend who supported colonization of free black Americans to Sierra Leone. In the "dialogues on the African colony," Jones rejected repatriation as a deportation scheme designed to smother the efforts of abolitionists. Cuffe tried to convince him otherwise, and Penn, having consulted George Washington (also dead since 1799), reported that the founding father greatly favored the return to Africa for the good of black Americans. Finally, Absalom Jones swal-lowed his doubts that whatever pleased slave masters could benefit free blacks. "My objections have been refuted," he said in this mock debate; "my scruples vanquished. And all my doubts satisfied, Heaven speed the undertaking!"[45]

Few black Philadelphians hearing or reading the dialogues packed their bags, left the city, and headed home to Africa. Rather they remonstrated in

1818 and 1819 against the Colonization Society and spoke with their feet when the ACS dispatched the first two ships to establish the colony of Liberia in 1819 and 1820. Of about ten thousand free black Philadelphians, only twenty-two joined the expedition, though economic conditions in the city had worsened greatly. A few years later, another recruitment campaign netted only another handful for settlement in Liberia.

(2)

By 1818, Tench Coxe must have wished that Philadelphia's black masses had opted for immigration to West Africa. The deep depression that followed the end of the War of 1812, the most severe ever experienced in the northern cities, may have shattered his earlier optimism about the assimilation of free black people and their potential as respectable citizens. Or had he fallen in line with the Jeffersonian faith in state-centered democracy, which was leading toward restrictions on black citizenship? Or had Philadelphia's white workingmen, who formed the Jeffersonian party's spine, changed his mind as they grew increasingly rabid on race issues? Or had the essays of men such as Charles Caldwell and Thomas Branagan reconfigured his thinking? Whatever the causes, Coxe reversed course, now viewing free African Americans concentrated in northern cities as an impoverished, uneducated mass for whom the rights of full citizenship were inappropriate.

But if free black people were a pariah group, how could their exclusion be squared with the avowed principles of color-blind citizenship that had prevailed for nearly half a century? Founding members of the American Colonization Society, which included some of the nation's most admired political leaders and thinkers, were constructing an answer. At ACS's first meeting, Henry Clay had argued that free black people were "a useless and pernicious, if not dangerous portion of [the nation's] population."[46] Others knew that these gloomy characterizations promoted ideas about a fractured American identity. In following up on Clay's address, Elias Boudinot Caldwell, scion of a wealthy New Jersey family and clerk of the Supreme Court, brooded about this. Quoting the founding fathers' axiom "that all men are created equal and have certain unalienable rights," Caldwell warned that the ACS was leading a cause ready to deny that *all* free Americans acquired citizenship by birthright. But Caldwell stumbled. Regrettably, he confessed, white hatred of black Americans made it impossible that "they can ever be placed upon this equality, or admitted to the enjoyment of these 'unalienable rights' while they remain mixed with us." "Some persons may declaim and call it prejudice," Caldwell admitted. But "no matter," he answered. "Prejudice is as powerful a motive, and will as certainly exclude them, as the soundest reason."[47] The idea of moving black Americans rather than removing white prejudice was winning the day. Caldwell was one of many leading white figures who chose to bow to popular feeling rather than seek to change it.

The task of finding a rationale for denying citizenship to free black Americans without sacrificing principles to prejudice captured Tench Coxe's attention in 1820. Could he find a "theoretically consistent way to deny [free black people] the rights and privileges of citizens"?[48] This was precisely the question raised in Congress when the admission of the Missouri Territory to the union as a slave state, first broached in 1819, became a fiery, deeply divisive, and destabilizing issue. Slavery, the pro-southern argument went, had to be protected to preserve the nation's unity. In fact, however, a North-South unity purchased through the expansion of slavery into the western territories proved to be a tenuous unity, indeed a counterfeit recipe for union and a ticking time bomb of sectional tension.

By March 1820, after some of the most fiery debates in Congressional history, Congress decided it did not have the power to forbid slavery in a state applying for entry into the Union. By admitting Maine as a free state while Missouri entered as a slave state, Congress maintained sectional parity in the Senate. Congress hoped to settle the issue by drawing a line through the rest of the Louisiana Territory at 36 degrees, 30 minutes, a fateful marker for defining slave and free territory for the future. But on the heels of this compromise, a second issue arose—a Missouri constitution passed in St. Louis in July 1820 that forbade the entry of free black Americans into the new state. Many northern Congressmen strongly objected to this denial of a prime citizenship right of free movement. Southerners vigorously defended the offending clause, denying explicitly that free blacks in the United States were citizens. This conflict brought the entire question about black citizenship to a head, investing it with "tremendous political and ideological significance."[49]

If Congress supported the southern position that free black people were not citizens (the position the Supreme Court avowed forty years later in the Dred Scott decision), then free black adults in the North, as many northern Congressmen pointed out, would be vulnerable to losing the right to move freely, acquire property, worship freely, and, correlatively, would be relieved of their obligation to pay taxes and defend their country. Pennsylvania's representative Joseph Hemphill put it bluntly: "If being a native, and free born, and of parents belonging to no other nation or tribe, does not constitute a citizen of this country, I am at a loss to know in which manner citizenship is acquired by birth."[50] Senator Justin Morrill of New Hampshire argued that if Congress endorsed Missouri's constitution, making a distinction between citizens simply on the basis of color, then the precedent would be set for every state to grant or withhold rights similarly. In this case, "your national existence is lost; the Union is destroyed; the objects of confederation annihilated, and your political fabric is demolished."[51] Secretary of State John Quincy Adams agreed that the Missouri constitutional clause would strip thousands of citizens of constitutionally guaranteed rights. "Already cursed by the mere color of their skin," he argued, "already doomed by their complexion to drudge in the lowest offices of society, excluded by their color from all the refined enjoyments of life accessible to others . . . this barbarous article deprives them of the little remnant of right yet left them—their rights as citizens and as men."[52] Southerners responded, with withering facts at their disposal: every day of the week northern states discriminated against free black men and women and denied them full equality. Free black people were not in fact citizens—and were not treated as such throughout much of the North. Especially, southerners argued, emancipated slaves were not free born and were therefore incapable of acquiring citizenship simply because their masters relinquished claims to their labor.[53]

Into the midst of this heated argument over whether free black Americans were citizens, aliens, residents, or something else, Tench Coxe, writing at a blistering pace, submitted thirteen essays to the Philadelphia newspaper most popular among Jeffersonian workingmen and shopkeepers, the Negrophobic *Democratic Press*.[54] He titled the essays "Considerations respecting the Helots of the United States, African and Indian, native and Alien, and their descendants of the whole and mixed blood." This was a tip-off since "helots" referred to a class of serfs in ancient Sparta who were neither slaves nor citizens; Coxe aimed to tilt Congress toward the southern view of black non-citizenship. Certainly his essays must have been greeted enthusiastically in the South, coming as they did from a "Philadelphia grandee" and a man who had served both as an important Federalist and Jeffersonian officeholder.

At the heart of his essays, Coxe argued that free black Americans, Indians, and all people of mixed blood had never been considered a part of the social compact before the American Revolution and that in the Declaration of

Independence and the state constitutions passed thereafter had never "been admitted to the rights of Citizenship."[55] This assertion blatantly disavowed what he had argued a few years before. Coxe did not relinquish the idea that slavery must end at some time in the future, and he was critical of northern states and municipalities for crippling the chances of free black people by denying them public education. But while hedging this hint that free black Americans were potentially worthy, he argued that the "Helots of America" were descended from "uncivilised or wild men without our moral sense . . . [or] our notions of moral character," a people "not yet evinced, by the actual facts, to be capable of genuine modern civilization." "Are we all willing to give them the whole substance of the liberty, wherewith heaven has made us free" he asked rhetorically; "or are the Helot people deemed unworthy to be made as consummately free citizens as ourselves; or are they considered incapable of attaining the characteristics, moral and intellectual, which belong to the least qualified portion of the white citizens in the states which admit to suffrage and office all but paupers and insane persons?"[56]

With this language, Coxe turned his back on the environmentalist beliefs espoused by the Pennsylvania Abolition Society and aligned himself with the speculations about biological inferiority that Jefferson had spun out in his *Notes on Virginia* a quarter of a century before. Choosing the loaded word "helot" to punctuate his essays, he joined the new pseudo-scientific school to revive the old views of how black people of purportedly savage backgrounds could never overcome immutable traits that made them forever unsuitable for citizenship. "Are we ready to put the trials of the black and colored men into the hands of juries of their true and proper peers, full black and colored citizens, without limitation," Coxe asked. "Are we ready to put the defence of the characters of our sons and chaste honor of our wives & daughters, upon such panels, uninstructed as they come to us, from the slave estates?" Put this way, only one answer would serve: it was right, Coxe pronounced, that free black men were "excluded . . . from the rights, qualities, and character of citizens."[57] Free black Americans would have to be removed to a "new Africa" somewhere in the remote West where they would be policed, reservation style, by the federal government.[58] Those still enslaved must remain so because injecting additional innately and incapable men and women into southern communities as free people would bring on the "horror . . . of a *Helot convulsion*" and "the prostration of everything from the cradle of the infant to the couch of age, the bed of virgin purity, and the half sacred connubial chamber."[59] Coxe's biographer Jacob Cooke calls this a defense of slavery "that not even southern hard liners . . . could have bettered."[60]

Coxe's essays reflected the growing white doctrine of innate black inferiority but also contributed to undermining the belief that American nationality was based on laws and institutions, not skin color.[61] He remained a nominal opponent of slavery, believing that "providence doubtless intends them [slaves]" for freedom. But he sternly lectured those who challenged slavery in the South, warning that this was reckless and would fatally wound the economic interests of the North that were becoming closely tied to the South's cotton-based slave economy.[62]

Why did Tench Coxe beat such a rapid retreat from his earlier position on free black entitlement to full citizenship? How came it, as his biographer puts it, that "he had only to contemplate fleetingly the notion of [racial] equality to be thrown into frenzied terror."[63] By Coxe's own account, it was the wretched condition of free African Americans in the North that had "raised in the most favorable minds fears that even gradual emancipation has lost much of its supposed facility among men who consider the present and probable results of that interesting operation."[64] Given the hapless condition of free black northerners and the unwillingness of whites to educate them, he argued, black people must be "bound to obey the exclusive legislative authority of the white people."[65] Yet Coxe's change of attitude toward black capability and entitlement to citizenship occurred during precisely the years when African American churches, schools, mutual aid associations, and literary societies had built the foundations for an estimable black citizenry while many black urban dwellers had carved out respectable niches in the economy. Also indisputably, as Coxe had witnessed and welcomed along with all Philadelphians, the shovel brigades of black Philadelphians, along with Irish, German, and other men with roughened hands, had marched out of town at the height of the War of 1812 to strengthen the fortifications protecting the city against an attacking British navy. A careful auditor of statistical information, Coxe also knew what the census of 1820 revealed—that among the city's two thousand black householders about one in eight was a property owner and many had achieved middle-class status. Many were his neighbors, men and women with whom he exchanged greetings on the streets from day to day.

Was it deliberate self-deception that led Coxe to argue that giving free black people full citizenship was misguided benevolence because it would "render the unfortunate black people objects of endless litigations, awful terrors, and fatal injuries?"[66] The origins of Coxe's stunning turnabout are multiple. Certainly his change of heart partakes of the American Colonization Society's rise and its embrace by many white Philadelphians, including many of Coxe's friends and even some members of the Pennsylvania Abolition Society.[67] In a few short years since its founding in 1816, the ACS had crystallized the latent feeling—in white churches, in salon life, and in the counting houses of Philadelphia—that black people were not assimilable either because of innate black inferiority or because of obdurate white prejudice. Coxe's essays on "the American Helots" dovetailed neatly with the ACS's arguments, providing what historian Charles Sellers calls "a moral fig leaf to claim antislavery virtue without disturbing the economic/political status quo."[68]

Coxe's reversal of a deeply held commitment to racial equality also jibes with Rogers Smith's analysis of how northern industrial development altered ideas of citizenship. The slave- produced cotton from the South that set the spinning wheels of northern textile factories humming put a premium on men such as Coxe to change their views. Always a man with an eye toward political economy, Coxe was particularly attuned to how the wheels of industry, banking, and commerce turned in Pennsylvania. "To assuage their liberal consciences," writes Smith of northerners, "white Americans . . . began elaborating . . . defenses of their civic inequalities, buttressed by pseudo-scientific Enlightenment and Protestant religious doctrines of racial and cultural superiority. In so doing they tacked white supremacist qualifications onto a basically Lockean understanding of American political identity."[69] When a Jacksonian senator from Ohio in 1839 thundered that "the slave power of the South and the banking power of the North are now uniting to rule the country," he echoed the rhetorical stance newly adopted by Tench Coxe nearly twenty years before.[70] In the early stages of the cotton revolution, which would soon turn Philadelphia and other northern cities into textile processing centers, Coxe, the herald of capitalist development, simultaneously became a herald of white supremacy.

Beyond the broader current of industrial change that was carrying men like Coxe toward an alliance with southern slaveholding interests, the controversy over the Missouri Compromise provides a more specific context for his turnabout on black citizenship. The Missouri agitation, wrote Elias Boudinot, the grizzled New Jersey revolutionary leader now in his eighties, "seems to have run alike a flaming fire thro our middle states and causes great anxiety."[71] Pennsylvania was of critical importance to proslavery southern Congressmen working for the admission of Missouri as a slave state, and Philadelphia was the center of the manufacturers, bankers, and merchants with close southern ties. Coxe plunged into the Missouri controversy, after observing the founding of the Philadelphia antislavery newspaper *National Gazette* in 1819, the strident attack on slavery by its editor Robert Walsh, and the heightened antislavery rhetoric of James Duane, editor of Philadelphia's *Aurora* in late 1820. Even more disturbing to Coxe was the unanimous resolution of the Pennsylvania legislature late in 1819 urging the state's congressmen in Washington to vote against admitting Missouri to the Union if slavery was sanctioned there. "The whole will depend on Pennsylvania," wrote Jefferson to Albert Gallatin, Coxe's close friend, on December 26, 1820.[72]

By this time, Coxe was already composing his essays on "the Helots of America," which, as his biographer maintains, were precipitated by the Missouri controversy. Viewed as an extended counterattack on Pennsylvanians and other northerners opposed to the extension of slavery to Missouri, they became an important cog in what New Jersey's Elias Boudinot believed was "a wheel within a wheel . . . some bargaining taking place between the East and Southern interests."[73] Written in the pivotal state of Pennsylvania, Coxe's essays were meant to tilt Pennsylvanians and other northerners toward accepting the extension of slavery into Missouri and pacify proslavery southerners.[74]

No one can measure the exact effect of Coxe's essays on "The Helots of the United States." But surely they fed the tide of anti-black sentiment coursing through James Forten's Philadelphia and throughout the North.[75] One year after Coxe's essays appeared, New York's legislature imposed a race-specific property qualification that disenfranchised most free black men.[76] Within a few more years, white marauders in Boston, New Haven, and Pittsburgh attacked the most tangible markers of free black accomplishment and respectability—African American churches and the homes of successful black urban dwellers. In 1829, whites attacked black churches and neighborhoods in Philadelphia and Cincinnati. Two years later, Philadelphia's leading Quaker reformer, Roberts Vaux, wrote discouragingly that "the policy, and power of the national and state government, are against [free black people]. The popular feeling is against them—the interests of our citizens are against them. The small degree of compassion once cherished toward them in the commonwealths which got rid of slavery, or which never were disfigured by it, appears to be exhausted. Their prospects either as free, or bond men, are dreary, and comfortless."[77] The way was paved for Pennsylvania's Constitutional Convention in 1837–38, which, as in most northern states, conferred universal white manhood suffrage for the first time while stripping black men of their vote. It was under this new definition of color-coded citizenship that thousands of black Pennsylvanians fought for the Union a quarter century later.

Though Coxe's essays fed the virulent proslavery, white supremacist campaign and contributed indirectly to southern slaveowning power in Congress, his literary productions became part of the proslavery stridency that spurred black organization, self-expression, and militancy. If it was not already clear before their publication, his essays showed free black Americans after 1820 that they faced a cruel double paradox. With the growing free black population demonstrating that slavery and blackness were no longer synonymous, white northerners "placed a premium on racial demarcation" to the disadvantage of blacks. At the same time, the more free black people achieved in building churches, schools, and mutual aid societies, the more white people resented them.[78] No black American in the North could escape this paradox. But resolving paradoxes is often the work of those who suffer its inequities and wounds. With civic-mindedness and moral rectitude, the earnests of good citizenship, no longer counting for much, black Americans had reached a watershed. Not given to despair and capitulation, they channeled anger, frustration, and disappointment into mobilization, where improvisation had to replace reliance on sweeping, clear-cut principles derived from the nation's founding documents. Before, the black preacher was—to use the words of W. E. B. DuBois—"the most unique personality developed by the Negro on American soil."[79] But now, after 1820, while black clergymen still stood as pillars of the black community, it was the secular leader, defiant rather than moderate, politically more than religiously attuned, who stepped toward center stage as a race-proud and uncompromising man. And as for black clergymen, they turned steadily from explanations of slavery and the slave trade as the mysterious workings of God's will to "free-will evangelicalism" that placed the blame for slavery squarely on ungodly human actors.[80]

(3)

Within a few years of Coxe's death in 1824, the first black newspaper in the United States, *Freedom's Journal,* launched a new era of black political consciousness and inter-city organization, all fueled by a growing stream of published sermons, speeches, and proceedings from inter-city black conventions.

This showed that the Missouri Compromise, often said to take the question of slavery off the table for wearied Americans, did not quiet the controversy at all. Though white Americans reluctantly admitted it, or pretended it wasn't happening, a "river of struggle," as Vincent Harding has put it, "slowly, steadily developed its black power beneath the rough surfaces of the new nation."[81] James Forten, now in his sixties, stands as an apt example. Becoming evermore active, as if to finish his life with a flourish that would counteract the effects of his neighbor Tench Coxe's corrosive formulations about race and citizenship, he penned an early contribution in 1827 to *Freedom's Journal*, indicting Henry Clay's dishonesty in pretending to be the friend of oppressed black Americans when his real intention, in promoting the American Colonization Society, was to rid the South of free black men and women whose presence threatened slavery.[82] In 1829, Boston's David Walker published the *Appeal to the Colored Citizens of the World*, which encouraged free black citizens to challenge white arguments such as those published by Coxe. Especially, he nourished the belief, in prose that fairly leaped off the page, that if America was truly to be a redeemer nation, redemption of the nation's sins would have to be the work of black, not white, Americans. Thus, in his "volume of fire," Walker called not only for black Americans to "think and feel and act as one solid body" but to see themselves as God's chosen people, a people whose resistance to slavery and white discrimination was divinely sanctioned.[83]

Two years later, as William Lloyd Garrison was preparing to launch his fiery abolitionist paper *The Liberator*, James Forten sent money for twenty-seven subscriptions that bought the ream of paper for the first issue. In the first month of publication, Forten contributed another essay attacking colonization as a wicked scheme based on the noxious notion that "a [black] man is an alien to the country in which he was born." Forten carried on his struggle for another decade. When he died in 1841, he had given not an inch from his belief that "to separate the blacks from the whites is as impossible as to bail out the Delaware [River] with a bucket."[84]

Of course, white legislators *were* able to separate white and black Americans in civil and legal terms, at the cost of compromising the founding fathers' belief in birthright citizenship. But James Forten, black citizen and patriot of the revolutionary generation, passed the torch to a new generation of black leaders, who occupied the anomalous status of free *non*-citizens in a white man's country. They would have to cope with the northern support for pro-slavery southerners that Tench Coxe had helped to galvanize; and in Forten's

Philadelphia they would have to gird their loins against the ever-strengthening nexus that linked the city's textile production with cotton-producing southern states. Yet whites, for all their power, whether in Philadelphia or elsewhere, could never sever free black Americans socially, economically, physically, or ideologically from American society at large. A people within a people perhaps, a nation within a nation, but nonetheless they were Americans. That this would remain overwhelmingly the commitment among African Americans was in no small part attributable to their remembrance and veneration of the black founding fathers and mothers of the revolutionary age, figures such as Richard Allen and James Forten of Philadelphia, Prince Hall and Phillis Wheatley of Boston, and similar touchstone figures whose names were invoked wherever free black people gathered in the young American nation.

NOTES

1. Rogers Smith, *Civic Ideals: Conflicting Visions of Citizenship in U.S. History* (New Haven: Yale University Press, 1997), 167.

2. Ibid., 165.

3. Quoted in Gary B. Nash, *Forging Freedom: The Formation of Philadelphia's Black Community* (Cambridge, Mass.: Harvard University Press, 1989), 47.

4. Ibid.; the quotation on Forten is from William Nell's *Colored Patriots of the American Revolution* (Boston, 1855), where a florid account of Forten's naval experience is given, 167–70. The fullest account of Forten's early life is in Julie Winch, *A Gentleman of Color: The Life of James Forten* (New York: Oxford University Press, 2002), chaps. 1–3.

5. Quoted in Gary B. Nash and Jean R. Soderlund, *Freedom by Degrees: Emancipation in Pennsylvania and its Aftermath* (New York: Oxford University Press, 1991), 112.

6. James H. Kettner, *The Development of American Citizenship, 1608–1870* (Chapel Hill: University of North Carolina Press, 1978), 288. For affirmations of racial equality and the use of July 4 to attack the national sin of slavery in the 1790s and early years of the nineteenth century, see David Waldstreicher, *In the Midst of Perpetual Fetes: The Making of American Nationalism, 1776–1820* (Chapel Hill: University of North Carolina Press, 1997), 308–14.

7. Gary B. Nash, "Reverberations of Haiti in the American North: Black Saint Dominguans in Philadelphia," *Pennsylvania History* 65 (1998): 44–73. For the Haitian Revolution as "a critical juncture in attitudes and policies toward slavery and race relations," see Tim Matthewson, "Jefferson and the Nonrecognition of Haiti," *American Philosophical Society Proceedings* 140 (1996): 22–48. Forten must have witnessed the Philadelphia crowd that roughly treated the five delegates from revolutionary Saint Domingue who arrived in the summer of 1793 while in transit to Paris. See Laurent Dubois, *Avengers of the New World: The Story of the Haitian Revolution* (Cambridge, Mass.: Harvard University Press, 2004), 168–69.

8. Gary B. Nash, *Race and Revolution: The Inaugural Merrill Jensen Lectures* (Madison, Wis.: Madison House, 1988), 78; Winch, *A Gentleman of Color*, 134–35, 152–53.

9. Don E. Fehrenbacher, *The Slaveholding Republic: An Account of the United States Government's Relations to Slavery* (New York: Oxford University Press, 2001), 259–61.

10. James Forten, *Letters from a Man of Colour* (Philadelphia, 1813), 8. Excerpts from Forten's letters are republished in Herbert Aptheker, *A Documentary History of the Negro People* (2 vols.; New York: Citadel Press, 1951), vol. 1: 59–66. The date of 1804 is tentative but is suggested by the report in *New-York Evening Post* on July 10 and 12, 1804, that black Philadelphians had been driven from the July Fourth celebrations, retreated to form their own militia units, and then marched through the streets "damning the whites and saying they would shew them *St. Domingo.*"

11. Forten, *Letters of a Man of Colour*, 8. In his study of "Birthright Citizenship and the Status of Indians, Slaves, and Free Negroes" (chapter 10 of *The Development of American Citizenship*), Kettner does not treat any attack on free black citizenship before the Missouri controversy of 1819–21. In Boston, at least as early as 1814, white youth drove free blacks from the Boston Common on celebration days.

12. Forten, *Letters of a Man of Colour*, 10; for legislative proceedings, see *Journal of the Pennsylvania House* 23 (1813–14): 216, 388–89, 417, 481.

13. Forten, *Letters of a Man of Colour*, 1.

14. Ibid., 7, 10–11.

15. Ibid., 4; see Winch, *A Gentleman of Colour*, 169–74, for a discussion of Forten's letters.

16. One year later, a Federalist-controlled legislature in Connecticut disenfranchised free African Americans. See James Truslow Adams, "Disenfranchisement of Negroes in New England," *American Historical Review* 30 (1925): 543–47.

17. Richard Newman, *Transformation of American Abolitionism: Fighting Slavery in the New Republic* (Chapel Hill: University of North Carolina Press, 2002), 48.

18. Tench Coxe, "America," in *The American Edition of the New Edinburgh Encyclopaedia, Conducted by David Brewster . . . First American Edition* (Philadelphia, 1813), vol. 1, pt. 2: 667. According to Coxe's biographer, the "America" essay was a slight revision of the original essays on "The New World" published in the *Democratic Press* in 1809. See Jacob E. Cooke, *Tench Coxe and the Early Republic* (Chapel Hill: University of North Carolina Press, 1978), 504.

19. Coxe, "America," 667–68. Italics are in the original. Coxe took note of the work going on to inculcate in Native Americans a desire "to embrace our political economy, our civil institutions, our morals, and our religion," and the same was true with black Americans, though their numbers and condition made this a costly and difficult process that was "gradual, deliberate, and arduous." But he had no doubt that "the humanity of our white people" was elevating freed slaves "from their African condition" ("America," 507).

20. Ibid., 507. Cooke describes other parts of the "New World" essays, pp. 504–7.

21. Caldwell became a member of the medical faculty at the University of Pennsylvania in 1810, though by now he was estranged from Rush. Caldwell's essays were provoked by the reissue of Samuel Stanhope Smith's *Essay on the Causes of the Variety of Complexion and Figure in the Human Species* in 1810, where Smith argued for the unity of humankind and averred that "the Negro is in every respect similar to us, only that his skin, or rather the skin of his ancestors, had

been darkened by the sun." For a detailed account, see Bruce Dain, *A Hideous Monster: American Race Theory in the Early Republic* (Cambridge, Mass.: Harvard University Press, 2002), chap. 2.

22. Winthrop D. Jordan, *White Over Black: American Attitudes Toward the Negro, 1550–1812* (Chapel Hill: University of North Carolina Press, 1968), 533–34.

23. Dain, *A Hideous Monster,* 72.

24. Jordan, *White Over Black,* 530–38.

25. Ibid., 542–43.

26. Quoted in Jordan, *White Over Black,* 544.

27. Jefferson, *Notes on the State of Virginia* (1786), quoted in Jordan, *White Over Black,* 546.

28. Ibid., 547.

29. Quoted in Nash, *Forging Freedom,* 180.

30. Ibid., 180.

31. Quoted in Noel Ignatiev, *How the Irish Became White* (New York: Routledge, 1995), 52.

32. Quoted in Nash, *Forging Freedom,* 179.

33. Ignatiev explains Branagan's turnabout as a reaction to the climactic victory of the black Haitian revolutionaries and the campaign of Dessalines, Touissant L'Ouverture's successor, to rid the island of white people altogether. *How the Irish Became White,* 56.

34. William B. Gravely's "The Dialectic of Double Consciousness in Black American Freedom Celebrations, 1808–1863," *Journal of Negro History* 69 (1982): 302–17, is the pioneering study of this phenomenon. The literature on this topic has grown steadily since then. For a recent discussion with citations to other work see Waldstreicher, *In the Midst of Perpetual Fetes,* 323–36, and Mitch Kachun, *Festivals of Freedom: Memory and Meaning in African American Celebrations, 1808–1915* (Amherst: University of Massachusetts Press, 2003).

35. For a discussion of white ridicule of black Americans celebrating the end of the slave trade–the so-called "Bobalition broadsides"—see Waldstreicher, *In the Midst of Perpetual Fetes,* 337–44, and Joanne Melish, *Disowning Slavery: Gradual Emancipation and "Race" in New England, 1780–1860* (Ithaca, N.Y.: Cornell University Press, 1998), 166–83.

36. Shane White, "'It Was a Proud Day': African Americans, Festivals, and Parades in the North, 1741–1834," *Journal of American History* 81 (1994): 13–50.

37. For an extended discussion of the early "freedom festivals," see Kachun, *Festivals of Freedom,* chap. 1.

38. Parrott, *Two Orations on the Abolition of the Slave Trade Delivered in Philadelphia in 1812 and 1816,* quoted in Kachun, *Festivals of Freedom,* 32.

39. Paul Goodman, *Of One Blood: Abolitionism and the Origins of Racial Equality* (Berkeley: University of California Press, 1998), 19. The ACS has been the subject of a tangled debate over its origins, composition, leadership, and motives. See Douglas R. Egerton, "'Its Origin Is Not a Little Curious': A New Look at the American Colonization Society," *Journal of the Early Republic* 5 (1985): 463–80. A revised version appears in Egerton's *Rebels, Reformers, and Revolutionaries: Collected Essays and Second Thoughts* (New York: Routledge, 2002), 107–19.

40. Forten had been in close touch with New Bedford's Paul Cuffe, an ardent emigrationist who in 1810 and 1815 had taken northern black people, disillusioned with the white man's republic, to Sierra Leone on several voyages. In about 1812, Forten himself had become president of the Philadelphia African Institution—a local adjunct of Cuffe's Friendly Society of Sierra Leone.

41. Accounts of this dramatic meeting are in Nash, *Forging Freedom*, 237–39, and Winch, *A Gentleman of Color*, 190–92.

42. Forten to Cuffe, Jan. 25, 1817, in Rosalind Cobb Wiggins, *Captain Paul Cuffe's Logs and Letters, 1808–1817* (Washington, D.C., Howard University Press, 1996), 502, and Forten's later account of the meeting in *The Emancipator*, June 30, 1835.

43. Ibid.

44. "The Protest and Remonstrance of the People of Color in the City and County of Philadelphia," in Aptheker, *A Documentary History* 1: 71–72; and James Forten and Russell Perrott, "An Address to the Humane and Benevolent Inhabitants of the City and County of Philadelphia, Aug. 17, 1817 in Dorothy Porter, ed, *Early Negro Writing, 1760–1837* (Boston: Beacon Press, 1971), 265–68. Forten and Parrott emphasized that free blacks were entitled to "share the protection of the excellent laws and just government . . . in common with every individual of the community."

45. *Philadelphia Union*, June 6 and 10, 1818, published in Isaac V. Brown, ed., *Memoirs of the Rev. Robert Finley* (New Brunswick, N.J.: Terhune and Letson, 1819). The author of the dialogues was Robert Finley, president of the Princeton Theological Seminary and publicist of the American Colonization Society.

46. Quoted in P. J. Staudenraus, *The African Colonization Movement, 1816–1865* (New York: Columbia University Press, 1961), 28.

47. Caldwell in *National Intelligencer*, Dec. 24, 1816. "It has been a subject of unceasing regret, and anxious solicitude, among many of our best patriots, and wisest statesmen, from the first establishment of our independence," he confessed, "that this class of people [free black Americans] should remain a monument of reproach to those sacred principles of civil liberty, which constitute the foundations of all our constitutions."

48. Kettner, *The Development of American Citizenship*, 311.

49. Ibid., 312.

50. *Annals of Congress*, 16th Cong., 2d Sess., 596–99.

51. Ibid., iii, quoted in Kettner, *The Development of American Citizenship*, 313.

52. Quoted in Leon Litwack, *North of Slavery: The Negro in the Free States, 1790–1860* (Chicago: University of Chicago Press, 1961), 35.

53. Litwack, *North of Slavery*, 36–39; Kettner, *The Development of American Citizenship*, 313–14; Smith, *Civic Ideals*, 179–81.

54. Coxe published his first two essays on November 25 and 28, 1820, and followed them with nine others in December. The final two essays appeared on January 4 and 8, 1821. The essays were precipitated by the Missouri controversy—and more particularly by the second Missouri controversy over the right of free black people to enter the state—a measure that Pennsylvania's legislature contemplated from 1805 to 1813 in regard to sealing its own borders. Cooke, *Tench Coxe and the Early Republic*, 513. Cooke points out that Coxe was a frequent contributor to Binns's *Democratic Press* and sometime manager of the paper. Coxe continued his attacks on black capabilities in "A Democratic Federalist," "To the People of the United States of America; concerning the Colored Population," *Democratic Press*, Feb. 6, 8, and 12, 1821 and the essay "Les Noires" on June 26, 1821.

55. The quoted phrase is from the first "Helot" essay in *Democratic Press*, Nov. 25, 1820.

56. Ibid.

57. Ibid.

58. Quoted in Cooke, *Tench Coxe and the Early Republic*, 515 (apparently from an essay by Coxe signed "Columbus" in *National Recorder*, Feb. 26, 1820). Coxe soon altered his plan. Creating reservations for free African Americas would be too expensive, he decided, putting aside the question how free black people might have sustained themselves in this kind of situation.

59. Quoted in Cooke, *Tench Coxe and the Early Republic*, 514. James Brewer Stewart, in "The Emergence of Racial Modernity and the Rise of the White North, 1790 1840," *Journal of the Early Republic* 18 (1998): 183n2, argues that the 1830s represent the crucial decade when "a reflexive disposition on the part of an overwhelming number of northern whites (intellectuals and politicians as well as ordinary people) to regard superior and inferior races as uniform, biologically determined, self-evident, naturalized, immutable 'truths'—and, the development of integrated trans-regional systems of intellectual endeavor, popular culture, politics and state power that enforced uniform white supremacist norms as 'self-evident' social 'facts.'" Coxe's essays on the "Helots of the United States" indicate that the hardening of white social thinking on matters of race took form at least a decade earlier.

60. Cooke, *Tench Coxe and the Early Republic*, 514.

61. Coxe may also have been influenced by the graphic racial caricatures produced by David Claypool Johnston and William Thackera, which adorned the walls of the city's genteel white citizens in about 1819. See Nash, *Forging Freedom*, 254–55. The cartoons used pseudo-black dialect and pictured pretentious dress to mock the vanity and stupidity of free black people in Philadelphia. Beneath the humor lay the deadly message that black people were by nature incapable of exercising the rights and responsibilities of citizenship. See Joanne Melish, *Disowning Slavery*, chapter 5, for the emergence of a series of broadsides in Boston that ridiculed free black aspiration to citizenship and turned free people of color into "counterfeit citizens" (167). Patrick Rael, in *Black Identity and Black Protest in the Antebellum North* (Chapel Hill: University of North Carolina Press, 2002), 73, observes that the racial caricatures "sought to undermine blacks' new claims to participate legitimately in public sphere discourse by pulling those claims against the stream of progress, back into the realm of a passing age of patron-client relations."

62. "Helots of the United States," nos. 7 and 11, *Democratic Press*, Dec. 22, 30, 1820.

63. Quoted in Cooke, *Tench Coxe and the Early Republic*, 513.

64. "Helots," no. 3, *Democratic Press*, Dec. 2, 1820.

65. "Helots," no. 11, *Democratic Press*, Dec. 30, 1820.

66. "Helots," no. 6, *Democratic Press*, Dec. 20, 1820.

67. Roberts Vaux and Rev. Charles Milnor were among the important PAS leaders who supported the ACS. By the early 1830s, when the influence of the PAS had waned, Pennsylvania had more than eighty local auxiliaries of the ACS, about one-third of all those spread across the country. See Newman, *Transformation of American Abolitionism*, 117–19.

68. Cooke, *Tench Coxe and the Early Republic*, 515. Christ Church, where Coxe worshiped, contributed to the Philadelphia branch of the ACS. The Episcopal bishop in Philadelphia, William White, and Robert Ralston, president of the United States Bank, with whom Coxe interacted frequently, were both early members of the ACS. For Sellers, see his foreword to Goodman, *Of One Blood*, xi. Some of Coxe's language in the essays is redolent of that of Henry Clay, a prime leader of the ACS who argued that colonization would "rid the country of a useless and pernicious, if not dangerous, portion of its population."

69. Smith, *Civic Ideals*, 167.

70. Thomas Morris, quoted in Wilentz, "The Details of Greatness," *New Republic*, March 29, 2004, 27.

71. George A. Boyd, *Elias Boudinot: Patriot and Statesman* (Princeton, N.J.: Princeton University Press, 1952), cited in See Robert P. Forbes, "Slavery and the Meaning of America, 1819–1837," Ph.D. diss., Yale University, 1994, 182.

72. Forbes, "Slavery and the Meaning of America," 176–78, 238–40; Jefferson quoted at 264.

73. Cooke, *Tench Coxe and the Early Republic,* 513; Forbes, "Slavery and the Meaning of America," 182.

74. Forbes treats Pennsylvania's role in the Missouri controversy in "Slavery and the Meaning of America," 196–97, 176–82, 224–26, 239–40, and 264–65.

75. Cooke observes that the "precise effect" of Coxe's writings "is difficult to assess" because "literary or journalistic influence cannot be precisely determined by any known method. . . . It is impossible to say how large an audience Coxe's articles commanded," Cooke concludes (*Tench Coxe and the Early Republic,* 507).

76. The requirement of property worth 250 dollars disfranchised many free black New Yorkers. Five years later, all property requirements for white men were eliminated. Leon Litwack, *North of Slavery: The Negro in the United States, 1790–1860* (Chicago: University of Chicago Press, 1961), 82–83. Black Connecticut freemen had lost the franchise in 1818.

77. Vaux to Samuel Emlen, May 31, 1831, quoted in Litwack, *North of Slavery,* 64. Attempts to revive bills to ban the entry of free black people reached Pennsylvania's legislature after 1820 but were rebuffed by those who insisted that the criterion of citizenship was not skin color.

78. Rael, *Black Identity and Black Protest,* 48. The first historian of Philadelphia, John Fanning Watson, wrote in his 1830 *Annals of Philadelphia, and Pennsylvania in the Olden Time* that "Their aspirings and little vanities have been rapidly growing since they got those separate churches, and have received their entire exemption from slavery. . . . Thirty to forty years ago, they were much humbler, more esteemed in their places, and more useful to themselves and others" (rpt. Philadelphia: Edwin S. Stuart, 1900), vol. 2: 261.

79. *The Souls of Black Folk, Essays and Sketches* (1903; rpt. Greenwich, Conn., 1961), 141.

80. John Saillant, *Black Puritan, Black Republican: The Life and Thought of Lemuel Haynes, 1753–1833* (New York: Oxford University Press, 2003), 177–80.

81. Harding, *There Is a River: The Black Struggle for Freedom in America* (New York: Vintage Books, 1983), 75.

82. "Original Communication" from "A Man of Colour," *Freedom's Journal,* May 18, 1827.

83. For the fullest treatment of Walker's *Appeal*, see Peter P. Hinks, *To Awaken My Afflicted Brethren: David Walker and the Problem of Antebellum Slave Resistance* (University Park, Pa.: Penn State University Press, 1997). Walker's message of black Christians as "a chosen people" was far from new. Richard Allen had used this phrase as early as 1794 in Philadelphia, and Absalom Jones, Allen's close colleague and fellow church leader, had a poignant passage from Isaiah inscribed on the inside wall of St. Thomas's African Episcopal Church: "But ye are a chosen generation, a royal priesthood, and an holy nation, a peculiar people; that ye should shew forth the praise of him who hath called you out of darkness into his marvelous light; which in time past were not a people, but are now the people of God." Similarly, in 1805, Daniel Coker in Baltimore

published on the theme of blacks in America as "the people of God," a "chosen generation," and a "holy nation" which had a biblical sanction, comparable to the Hebrew exodus from Egypt, to cleanse white Christians who were mired in the sins of slaveholding and racism and had trapped themselves in the logical contradiction of trying to build a republic of slaveholders. See Albert Raboteau, *A Fire in the Bones: Reflections on African-American Religious History* (Boston: Beacon Press, 1995), chapter 2, "'Ethiopia Shall Soon Stretch Forth Her Hands': Black Destiny in Nineteenth-Century America."

84. *The Liberator,* Jan. 22, 1831.

CHAPTER 5

The Pennsylvania Abolition Society and the
Struggle for Racial Justice

RICHARD NEWMAN

No abolitionist group was more famous than the Pennsylvania Abolition Society. Founded in the hallowed American year of 1775 (when revolutionary
Minutemen fired the shot heard 'round the world) and dedicated to the proposition that slavery was not merely a moral problem but an insidious institution
that must be vigorously uprooted, the Pennsylvania Abolition Society (PAS)
defined American abolitionism for over fifty years. Indeed, until the Garrisonian assault on bondage and racial injustice utterly transformed abolitionism
in the 1830s, PAS members constituted, as William Lloyd Garrison admitted,
one of the most dedicated group of reformers anywhere. Abolitionists throughout the Atlantic world lauded the group's activities too, from its petition efforts to state and federal governments to its legal aid system for endangered
African Americans. For many statesmen and reformers, PAS membership was
a crowning achievement. "I have just received [a note] . . . admitting me as a
member of the PAS," a London man excitedly wrote the group in 1795. "I take
the opportunity to assure you that no honor or distinction could have been
more acceptable to one . . . [and] I will always endeavor to . . . promote that
benevolent and righteous design which constitutes the leading object of this
respectable society."[1] African Americans remained eternally grateful to PAS
lawyers. In 1841, for example, Philadelphia's black community gathered en
masse at Bethel Church to celebrate the unmatched legal exertions provided
by PAS member David Paul Brown, a white lawyer and longtime legal consul-
tant to Afro-Philadelphians. As Robert Purvis shouted in the crowded church,
no one had done as much "advocating the . . . liberties of the oppressed of this
country" than that PAS legal eagle, David Paul Brown.[2]

Although abolitionism's gold standard during the early national period,
the PAS has received surprisingly little historiographical treatment. Even

textbooks devoted to antislavery movements, or early African American history, skip over the group's formation and evolution, focusing instead on later periods and people. Perhaps, as the noted nineteenth-century historian Francis Parkman once wrote, "it is the nature of great events to obscure the great events that came before them."[3] But must the PAS perennially take second place to those justly famous post-1830s abolitionists—Garrison, Frederick Douglass, Lydia Maria Child, Maria Stewart?

The answer, of course, is no. Indeed, the PAS's marvelously long institutional history—the group remains operational in our own time—illuminates much about the earliest antislavery movements in America. Inaugurated during a time when Thomas Jefferson and other founders wished slavery away but often refused to take literal abolitionist steps, the PAS had a coherent abolitionist strategy to destroy bondage: the adoption of state-sponsored gradual abolition plans. And in a time when endangered African Americans—from kidnapping victims to duped indentured laborers—could attain only spotty support, the PAS created a legal aid system that rendered aid to hundreds, perhaps thousands, of black men and women, including many fugitive slaves. The PAS issued the first federal petition to Congress in 1790, and was among the first groups to call for slavery's end in the federally controlled District of Columbia. As southern secessionists of the 1860s made clear, organized abolitionism pre-dated even the "fanaticism" of Garrison and Douglass; it dated from Pennsylvania abolitionists' activism during the nation's founding era. Georgia disunionist Thomas R.R. Cobb declared that, ever since those pesky Pennsylvania reformers organized an abolitionist society, slavery had been under assault.[4]

The organizational history of the PAS also illuminates the limits of interracial activism. It is axiomatic in contemporary scholarly circles that black and white abolitionists vehemently disagreed about a range of issues, from politics to the use of violent tactics to the very leadership of the abolitionist struggle. As historians Jane and William Pease argued in "two abolitionisms," a much under-rated book chapter from the 1970s, a deep "conceptual chasm separated black from white [abolitionists]."[5] This perceptual gap, borne of the obviously divergent social experiences of black and white reformers, translated into differing perceptions over tactics, strategy, and the very definition of the abolitionist project in antebellum culture. In short, they concluded, abolitionism could only be studied as a fragmented movement, not as a single entity.

Pease and Pease's Duboisian framework of two abolitionisms—a white reform movement and a black reform movement often irreconcilably opposed to one another—has compelled a generation of scholars to re-examine the promise and prospect of interracial activism. But because their work, like that of many scholars following in their footsteps, refers mostly to the antebellum period, an important aspect of that question often goes unanswered: how did black and white reformers interact *prior to* the 1830s?[6] Were there "two abolitionisms" even before Garrison and Frederick Douglass parted ways? On these questions too, the PAS's institutional history provides a critical analytical perspective for historians to consider. As the nascent abolitionist movement's leading group, the PAS was the first antislavery organization to confront the day-to-day realities of the color line. In fact, Pennsylvania abolitionists created a rich and varied relationship with free black activists and communities along the mid-Atlantic coast. While often serving as blacks' ally in political and legal venues, however, the group did not admit African American members to its ranks until much later, during the antebellum era. Moreover, although the PAS often served as free blacks' educational patrons, it did not advocate interracial schooling, nor did it publicly support African Americans' claims to equality during debates over colonization in the early nineteenth century. While the PAS did much to launch the formal abolitionist movement in early national society, its institutional conservatism also convinced many African Americans to create their own autonomous conception of abolitionism—one that directly influenced the Garrisonian generation of radical reformers.

(1)
THE PAS AND AMERICAN ABOLITIONISM

The Pennsylvania Abolition Society was the Atlantic world's very first antislavery group. Any analysis of the PAS, however, must begin with abolitionism's Quaker roots. Long before the PAS's official organization in 1775, the Religious Society of Friends had meditated on slavery's iniquity. Quaker writers produced the richest body of antislavery literature, and the earliest abolitionist codes, of any religious or secular group in colonial America. Between the 1730s and 1770s, a succession of Pennsylvania Quakers—Ralph Sandiford, Benjamin Lay, John Woolman, Anthony Benezet—issued antislavery missives. Late in his life, Benjamin Franklin proudly recalled printing much of this Quaker antislavery literature. When British reformers claimed credit for pushing antislavery into the mainstream, Franklin countered that "the good seed" of antislavery had been sown much earlier in Pennsylvania. Indeed, he noted, "I myself printed . . . [works] against keeping negroes in slavery" as early as 1729.[7]

By the American Revolutionary era, Quaker rhetoric had become reality, as the Religious Society of Friends in Philadelphia issued strict edicts against both slave trading and slaveholding. Thus, during a time when a considerable portion of Anglo-American culture considered slavery a normative institution, Pennsylvania Quakers labeled it a curse and told members that refusal to comply with abolitionist doctrines would result in banishment from the Society of Friends.

A select group of Pennsylvania Quakers hoped to expand upon this impressive, though localized, abolitionist foundation. And so in 1775 roughly a dozen men met at Philadelphia's Rising Sun Tavern to dedicate themselves to a new brand of antislavery activism. Though under the leadership of stalwart reformers like Anthony Benezet and Thomas Paine, this initial version of the PAS—called the "Society for the Relief of Free Negroes Unlawfully held in Bondage"—stalled for a couple of years during the Revolutionary War. The group reformed after peace with Great Britain in 1784. Now calling itself the "Pennsylvania Society for Promoting the Abolition of Slavery and for the Relief of Free Negroes Unlawfully Held in bondage," the PAS (as it then became known) had a new mission: not merely to aid people illegally held in bondage but to promote abolitionism locally and nationally. Two important documents from the time bolstered the PAS's mission. First, the Declaration of Independence had grounded American society in the principles of human equality. Second, Pennsylvania's new state government had passed the world's first gradual abolition law in 1780, guaranteeing that all slaves born after that date on Pennsylvania soil would be freed at the age of twenty-eight. Though the law had loopholes—and it did *not* liberate slaves born prior to 1780—it applied to slaveholders emigrating from other states. As Marylanders and Virginians would soon discover, failure to comply with the state's abolition act (for instance, by registering enslaved people if one was staying longer than six months) often resulted in successful black freedom claims.[8]

PAS ideology was grounded firmly in two worlds: that of the Enlightenment, and that of universalist religion. Like Enlightenment rationalists, Pennsylvania abolitionists believed that slavery must be put under the light of reasoned discourse and action. Once statesmen and citizens learned of slavery's horrible realities, they would find bondage to be anathema to republican government and take appropriate, if gradual, steps to destroy the cursed institution. Then too, like religious enthusiasts throughout the eighteenth-century world, they believed that neither the Lord nor the Bible sanctioned bondage. The Golden Rule was the PAS's credo: Do unto others, as you would have them do unto you. The PAS affixed this motto to its own constitution, written in 1787 after the society reorganized itself. "It having pleased the creator of the world," the group explained, "to make of one flesh all the children of men, it becomes them to consult and promote each others' interests as members of the same family, however diversified they may be, by color, situation, religion or different states of society." The PAS's constitution went on to note that it was "more especially the duty of those persons who profess to maintain for themselves the rights of human nature" to expand freedom and equality. If Americans wanted to remain liberty's leaders in the world, they must attack slavery.[9]

One other facet of PAS ideology revolved around race. For the group soon came to believe that its mission included wholesale racial uplift. In 1787, the PAS added a key phrase to its official title that indicated this new belief. To its mission of fighting slavery and aiding kidnapped free blacks, the group was now dedicated to "improving the condition of the African race."[10] In other words, PAS members became convinced of the need to make African Americans fit for freedom. The Pennsylvania Abolition Society was not alone in making such claims—the post-revolutionary age was ripe with programs of black uplift. Nor would this goal mark the PAS as unique among white abolitionist groups in America. What this plank did suggest, however, was Pennsylvania abolitionists' concern with blacks' fitness for freedom.

Such concerns notwithstanding, the PAS continued to strike at slavery where it could. Just how did the group do this?[11] Early abolitionists believed first and foremost in the efficacy of gradual, not immediate, abolitionism. While the PAS certainly supported immediatism on occasion—in the liberation of kidnapped free blacks and some fugitive slaves—it more consistently supported gradual abolition schemes at the state level. It is important to remember time and place here, for the PAS operated at a time when federal union was a new concept and slavery a national institution. PAS members worried that abolitionist agitation, if too radical, could wreck both antislavery and union. This they learned first from Pennsylvania politics. The Quaker state contained roughly seven thousand enslaved people when the gradual abolition act took effect in 1780. Masters did not universally cheer the law; in fact, there were efforts to rescind it through the 1790s.[12]

Moderation became even more important as the PAS looked at the national and even international scene. The Haitian Revolution (1791–1804) and a series of attempted North American slave uprisings (reports of a Virginia conspiracy in 1794, Gabriel's Rebellion of 1800, and the Louisiana Uprising of 1811) struck a powerful blow against the idea that slaves would not fight for their liberty. But slave rebellions also convinced many white politicians and masters that abolitionism—to say nothing of racial equality—was foolhardy. Many slaveholders doubted the efficacy of even gradual abolitionism. In Virginia, the PAS knew that private emancipation had only recently been permitted by the state legislature in 1782, while northern states with relatively small enslaved populations had often fierce debates over the adoption of gradualist laws through the 1800s. While every northern state would eventually abolish slavery via gradualist edicts, the road to northern emancipation was anything but smooth. New Yorkers contested gradual abolition schemes all the way up to 1799, when the legislature finally adopted a plan to manumit nearly twenty-one thousand slaves; New Jersey adopted such a plan only in 1804. Even after these states adopted abolitionist laws, slaveholders found ways to evade them. Shane White has estimated, for example, that New York City masters sold to southern slave markets nearly a third of their to-be-emancipated slaves.[13]

In such a climate, Pennsylvania abolitionists believed that gradualism was the soundest antislavery policy. At the same time, they knew deep in their bones that gradualism did not translate into passivity. Indeed, PAS activists were fired not only by religious morals and ideological precepts of equality but by a firm belief that abolitionism must become a firm part of American civic culture to be successful. Tactically, the group targeted public men (statesmen, jurists, legislators) as key potential supporters of their cause. Thus did the PAS appeal to Virginia Governor Edmund Randolph in 1788 as a potential abolitionist ally. Would he be both a corresponding member and an advocate of abolitionism within the largest slaveholding polity in America? Randolph's response illuminates some of the problems even gradualists faced in the post-revolutionary era. No, no, Randolph wrote back to the PAS, he could never be an official sponsor of PAS-style abolitionism in his own state, for he believed that slavery was a private matter. He could only wish the Pennsylvanians well—and hope they did not meddle with slavery in his state. The group received a better reception that same year from Governor John Collins of Rhode Island. Pennsylvania abolitionists had sent him "a few copies of their constitution, and the laws of Pennsylvania which relate to [abolition]," hoping that Collins would use his elevated station to crack down on the slave trade in his state. Collins pledged to do just that. The PAS hoped that Collins would be an example to all public men.[14]

In this manner, the PAS steadily expanded its institutional base and reach. In 1787, the group re-organized and wrote a formal constitution. Not merely an advocacy group, the PAS looked like, and worked like, a mini-government. There was a "president," treasurer, secretaries, and various "counselors." The group operated through a series of departments (known as committees) dedicated to specific abolitionist tasks. There was an acting committee, which kept track of PAS activities on a quarterly basis; a committee of guardians, which dealt specifically with black educational and apprenticing concerns; an electing committee, to nominate new members and keep track of an expanding membership base; and a committee of correspondence, charged with not merely secretarial duties but promoting the cause among a broad range of contacts in Britain, France, and the Caribbean, not to mention governing officials and statesmen in nearly every American polity and many territories.[15]

Post-revolutionary society's emphasis on civic virtue and activism became discernable influences on PAS style too. Just as philanthropists and civic-minded officials formed benevolent societies to focus attention on key issues, so too did the PAS picture itself as a respectable society of civic-minded men. And just as banks and churches sought official incorporation from the state as a seal of their public-mindedness, so too did the PAS seek and gain a charter from the state in 1789. As Benjamin Franklin, probably the spearhead behind the incorporation attempt, knew, state backing would provide both civic respectability and institutional integrity. Incorporation, the PAS argued, would give a "permanency and security" to abolitionism, while philanthropists could donate money (to black schools, say) confident in the knowledge that the Commonwealth of Pennsylvania was behind the group.[16] In short, in the hands of the PAS, abolitionism would be no fly-by-night concern. If, as John Stauffer has written, subsequent abolitionists would revel in their status as "passionate outsiders," then Pennsylvania reformers reveled in the notion that they were felicitous insiders.[17]

Despite its grounding in Pennsylvania, the PAS pitched itself as an organization of national and international import. The group hoped that by cultivating national contacts the PAS would become a model for the formation of many other abolitionist societies. Together, these groups would form an ever-expanding abolitionist front that would pressure governing officials and jurists into enacting abolitionist laws. Antislavery would then become a national movement grounded in local institutions. The PAS became the leader of the first clearinghouse for the myriad abolitionist groups appearing in the 1780s and 1790s, the American Convention of Abolition Societies. Meeting biennially from 1794 through 1836, the group included institutions from New York, Maryland, Delaware, and even Virginia. Though many southern abolition societies in particular had trouble operating in PAS fashion, the American Convention nevertheless issued national calls to curtail the slave trade and domestic slave trade. Nevertheless, this first national antislavery body was clearly limited in scope. Several abolition societies beyond the PAS admitted slaveholders; some favored colonization schemes as well. For this reason, the group continued to operate as a quasi-national organization.[18]

As it grew steadily during the 1780s and 1790s, the PAS also cultivated international contacts. While Ben Franklin became a focal point of the PAS's overseas outreach during his presidency of the group, Anthony Benezet deserves credit for instilling in the early PAS members an international ethic. His correspondence with British reformers and politicians sparkled with hopes that American-style abolitionism—shining a light on injustice and then steadily working to eradicate it—would spread around the world. Franklin sharpened Benezet's focus and expanded its reach in his brief reign atop the organization. By the 1800s, PAS files bulged with correspondence to and from the brightest minds—Condorcet, Abby Raynal, Granville Sharpe, Richard Price, Edmund Randolph, St. George Tucker, Noah Webster, John Adams.

It pays to shine just a bit more light on Franklin, an abolitionist convert at the very end of his life and PAS president from 1787 to 1790, who corresponded with a bevy of reformers in both Paris and England. Indeed, no one offers a better glimpse into the hopes of PAS activists than Poor Richard himself. A former northern slaveholder, as David Waldstreicher has wonderfully shown, Ben Franklin accommodated to slavery for most of his life.[19] Yet Franklin also came to see abolitionism as part of a momentous change sweeping through western society. Slavery, Franklin knew by the 1780s, was a dirty word. For much of his life, "abolition" had nothing whatsoever to do with racial slavery. Franklin initially used the word when referring to things like colonial fears that England would abolish trial by jury. After Franklin joined the PAS, however, he used "abolition" only in reference to battling bondage.

And he excitedly wrote to friends around the world about the wonders of the PAS. Its exertions, he hoped, would put slavery forever on the defensive. Who knows, he thought, someday it might be abolished altogether.

(2)

**BUILDING A TACTICAL ASSAULT ON SLAVERY
WITH AFRICAN AMERICAN SUPPORT**

The PAS earned its activist reputation by attacking slavery both in courts of law and in the halls of representative government. Indeed, while it circulated antislavery missives and spent considerable funds on schools for free black children, the group was best known for its legal and political initiatives. While antebellum abolitionists often get the credit for launching petitioning efforts, Pennsylvania abolitionists were in fact the first group of American reformers to utilize consistently the sacred mode of petitioning for antislavery purposes. No sooner had the Constitutional Convention met in 1787 in Philadelphia than the PAS sought to infiltrate this nascent federal government by giving Benjamin Franklin an anti–slave-trading petition. Although Franklin pocketed the memorial—fearing that it would create tension between slaveholding and emancipating sections of the new federal union—the PAS was not deterred. Over the next decade, the group became a familiar presence at Congress (which met, conveniently, in Philadelphia from 1790 until 1800), offering memorials against the slave trade. By the early years of the nineteenth century, PAS petitions were aimed at restricting slavery's expansion to western territories and eliminating bondage in the federally controlled District of Columbia. At the state level, Pennsylvania abolitionists launched similar offensives, petitioning to end the domestic slave trade through and around the state, to protect free blacks from kidnapping threats, and even to convert gradual emancipation plans into immediate ones.

If the group was far from successful in achieving its grandest plans—Congress did not ban slavery or slave trading in the District of Columbia, nor did the state of Pennsylvania adopt immediate emancipation laws—it nevertheless pushed governing officials to take abolitionism seriously. In short, the PAS put abolition on the radar of state and federal legislatures.

Pennsylvania abolitionists' first congressional petition best illuminates this strategy. Presented to the federal government in February 1790, the memorial asked congressmen to craft abolitionist laws commensurate with new federal powers. "We have observed with great satisfaction," the petition stated, "that many important and salutary powers are vested in you for 'promoting the welfare' and 'securing the blessings of liberty' to the people of the United States." Both slavery and the slave trade were a blight on Americans' liberty-loving character. Perhaps, the PAS prodded, federal officials would use such powers to end the overseas slave trade—or to take aim at domestic slavery itself. The sooner the federal government became involved in abolitionism, the better.[20]

Many southern congressmen were aghast, particularly members from the Deep South. Those pesky Pennsylvania abolitionists, James Jackson of Georgia thundered, would swing from a rope if they ever entered his state carrying such a memorial. Years later, on the eve of his state's secession from the union, Georgian Robert Toombs would recall that this Pennsylvania petition had forever put southern slaveholders on notice about meddling northern fanatics. From that time onward, in Toombs's reckoning, southern masters sought to seal off the federal government from abolitionist intrusions. Suffice it to say that in 1790, with the union so preciously new and Deep South officials complaining so loudly, the PAS memorial did not gain many converts. The petition was in fact neutralized by a congressional committee, which accepted the memorial but affirmed slaveholders' property rights in the American union. In subsequent years, the PAS would tone down its rhetoric even as it remained a steadfast advocate of anti–slave-trading laws or other federal measures limiting slavery's growth.[21]

Despite the setback in 1790, the PAS was not being naïve in presenting so challenging a memorial to Congress. Indeed, when one considers a petition effort at the state level at roughly the same time, it is clear that the group believed its petitioning efforts could make a difference in the struggle for black liberty. When the state of Pennsylvania revised its constitution in 1790, some statesmen proposed inserting the word "white" before the enumeration of rights and liberties. Thus, "white" citizens would be ensured constitutional protections, not free black citizens. The PAS jumped to blacks' defense, urging the state constitutional convention to sack the proposed racialist rhetoric. Fortunately on this occasion, statesmen listened: The constitution of 1790 did not differentiate black from white rights. As James Forten would later write, this "estimable" decision made the Pennsylvania constitution a model for all Americans.[22]

In the legal realm, PAS lawyers worked in a similarly diligent manner for black freedom. PAS lawyers and legal aid counselors represented blacks who negotiated indentures with former masters and sought apprenticeships for their children; they aided black families trying to liberate kidnapping victims; and they even helped fugitive slaves from other states gain freedom when and where facts or legal loopholes permitted. Indeed, the legal arena provides one of the most illuminating perspectives for understanding the day-to-day operating objectives of Pennsylvania abolitionists. For PAS legal action might be described as gradualist in intent and deployment: abolitionist lawyers aimed at hindering slavery's operation in the early republic, not eliminating it in one fell swoop. Unlike second-wave abolitionists, who often extrapolated big antislavery lessons from the smallest of legal cases, PAS lawyers did not usually make grand demands for universal human freedom. They cared more about the facts of individual black freedom claims and on the technicalities and loopholes offered by state and federal law. Thus, as one Pennsylvania re-former would note in 1822, PAS activists would always be torn between the heart and head. "If it were in my power," this PAS member wrote, "I would declare without hesitation that every fugitive slave setting foot on the soil of Pennsylvania should be free and emancipated at once. Born and educated in Pennsylvania, the sentiments are so deeply rooted in my heart that they can never be . . . shaken." But, he went on, the American constitutional order protected southern slaveholders' property rights. No Pennsylvania abolitionist could therefore seek to liberate fugitives and runaways in an unquestioned manner.[23]

Nevertheless, by creating a legal aid system that helped blacks from around the nation (not just Pennsylvania), the PAS hoped to accumulate enough vic-tories in court that slavery lost its judicial sanction in key locales or became an inefficient and legally troublesome institution for masters to maintain. The group was not afraid to go to court against southern masters who flouted or ignored the state's abolition law, or to aid blacks who had certain legal loop-holes on their side. In 1825, for instance, a Maryland master lost his slave in Pennsylvania courts on grounds that he willingly let a bondman visit the Quaker State. When the enslaved man refused to return, PAS lawyers backed his freedom claim—and won on grounds that the black man was not a fugitive slave but a formerly enslaved person who had resided in Pennsylvania with his master's consent long enough to be free! While latter-day readers might marvel at the judge's decision in this case, Maryland masters fumed at PAS meddlers, going so far as to petition against abolitionist legal exertions.[24]

It did not take that long for the PAS to make its mark on Chesapeake masters. One of the most famous abolitionist cases occurred in the 1790s and involved a Virginia master's two freedom-seeking slaves and the PAS. Known in legal circles as *Respublica v. Blackmore*, the case revolved around two frontier counties once part of the Old Dominion. Some slaveholding migrants did not know—or claimed not to know—that by the 1780s they now lived in Pennsylvania, an emancipating state. Recall that the gradual abolition law of 1780 had decreed that out-of-state masters who did not register slaves within a certain period were at risk of losing them. That was a fine law for the books, but abolitionists wondered whether it would hold up in court.

Intriguingly, abolitionists discovered that many enslaved people knew that they had come to a free state. And that is precisely what happened to a Maryland master named Samuel Blackmore, who had visited the disputed counties in 1780 and then moved there in 1782 with his two slaves, but did not register them. Blackmore's slaves eventually sued for their freedom. The Pennsylvania Abolition Society served as the black women's lawyers when the case finally went to court in 1797. When Blackmore's legal counsel claimed that his client had attempted to comply with Pennsylvania's abolition law after he discovered his error, the PAS would have none of it. They used the technicality (the master's late compliance with the abolition act) to secure both women's freedom. As soon as Blackmore made his mistake (and failed to register his slaves), the PAS lectured the court, the two women were free. Knowing that the facts were on their side, PAS lawyers ventured out further, noting that Blackmore's slaves were not temporarily free but forever free. No court could ever justly re-enslave them. "Can the legislature by a law, declare a free person to be a slave when the [state] constitution declares all men [or in the case, women] free?" PAS counsel wondered? Certainly not, the court agreed, and the two women were set free. Blackmore's lawyers complained that the case boded ill for southern slaveholders.[25]

As the Blackmore case showed, Pennsylvania abolitionists were a palpable presence in mid-Atlantic courts of law. But the case showed something else too: both legal work (and petitioning, to some extent) stemmed from black activism on the ground. No sooner had Pennsylvania passed its gradual abolition law than slaves from Maryland, Virginia, and Delaware attempted to get to "free Pennsylvania." A good number of these fugitives sought—and often received—abolitionist counsel. And within Pennsylvania itself, of course, the PAS confronted an ever-increasing caseload of black kidnapping complaints. For these reasons, the PAS had to steadily increase its legal aid cadre in the

1780s and 1790s. The parallelism, in fact, between the rise of black kidnapping complaints and the PAS's assigning of more legal aid representatives is striking. Moreover, group lawyers quickly learned that African Americans needed legal aid when bargaining with masters over indenture contracts, which some lucky and crafty runaway slaves used to shorten slavery for life sentences into a five- or seven-year apprenticeships of sorts. Abolitionists and free blacks had to remain vigilant, though, for devious masters tried to re-enslave unsuspecting blacks before their freedom agreement came due. The PAS kept a massive file of emancipation and indenture certificates on hand in Philadelphia, which it found useful when dealing with kidnapping complaints about masters accused of violating freedom agreements.

Sadly, the PAS found, tales of kidnapping abounded. Between 1796 and 1798, for example, Pennsylvania abolitionists secured the release of five free black man detained illegally. In 1800, Pennsylvania abolitionists helped liberate a free black man in Winchester, Virginia. He too had been illegally detained, this time by a mistress who claimed that she could dispose of her property in any manner she saw fit, former agreements be damned. Working again with family and local reformers, the PAS discovered that an indenture agreement had been brokered and that the woman had no claim on the man's liberty. He too was soon freed.[26]

The PAS's caseload multiplied in just this way: working with African American family members and friends who came to know of its legal aid system, the group liberated a good number of kidnapped free black people. Still, many others were never found. Pennsylvania abolitionists noted in various reports to the American Convention of Abolition Societies that the domestic slave trade swallowed up a much larger number of black victims than abolitionists ever were able to help. In a particularly vexing case from the early 1800s, the PAS tried to trace the whereabouts of a free black man named William Coachman from New Jersey. Coachman had made an indenture agreement with his former master, only to disappear shortly before his liberation day. In-depth interviews with his friends, family, and neighbors filled a PAS file and brought many leads. But there were no answers to his disappearance. Abolitionists guessed that Coachman might have been sold into Maryland bondage by his former master.[27]

If these legal and political tactics are a guide, the PAS and African American reformers forged a complex relationship—or, as one might more properly refer to it, an inter-relationship. For many African Americans, white abolitionists served as an extension of their own voices. The PAS could take black complaints about, say, kidnapping, where they traditionally had little weight: in courts of law and statehouses. Thus when Pennsylvania masters tried to circumvent abolitionist codes, African Americans complained not only to local justices of the peace but to white abolitionists. The PAS responded by supplying legal expertise to endangered blacks, from kidnapping victims to fugitive slaves who, Pennsylvania abolitionists believed, may have had legitimate claims to freedom. Similarly, when white settlers from Maryland or Virginia came to the Quaker State with no intention of complying with abolitionist provisions, blacks did not simply run away; they found abolitionist lawyers who represented them in Pennsylvania courts. For these reasons, Richard Allen and Absalom Jones famously celebrated Pennsylvania abolitionists as "the Friends of him who hath no helper."[28]

Allen and Jones's phrasing not only offers an apt description of what early abolitionists sought to do for African Americans—provide practical advice and legal aid—it also suggests the broader relationship between early black and white reformers. For black activists and communities often utilized PAS members as patrons. Why? For one thing, white patronage offered African Americans momentary opportunities to break into formal political and legal venues. To gain a hearing in the U.S. Congress in December 1799, for example, Philadelphia's black community probably used a PAS member and federal representative named Nicholas Waln as a key contact. Signed by over seventy free blacks, the petition sought congressional support for both gradual abolition schemes and anti-slave trading laws. Though presented, the memorial was quickly rejected and returned. "We the People did not mean them," a Georgian exclaimed. The point here is that white abolitionists supplied the contacts that allowed free black leaders a congressional hearing. Interestingly, while that free black petition was never formerly accepted, it did become part of the congressional record. (Northern newspapers recounted the black petition effort.) James Forten, writing to the lone congressional member who eventually supported black petition rights, highlighted the importance of white patronage. Your aid, he said, allowed African American voices to speak "unfettered" in Congress, at least for a brief moment.[29]

White patronage was one side of the coin. On the other side, African American "clients" supplied local knowledge to white abolitionists intent on pursuing their own petitioning tactics and legal challenges. When the PAS sought to stand up to anti-abolitionist calls to rescind Pennsylvania's emancipation act during the 1790s, it needed information on the free black community's status—to tout, as it were, the virtues and accomplishments of abolition. PAS officials utilized their contacts in Philadelphia's free black community to gain information on the numbers of black homeowners (one hundred out of two thousand people survey), black job opportunities, and the establishment of black benevolent groups like the Free African Society. These contacts helped whites take what was in essence the first census of African American society. Abolitionists could then make the case that emancipation was indeed working in Pennsylvania—and could work nationally. Anti-abolitionist calls to halt the state's emancipation act were cut off, and hope for state-sanctioned abolitionist laws elsewhere were bolstered.

Apprenticing and indenture opportunities offer more poignant examples of this "patron-client" relationship. The PAS's steady support of black freedom claims in courts of law and legislatures gave the group a public standing that spread well beyond Philadelphia. African Americans came to rely on abolitionists for expert advice on, and communications about, apprenticing opportunities and indentured servitude. At one level, then, the PAS supplied institutional support to African Americans, helping them sign an indenture or apprentice contract. One Maryland woman—perhaps a slave—came to Philadelphia in the early 1800s just to apprentice her son through the PAS. She movingly told the group that she had to return to Maryland but wanted the PAS to zealously guard her son's life as if it were her own. This the organization did, just as it hoped to do for hundreds of other blacks. At another level, African American leaders often served as go-betweens, linking abolitionists to black people in need of apprenticing opportunities and white employers seeking laborers. In 1795, Richard Allen helped white abolitionists place over two dozen emancipated slaves in apprenticeship positions. The lot of enslaved people had come from Jamaica to Philadelphia when a British banker came into the possession of a Caribbean estate but wanted no part of bondage. He wrote to the PAS, hoping the group could make freedom possible for so many bond people. Pennsylvania abolitionists pledged aid and support, and then turned to Philadelphia's black community. Working together, the PAS and African Americans found apprentice opportunities for all twenty-eight men and women, boys and girls. Richard Allen became the key contact person, providing all manner of aid to the emancipated slaves, from spiritual to economic, blankets to bibles.[30]

For black clients and white patrons, the prospect of interracial alliance was

not only salutary but expedient. It flowed from a sense that very practical interracial cooperation—not idealistic calls for true social or political equality—
solved pressing problems: black leaders and communities raised consciousness
about certain problems, white activists provided legal and political expertise
to help solve them. But there was more. Moral uplift ideologies helped forge a
deeper sense of interracial connection among early black and white reformers.
A precursor to moral reform movements of the 1830s—a much more rigorously
defined reform program involving temperance, piety, education, and universal
equality—eighteenth-century moral uplift strategies emphasized godliness,
industriousness, and deference to community leaders. Moral uplifters believed
firmly that the individual self contained the seeds of one's social, educational,
and economic uplift. Indeed, just as Quakers believed in the "inner light," so
too did proponents of moral uplift assert that individuals had the capacity to
remake their lives—and the lives of those around them—by working hard,
praying, and paying heed to leadership figures. In this sense, moral uplift was
not completely racialized. Indeed, the PAS happily took note of black moral
uplift endeavors and attempted to bolster them by issuing their own uplift
broadsides in the black community during the 1790s and early 1800s.

Importantly, black leaders believed that moral reform must take aim at
slavery and define free blacks as equal citizens. To make sure this issue remained on statesmen's agenda, black leaders argued for their own relevance
as activists in the cause of racial justice. Early white abolitionists weren't so
sure about this. To be a legitimate public activist, PAS members emphasized,
one had to have standing in courts of law or in the halls of congress—venues
of power. With no formal standing as citizens in most locales, African Americans' were not legitimate abolitionists. Of course, black reformers disagreed.
After all, they argued in a steady stream of sermons, newspaper essays, and
pamphlets of protest issued during the early national period in Philadelphia
(and elsewhere), black reformers had the moral compass that served as abolitionism's very foundation. James Forten, the celebrated free black Philadelphia sailmaker and Revolutionary War veteran, perhaps best exemplified this
emerging tradition. His 1813 pamphlet, Series of Letters by a Man of Color,
used the one venue open to blacks—or rather, the one which African Americans successfully invaded and made their own—printed discourse. Forten's
celebrated publication argued vigorously against a proposed Pennsylvania law
requiring emigrating blacks to register, lest they be fined, jailed, or sold into
bondage.[31]

Drawing on the black jeremiad tradition, Forten declaimed against such a law. "'We hold these truths to be self-evident,'" Forten began, "that GOD created all men equal." This concept undergirded American society, embracing not merely white men but "the Indian and the European, the savage and the saint, the Peruvian and the Laplander," and of course, black as well white men. Yet it seemed that Pennsylvanians might no longer be willing to uphold such truths. "We sincerely hope," Forten wrote with a tactical nod to white patronage, "[that] the white men, whom we should look upon as our protectors, will have become convinced of the inhumanity and impolicy of such a measure," and drop the proposed racist law. Forten boldly asked whether Pennsylvania would once again become the "only state in the union" where "rational liberty" applied across racial lines.[32]

Forten's consciousness-raising pamphlet helped articulate the moralistic case against the proposed law. But PAS reformers did their bit by working behind the scenes at the state capital. Working together, they scuttled the law. This was prima facie evidence that, though black and white often operated in two different realms—African Americans in the public arena, white abolitionists in seats of power—interracial cooperation could make a difference.

(3)
THE PAS AND THE FAILURE OF INTERRACIAL REFORM IN THE AGE OF COLONIZATION

Despite this rich legacy of interracial cooperation, Pennsylvania abolitionists' relations with black activists were put under considerable strain during the first two decades of the nineteenth century. For one thing, key white abolitionist leaders—Benjamin Rush, the Pemberton brothers, Warner Mifflin—had passed on while others began to express doubt about blacks' ability to rise in American culture. Secondly, immigration patterns shifted in Pennsylvania, with Europeans outpacing black settlers by the 1810s. This development reshaped blacks' economic possibilities. Apprenticing opportunities declined during the 1800–1820 period. Even black leaders like Richard Allen began to fret about young African Americans' dismal future in the so-called free North. Thirdly, American slavery grew substantially in the southwest, with nearly two million—almost triple the number that had existed in 1790—held in bondage by the 1830 census. How would the PAS react? Finally, the colonization movement ascended in American culture, dredging up as much anti-black feeling as it did antislavery possibility. In sum, by the 1820s, as Pennsylvanians looked forward to the fiftieth anniversaries of both the PAS's inauguration (1825) and the state's gradual abolition act (1830), a palpable sense of despair gripped white as well as black abolitionists.[33]

As both the PAS and black activists would learn during these challenging years, interracial cooperation was not tantamount to universal brotherhood. Indeed, though they worked together on many occasions, black and white abolitionists (clients and patrons, respectively) occupied essentially segregated universes. At one level lay tactical divisions: where African Americans continued to utilize public appeals (because they offered direct access to white citizens' hearts and minds), the PAS did not—would not—politicize black voices or publicize antislavery action in any major way. What did this mean for the American abolition movement in the first two decades of the nineteenth century? PAS activists often muted African Americans' calls for freedom. As James Green has intriguingly written, one of the western world's first slave narratives went out of print during the PAS's reign. Olaudah Equiano's autobiography, a moving and wrenching account of his struggles both in the Middle Passage and in bondage (now celebrated as one of the leading examples of the genre) actually slipped from the public's consciousness between the 1790s and 1830s because abolitionists did not think it a valuable tool for attacking bondage. The document was finally restored to print by Garrison's partner Isaac Knapp in 1837. Though it disseminated all manner of abolitionist information to reformers throughout the Western world, the PAS would not circulate Equiano's first-hand account of slavery to demonstrate the horror of bondage.[34] Similarly, the PAS later refrained from reprinting and circulating David Walker's incendiary call to mass black organizing, "The Appeal," after it debuted in 1829. Nor did the PAS mine its incredible collection of first-person interviews with black kidnapping victims, fugitive slaves, and free black activists (which became the bedrock of PAS legal challenges) for propaganda purposes. Any such tactics, the group worried, might well foment anti-abolitionist sentiment and even disunion among southerners. And when the PAS decided to commission the first history of abolitionism, it never even considered black authors before settling on white novelist Charles Brockden Brown.

Tactical divisions over how to prosecute abolition gave way to deeper problems. The PAS did not admit black members during the early national period. Robert Purvis (who was the freeborn son of a white father and a "mixed race" mother) would become the first African American member of the group in

1842, but he was the last black person admitted until Frederick Douglass was offered a ceremonial admission after the Civil War.[35] Nor did the PAS believe that social equality was an important goal of the movement. On the matter of schooling, for instance, the PAS did not push for interracial educational institutions but remained content with the establishment of autonomous free black schools. In the post-revolutionary era, when there were few such schools save those provided by abolitionist groups and/or religious societies (not only Quakers but Anglicans favored black education), black-only institutions were a milestone. Still, the PAS did not expand its educational vision during the 1810s or 1820s to encompass bi-racial schooling. Such visions did, of course, become foundational elements—if not a hard and fast reality—of subsequent abolition movements in Frederick Douglass's New York and William Lloyd Garrison's Massachusetts. Inattention to issues of social equality, in the eyes of the PAS's earliest historians, led to a certain limitation in early abolitionists' vision—a distance and reserve from African American concerns that infiltrated group activities. Writing in 1840, Edwin Needles observed that social equality was a difficult concept for the PAS to grasp, in large measure because group members did not daily interact with black reformers. Quite obviously, PAS members did not view African Americans as co-equals within the abolitionist movement. "Very few even of the abolitionists in those days," he observed of the PAS, "were free from the deep seated prejudice of caste." This meant that they might "act incoherently towards their colored brethren, as though they really were an inferior race of beings."[36]

Looking at early abolition societies' membership policies helps explain such attitudes. Although abolitionist groups up and down the Atlantic Coast mixed paternalistic attitudes towards blacks with philanthropic activity, no first-generation abolitionist group ever admitted blacks as equal members before the 1830s. Revealingly, many of these same organizations took varying stands on the admission of slaveholders into their ranks. Although early southern abolitionist groups struggled with slaveholders' admission in particular (and as a result eventually faded from the landscape in Virginia by the end of the 1790s), northern abolition societies could also admit slaveholders—an inconceivable position for subsequent groups of reformers (Garrisonians admitted black activists from the start). Both the New York Manumission Society and the American Convention of Abolition Societies (a biennial convention of state and local abolition groups which often met in Philadelphia) admitted slaveholders before the 1800s. Even the occasional PAS member could hold a slave, despite violating the very spirit of the group. Benjamin Rush purchased an enslaved person in the 1770s, maintaining his claims on the man even after he helped the PAS revive itself in 1784. Few abolitionists were as stalwartly in favor of free blacks' rights as Rush—he raised money for the establishment of free black churches in Philadelphia—but his vision of black equality was certainly compromised by his ownership of another human being.[37]

Early abolitionists' racial ideology deserves a closer look for yet another reason. The PAS evolved in a post-revolutionary world rife with debate over not just the meaning of universal freedom but social order and stability. Many American statesmen of the day wondered whether democracy would devolve into anarchy, class war, and social ruin. With august figures like Benjamin Franklin in their midst, not to mention officers of the federal government in Philadelphia between 1790 in 1800, the PAS could hardly escape such debates. Indeed, Pennsylvania abolitionists consistently and publicly registered their own concerns on this score, albeit with a racial twist: would mass emancipation lead to social disorder and racial mayhem? The very policy of gradual abolitionism, the group often asserted, provided an orderly plan of manumission, allowing Pennsylvania masters time to slowly acclimate to black freedom while at the same time providing them some return on a propertied investment. Pennsylvania abolitionists also emphasized their respect for the American constitutional order's protection of property rights in man. Although PAS members exploited loopholes for black freedom, they told fugitive slaves that they could not expect immediate freedom upon entering Philadelphia. Slaves were returned to bondage with PAS sanction. Furthermore, the PAS recognized that both indenture contracts and private manumission agreements with masters, although they bargained slavery for life down to a shorter term of labor, were nevertheless based on the legitimacy of masters' claims to the property of black bodies.

While firmly in support of black freedom, many PAS members also believed that African Americans required some form of social control beyond bondage. Benjamin Franklin, a slaveholder himself before joining the PAS, made explicit Pennsylvania abolitionists' concerns about the challenges of black freedom. "Slavery is such an atrocious debasement of human nature," he explained in a public missive in November 1789, "that its very extirpation, if not performed with solicitous care, may sometimes open a source of serious evil." An enslaved person who was accustomed to being treated as a "brute animal too frequently sinks beneath the common standard of the human species." With no civic identity in bondage, and wearied by slavery's ceaseless toil, the former slave could become reckless. In fact, Franklin warned, "freedom may often prove a misfortune to himself and prejudicial to society."[38] The PAS resolved, accordingly, to make oversight of freed people a cornerstone of the early abolition movement.

As gradual abolition statutes steadily worked their course between the 1780s and 1820s, and the free black population speedily grew in and beyond the Quaker State, Pennsylvania abolitionists remained quite concerned about black freedom—and by extension, about black character. The group's mission after 1787, of course, included not only aiding distressed blacks but "improving the condition of the African race." In public addresses aimed at Philadelphia's growing free black community during the 1790s and early 1800s, the PAS emphasized the continued importance of moral uplift, piety, and hard work to freed people's future. In 1800, for example, the group issued a pamphlet to free blacks claiming that it had long aided African Americans' "lawful claims to freedom." But how blacks lived after attaining their liberty was equally significant, the group declared. Thus, the PAS "now earnestly desire, that having [attended] to the enjoyment of this blessing, you may manifest a suitable sense of gratitude [to abolitionists] . . . by lives of rectitude and by exemplary attention to those duties which have always distinguished the honest good man and the upright Christian." These duties included attending church, foreswearing wicked acts, and refraining from "idleness, dissipation, frolicking, drunkenness, theft, or any other vice." Dress simply, the group further lectured free blacks, teach your children useful trades and "avoid association with those of any color whose lives are dissipated and immoral." Living in this manner would "remove the prejudices of many who are unfriendly to the African race."[39]

In making such pronouncements, early abolitionists walked a fine line between advocating universal liberty for enslaved African Americans and promoting social control of liberated blacks. David Brion Davis famously asserted that early abolitionists' humanitarian motives may have elided support of other exploitative forms of economic organization and social control sweeping through the Atlantic world in the eighteenth and early nineteenth centuries— namely, commercial capitalism. In fighting racial slavery but supporting wage labor systems (which many white reformers benefited from as a class), early abolitionists may have ushered in a harsh new world of labor relations. While some scholars have questioned Davis's reading of first-generation abolitionists' motivations, his critique offers an intriguing way to envision Pennsylvania abolitionists' racial discourse. For some Pennsylvania reformers registered as much concern over black freedom as they had with American bondage. The discourse they established in dismantling slavery may have simultaneously castigated blacks as a potentially threatening presence, unless properly monitored, educated, and watched. Although he may have been the extreme example, former PAS member Tench Coxe became one of the leading antiblack writers in early nineteenth-century Philadelphia. Decades of freedom, he observed in 1820, had shown that free blacks were "uncivilized or wild men, without a moral sense."[40]

Versions of this same racial discourse ultimately undid early abolitionism. According to Paul Goodman, James Brewer Stewart, and James and Lois Horton, among other scholars, the advent of the American Colonization Society in 1817, and black and white abolitionists' varying responses to it, drove a wedge into the first-generation antislavery movement.[41] The ACS became a juggernaut in the 1820s and 1830s, attracting impressive support not only among border-South slaveholders (who often tied emancipation schemes to African colonization) but many northerners too. The ACS also attracted the type of weighty supporters the PAS once fancied: James Madison, Henry Clay, future Harvard President Edward Everett. In Pennsylvania, the colonization movement garnered strong support from many local communities, with over eighty auxiliary societies in existence by 1830. The state's flagship group, the Pennsylvania Colonization Society, was formed in 1826, and its members fervently believed that colonization made abolition more palatable to southern slaveholders. Nationally, the ACS attracted supporters in non-slaveholding locales who viewed free blacks—and not merely bondage—as anathema to a white republic. In other words, for the first time since the early days of the American Revolution, white Americans north and south united behind a single "antislavery" movement: colonization.[42]

Perhaps most importantly for the PAS and black reformers, the ACS spawned a national debate on African Americans' character and condition. While some ACS supporters made the intriguing—to modern ears, anyway—argument that white society would never let black genius flourish, other colonizationists made clear that free blacks simply had no place in a white republic. Edward Everett, who served as congressman in the 1820s and Massachusetts governor in the 1830s, argued that free blacks were a vagrant class, responsible for a disproportionate number of crimes. Some Pennsylvania colonizationists asserted that free blacks were not capable of acting responsibly beyond slavery—and they undercut white laborers' wages by taking jobs at reduced prices. Far from lone voices, such cries were part of the first critical surveys of northern emancipation in the 1820s and 1830s. Northern abolitionism, such commentary ran, was a failure. Colonization was the best response.

To most African Americans, of course, colonization seemed like expulsion. And while some black leaders in Philadelphia flirted with the ACS, most firmly opposed it. Perhaps the most significant anti-colonization meeting took place at Richard Allen's Mother Bethel AME Church in January 1817. A packed house of nearly three thousand rejected African colonization as a reform cause (though, as he put it, not "every scheme" of emigration), and, in a public remonstrance, vowed to remain connected to southern slaves in America. "If the plan of colonizing is intended for our benefit," Philadelphia's black community proclaimed in a brief pamphlet in 1818, "it is not asked for by us." Beyond worrying about African colonization's benefits to expatriated blacks, Afro-Philadelphians saw the ACS as the proverbial wolf in sheep's clothing—a ploy to separate free black activists from southern slaves. "The bondage of a large portion of our brothers will thus be rendered perpetual." Abolition *within* American culture, and redress of racial injustices, was the only true remedy to the so-called slavery problem. Richard Allen, who would remain interested in black-led emigration schemes for the rest of his life, nevertheless spoke the keynote for black anti-colonizationists: "America is our mother country," he would argue in a famous newspaper article in 1828, "and we have watered it with tears . . . and blood."[43]

While Afro-Philadelphians led the anti-colonizationist charge—with black communities in other locales, north as well as south, adding stinging critiques of the ACS—the PAS stumbled on the colonization issue, refusing to take a strong public stand against the ACS until the late 1820s. Some PAS members actually favored colonization—not altogether surprisingly in an age when many white reformers embraced the cause—while others had important colonizationist friends and allies whom they did not want to upset. Both Roberts Vaux and the Reverend Charles Milnor were ACS supporters. On the other hand, Jonathon Roberts corresponded with colonizationists who believed that black expatriation was the only way to rid America of slavery (by enticing masters), even if it meant removing blacks. Vaux, a Philadelphia reformer who took an interest in everything from Pennsylvania's native American history to temperance, wondered about free blacks' future in America. He asked a group assembled for black education in 1824 whether emancipated slaves would be able to participate in American culture. Free black Philadelphians' lives were anything but encouraging, he noted. No reformer should thus seek to criticize the ACS goals or motives, he concluded.[44]

The PAS's official position was that colonization would not work, but that Pennsylvania abolitionists would do little good by criticizing the movement. Longtime President William Rawle predicted that colonization "will [not] be of much importance." Still, he knew that gradual abolitionists must not offend weighty colonizationists, for the movement had "many ardent friends" and benefactors.[45] Still other PAS members disagreed with these arguments. A vanguard of reformers believed that colonization *was* harmful and that abolitionists must defend African Americans from ACS propaganda. Thomas Shipley and Arnold Buffum, both of whom had been active on the PAS legal circuit (not as trained lawyers but as legal counselors), believed that colonization threatened abolitionism's very core. Why wasn't the PAS more confrontational on this issue? Not surprisingly, both men would join the Garrisonian movement in the 1830s. Such dissidents notwithstanding, the PAS did not make anti-colonizationism a centerpiece of its activism. In other words, in a period where not only slavery but anti-black prejudice was growing—in no small measure because of ACS rhetoric north and south—the PAS cooled its criticism.

Black activists took this as a lesson: no white abolitionist institution, not even the venerable PAS, would zealously plead blacks' cause in the face of the meteoric rise of the ACS. In pamphlets, public meetings, and declarations, and in the first black newspapers published during the 1820s, African Americans would offer an alternate vision of abolitionism, one based not on careful legal and political maneuvering á la the PAS but instead on declamatory public discourse. This form of abolitionism, fiery and angry and concerned with confronting slavery's evil head-on, became one of the foundations of subsequent abolitionist movements. The PAS's demise stemmed in large measure from its colonization stumble.

(4)

BEYOND 1830

Though early abolitionism is often pictured as a mere prelude to radical reform movements of the 1830s, the history of the Pennsylvania Abolition Society belies that simplistic portrait. Not only did the PAS put abolitionism on Americans' legislative and judicial radar during the early national period but PAS members remained a visible part of antebellum reform movements, becoming involved in Underground Railroad activities and fugitive slave rescues, the operation of black educational institutions, and even the organization of new "immediatist" abolition societies appearing in the country after 1830.[46] The PAS was also among the first white abolitionist groups to confront the realities of the color line. Yet the group's failure to integrate abolitionism created repercussions for the entire movement. Other factors certainly contributed to the transformation of American abolitionism—for example, the Garrisonians' rise in New England—after 1830, from the spread of market capitalism in the North to the onset of revivalist movements (with their mandate of immediately stopping sin). But the issue of race haunted the PAS, which faded from prominence in national abolitionist circles between 1830 and 1860.

The PAS did not admit black activists at any time before the 1830s, nor did it view racial vindication—arguing vigorously and publicly for free black claims to equality—as a key abolitionist strategy. The group's reaction to the formation and rapid expansion of the American Colonization Society laid this concern bare. While black activists registered immediate concern over the ACS's racist rhetoric and plan of exporting free black reformers, the PAS refused to publicly rebuke colonizationist supporters for over a decade. This apathetic response may have stemmed, as some PAS members claimed, from a view that the ACS would ultimately fail. But because ACS supporters often attacked free black claims to equality in America, and did so precisely at the moment when the fruits of gradual abolitionism were questioned by northern writers and statesmen, colonization served as an alarm bell to black activists. As the PAS's own Edwin Needles put it in the 1840s, many early members did not believe in social equality. This may have contributed to the group's conservative racial beliefs and to the PAS's public stand that media assaults on racial injustice were unworthy—or dangerous.

To meet the challenges of the antebellum era, when slavery and anti-black racism grew apace, black activists realized that they needed new allies in the struggle for equality. They found them in that rising generation of immediatist—or Garrisonian—white reformers in the Northeast and Midwest. As the New England Antislavery Society formed in 1832, and the American Antislavery Society in 1833, black reformers became for the first time "coadjutors" of the mainstream movement. William Hamilton, a black New Yorker who had known generations of white abolitionists dating back to the post-revolutionary era, declared in 1834 that prejudice itself was for the first time under serious attack now that biracial, immediatist abolition societies had appeared on the horizon. "That hitherto strong-footed but sore-eyed vixen, prejudice is limping off," he announced at a convention of black reformers, "[now] that the antislavery society and the friends of immediate abolition are taking a bold and manly stand in the cause of universal liberty."[47]

One of the great ironies of abolitionism's transformation after 1830, of course, is that black and white reformers would continue to clash over tactics, politics, and leadership. As historian Margaret Washington has nicely put it, though antebellum black activists like Frederick Douglass would recognize the seminal aid and contributions of radical white abolitionists, they believed that "what was [still] needed was a strong black voice" directing the movement.[48] Some black activists, like Martin Delany, went further still, asserting that African Americans must remain autonomous activists to truly achieve racial justice. And when one considers the "romantic racialism" (or paternalism), to borrow from George Frederickson, of many white Garrisonians, antebellum black activists had a salient point.[49] The PAS, in short, was not the only abolitionist group to stumble and even falter on the color line. The Reverend Charles W. Gardner probably put it most succinctly in 1837 when he declared that blacks had been abolitionists since Garrison was "a schoolboy."[50] Gardner's candid remarks stemmed from a sense that white figures—like Garrison—still garnered too much attention within the organized abolitionist community, while African American historical and present contributions were slighted.

But there was indeed a difference between the PAS and post-1830 abolitionists regarding true interracial possibility. During the early 1830s, black activists became perhaps *the* key supporters of Garrison's *The Liberator,* immediate abolitionism's standard-bearer: black writers provided at least 20 percent of the intellectual content of the paper during its inaugural year, and as much as 75 percent of its financial base. There was more. From 1833 to 1840, thirteen African Americans sat on the board of the American Antislavery Society. And during the 1830s and 1840s, African Americans shared lecture stages from New England to the Midwest with even the most prominent white activists. Moreover, African American women became founding members of groups like the Philadelphia Female Antislavery Society. If some black reformers nevertheless remained convinced of the need to maintain an autonomous abolitionist movement over the next few decades, such a belief did not stem from a few short years of troubled interracial activity with Garrisonians. Rather, it had roots dating back to the very founding of organized abolitionism in the late eighteenth century, when the PAS reigned supreme but could not yet imagine a world where black and white reformers operated as equals.

NOTES

1. W. Richards to Pennsylvania Abolition Society (PAS), March 26, 1795, PAS Papers, microfilm edition, reel 26, "Misc. Correspondence, 1788–1795."

2. Robert Purvis quoted in Richard S. Newman, *The Transformation of American Abolitionism: Fighting Slavery in the Early Republic* (Chapel Hill, N.C., 2002), 63–64.

3. Francis Parkman, *Montecalm and Wolfe: The French and Indian War* (rpt. New York, 1995), xxxiii.

4. For Cobb quotation, see William W. Freehling and Craig Simpson, eds., *Secession Debated* (New York , 1993), 16.

5. See Jane H. Pease and William H. Pease, *They Who Would Be Free: Blacks' Search for Freedom, 1830–1861* (New York, 1974), 3.

6. Among the best books on race and slavery in the early republic, see Mia Bay's first chapter in *The White Image in the Black Mind: African-American Ideas About White People, 1830–1925* (New York, 2000); Bruce Dain, *A Hideous Monster of the Mind: American Race Theory in the Early Republic* (Cambridge, 2002); Douglas Egerton, *He Shall Go Out Free: The Lives of Denmark Vesey* (Madison, Wis., 2000); Graham Russell Hodges, *Slavery and Freedom in the Rural North: African Americans in Monmouth County, New Jersey, 1665–1865* (Madison, Wis., 1997); Mitch Kachun, *Festivals of Freedom: Memory and Meaning in African American Emancipation Celebrations, 1808–1915;* Elizabeth McHenry, *Forgotten Readers: Recovering the Lost History of African American Literary Societies* (Durham, N.C., 2002); Joanne Pope Melish, *Disowning Slavery: Gradual Emancipation and "Race" in New England, 1780–1860* (Ithaca, N.Y., 1998). See also James Brewer Stewart's excellent essay, "The Emergence of Racial Modernity and the Rise of the White North 1790–1840," *Journal of the Early Republic* 18 (Summer 1998): 181–217, and Richard S. Newman, "Not the Only Story in 'Amistad': The Fictional Joadson and the Real James Forten," *Pennsylvania History* (Spring 2002): 218–39)

7. On Quaker antislavery debates, see especially Jean Soderlund, *Quakers and Slavery: A Divided Spirit* (Princeton, N.J., 1985). For Franklin's publication of Quaker antislavery literature, see Franklin to John Wright of London, June 4, 1789, unpublished letter, Franklin Papers, CD-ROM edition, American Philosophical Society.

8. On Pennsylvania's emancipation act and its consequences, see the fine book by Gary Nash and Jean Soderlund, *Freedom by Degrees: Emancipation and Its Aftermath in Pennsylvania* (New York, 1991).

9. PAS Constitution of 1787, republished in the Franklin Papers.

10. On this theme, see in particular Margaret Hope Bacon's fine essay, "The Pennsylvania Abolition Society's Mission for Black Education," *Pennsylvania Legacies* 5, no. 2 (November 2005): 21–26.

11. I have treated this theme more extensively in another context. See *The Transformation of American Abolitionism*.

12. Because the gradual abolition law operated in post-nati (after birth) fashion (i.e., laws released enslaved people born after 1780 at age twenty-eight), Pennsylvania still contained slaves into the 1840s.

13. See Shane White, *Stories of Freedom in Black New York* (Cambridge, Mass., 2003).

14. See Edmund Randolph to Benjamin Franklin, August 2, 1788, in PAS Papers, microfilm reel 11; see also Franklin (on behalf of the PAS) to Gov. John Collins of Rhode Island, July 12, 1788, in Franklin Papers.

15. For a reprinted copy of the PAS constitution of 1787, see the Historical Society of Pennsylvania's website, which includes an educational link to the papers of the PAS.

16. Benjamin Franklin signed the appeal to the Pennsylvania legislature in 1789.

17. John Stauffer, *The Black Hearts of Men* (Cambridge, Mass., 2001).

18. On the consideration of kidnapping by the American Convention of Abolition Societies, see Carol Wilson, *Freedom at Risk* (Lexington, Ky., 1995).

19. See David Waldstreicher's excellent book, *Runaway America: Benjamin Franklin, Slavery, and the American Revolution* (New York, 2004).

20. See John P. Kaminiski, *A Necessary Evil? Slavery and the Debate Over the Constitution* (Madison, Wis., 1995).

21. For fuller treatment, see Richard S. Newman, "Prelude to the Gag Rule: Southern Reaction to Antislavery Petitions," Journal of the Early Republic 16 (Winter 1996): 571–99.

22. Forten, "Series of Letters by a Man of Colour," rpt. in Richard Newman, Patrick Rael, and Philip Lapsansky, eds., *Pamphlets of Protest: An Anthology of Early African American Protest Literature, 1790–1860* (New York, 2000).

23. Meredith quoted in Newman, *The Transformation of American Abolitionism*, 85.

24. *Green v. Brickell* (1825). See Newman, *The Transformation of American Abolitionism*, 79.

25. The case was decided in 1797. See Newman, *The Transformation of American Abolitionism*, 76–78.

26. For information on the many PAS cases from the 1790s, see "Cases in Which Slaves Were Awarded Freedom in Court, 1773–1833," PAS Papers, microfilm reel 24.

27. See *William Coachman v. George Hand*, Cape May, N.J., 1802–4, PAS Papers, microfilm reel 24.

28. Allen and Jones, "To Him Who Hath No Helper," part of "A Narrative of the Black People During the Late Aweful Calamity in Philadelphia," rpt. in Newman, et al., eds., *Pamphlets of Protest, 33–42*.

29. See Julie Winch, *A Gentleman of Color: The Life of James Forten* (New York, 2002), 153–55.

30. For a fuller picture of the Barclay manumission and indentures plan, see PAS Papers, microfilm reel 6, "Committee for Improving . . . Free Blacks," 1796.

31. Forten, "Series of Letters by a Man of Colour," in Newman, et al., eds., *Pamphlets of Protest, 67–72*.

32. Ibid.

33. For a particularly insightful survey of the worsening racial situation during the 1810s and 1820s, see Gary Nash, *Forging Freedom: The Formation of Philadelphia's Black Community, 1720–1840* (Cambridge, Mass., 1988), chap. 7.

34. James Green, "The Publishing History of Olaudah Equiano's *Interesting Narrative*," *Slavery and Abolition* 16, no. 3 (December 1995): 362–75.

35. See Margaret Hope Bacon's wonderful recent mini-essay on Purvis and the PAS, "Robert Purvis: President of the Underground Railroad," *www.hsp.org/files/legaciespurvis.pdf.*

36. *The Pennsylvania Freeman*, September 14, 1840.

37. On Rush's slave purchase, see Gary Nash, *Race and Revolution* (Madison, Wis., 1990), 32.

38. Benjamin Franklin, *An Address to the Public from the Pennsylvania Society for Promoting the Abolition of Slavery, and the Relief of Free Negroes Unlawfully Held in Bondage* (Philadelphia, 1789).

39. *An Address From the Pennsylvania Abolition Society to the Free Black People . . .* (Philadelphia, 1800), 3–8.

40. Coxe, *Considerations Respecting the Helots of the United States, African and Indian, Native and Alien, and Their Descendants of the Whole and Mixed Blood* (Philadelphia, 1820). Coxe quotations in Nash, *Forging Freedom*, 225.

41. James Oliver Horton and Lois E. Horton, *In Hope of Liberty: Culture, Community, and Protest Among Northern Free Blacks, 1700–1860* (Oxford, U.K., 1997); Paul Goodman, *Of One Blood: Abolitionism and the Origins of Racial Equality* (Berkeley, Calif., 1998); James Brewer Stewart, *Holy Warriors: The Abolitionists and American Slavery* (1976; rpt. New York, 1997).

42. See Goodman, *Of One Blood;* Horton and Horton, *In Hope of Liberty.* See also James Brewer Stewart's excellent essay, "The Emergence of Racial Modernity and the Rise of the White North 1790–1840," *Journal of the Early Republic* 18 (Summer 1998): 181–217. See also Newman, *The Transformation of American Abolitionism*, chapters 4 and 5, for an extended treatment of this theme.

43. The memorial of free blacks is entitled, "To the Humane and Benevolent Inhabitants of the City and County of Philadelphia" (Philadelphia, 1818), rpt. in Dorothy Porter, comp., *Early Negro Writing* (Boston, 1971), 265–68.

44. See Roberts Vaux's unpublished manuscript, "Address on the Impolicy of Slavery . . . Delivered in Philadelphia Before an Association Formed for the Education of Men of Colour," January 1, 1824, 25–37, original at the American Philosophical Society, Philadelphia.

45. For comments on the ACS, see Rawle's plan on the formation of a "National Antislavery Society," May 20, 1833, in Rawle Family Papers, Historical Society of Pennsylvania, Philadelphia.

46. For example, PAS member Passmore Williamson was involvement in the celebrated 1855 fugitive slave case of Jane Johnson, a black women enslaved to a congressman from North Carolina who escaped with her two children when passing through Philadelphia. See Christopher Densmore, "Seeking Freedom in the Courts," *Pennsylvania Legacies* 17 (November 2005): 16–20.

47. Hamilton, "Address to the Fourth Annual Convention for the Improvement of the Free People of Colour" (New York, 1834), in Newman et al., eds., *Pamphlets of Protest*, 111–13.

48. Washington quoted in PBS documentary on Douglass, "When the Lion Wrote History," aired 1994.

49. On the concept of "romantic racialism" generally, see Frederickson, *The Black Image in the White Mind* (Middletown, Conn., 1971).

50. Gardener quoted in C. Peter Ripley et al., *The Black Abolitionist Papers* (5 vols., Chapel Hill, N.C., 1987–1992), vol. 1: 210.

III.

SHADES OF FREEDOM

Global Abolitionism, Religious Reform, and the Staging
of Race between the Revolution and the Civil War

CHAPTER 6

Philadelphia Abolitionists and Antislavery Cosmopolitanism

W. CALEB MCDANIEL

From its beginnings, abolitionism in Philadelphia was transatlantic in orientation. In the mid-1700s, Quaker abolitionists like Anthony Benezet helped forge a Quaker "Antislavery International" knitted together by religion, business, and kinship. Benezet and Benjamin Rush both corresponded with British abolitionist Granville Sharp in the 1770s, and the Pennsylvania Abolition Society maintained ties with abolitionists in Britain and France. After 1830, even as much about American abolitionism changed, activists in Philadelphia continued this established tradition of transatlantic cooperation. In 1840, when a group of American abolitionists crossed the Atlantic to attend a "World's Convention" on slavery in London, many of the delegates were from Philadelphia. Before leaving England, one delegate told a group of Dublin abolitionists she was glad that their "intercourse need not cease though an Ocean divide us." Such "Atlantic crossings," like those of later generations of reformers, were vital to American abolitionism in the 1700s and the 1800s. Transatlantic networks served as conduits for the exchange of information, ideas, and both moral and material support.[1]

Yet transatlantic networks may have been most important to abolitionists as sources of new identities and imagined communities. Ties with abolitionists abroad encouraged Philadelphia's abolitionists to identify as citizens of the world, whose allegiance to the global community of humankind superseded local attachments. In 1790, for example, an antislavery poem printed in Philadelphia eulogized Anthony Benezet as a cosmopolitan philanthropist: "the World [was] thy country, and thy Friends MANKIND." According to Joseph Sansom, the poem's author and an officer in the PAS, Benezet "considered himself as a citizen of the world, and regarded all Mankind as friends and countrymen." For proof, he cited a 1781 letter from Benezet to French abolitionist Abbé Raynal, which saluted Raynal as part of a "grand circle" of love, "unconfined by our parentage or country." Other early antislavery writers in

the city, such as Benjamin Rush and Thomas Paine, also claimed to be philanthropists whose love for humanity was unconfined by national boundaries. In
1792, two years after Sansom's poem was published, Paine published *Rights
of Man*, in which he too claimed, much more famously, "my country is the
world." Around the same time, Rush also wrote Granville Sharp that "our
Divine Master forbids us . . . to have either friends or country." According
to Rush, "the globe [was] the native country, and the whole human race the
fellow citizens of a Christian."[2]

Early Philadelphia abolitionists identified as citizens of the world partly because of their strong personal ties with European correspondents. By the mid-
1700s, Philadelphia was North America's central depot for the transatlantic
exchange of ideas and texts. Benezet, whose Huguenot parentage itself marked
him as cosmopolitan, was not only a friend of Rush, who met Hume and Diderot while pursuing his education abroad, but also knew Benjamin Franklin,
whose letters of introduction Rush carried to Europe. Franklin, in turn, knew
English Quaker John Fothergill, the renowned scientist, who knew radical
British thinkers like Richard Price, also one of Rush's friends. Friendship with
like-minded thinkers in other countries sharpened early abolitionists' images
of themselves as citizens of the world. Conversely, that self-image propelled
abolitionists out of their local spheres and into far-reaching intellectual and
reform networks.[3]

Eighteenth-century abolitionists also idealized world citizenship because many contemporary thinkers on both sides of the Atlantic criticized
patriotism as a basis for moral action. In continental Europe, Enlightenment
thinkers revived the ancient Greek ideal of cosmopolitanism as a nobler virtue
than patriotism, while a wide range of writers in the late eighteenth century
made a virtue of "liberality," defined partly as freedom from local customs and
prejudices. In Britain, Scottish Enlightenment philosophers argued before the
American Revolution that "universal benevolence" was more commendable
than narrow-minded love for country. Transatlantic debates about cosmopolitanism and universal benevolence were heightened in the 1790s by the French
Revolution, as British writers like Richard Price, Edmund Burke, and Paine
himself argued over the moral status of patriotism. Crucially, as historian J. M.
Opal has noted, eighteenth-century debates about the morality of slavery were
coeval with debates about the morality of patriotism.[4]

Eighteenth-century Philadelphia abolitionists like Benezet, Rush, and
Paine enlisted contemporary ideas about patriotism and universal benevolence

in their published attacks on slavery, developing a long-lasting set of arguments that I will call "antislavery cosmopolitanism." Antislavery cosmopolitans began with the premise that all human beings belonged to a common family with a common maker, so that national distinctions between natives and foreigners were irrelevant to one's moral duties. That premise was conjoined with the argument that excessive patriotism among Europeans was one cause of the African slave trade. Together, those arguments entailed that opponents of slavery had to be citizens of the world. According to antislavery cosmopolitans, abolitionists loved all nations equally, rather than one country exclusively.

The rhetoric of antislavery cosmopolitanism survived well into the antebellum period. To be sure, as historian Richard Newman has shown, many wide ideological gulfs separated eighteenth-century abolitionists, who tended to favor gradual emancipation and sometimes supported African colonization, from the antebellum followers of William Lloyd Garrison, who opposed colonization, demanded immediate emancipation, and encouraged interracial activism.[5] Yet antislavery cosmopolitanism was one thread of continuity connecting earlier abolitionists with the Garrisonians. Garrison published a version of Paine's famous motto on every issue of his newspaper, *The Liberator:* "Our Country is the World—Our Countrymen are All Mankind." Members of the American Anti-Slavery Society, organized in Philadelphia in 1833, and local auxiliaries like the Philadelphia Female Anti-Slavery Society (PFASS) and the Pennsylvania Anti-Slavery Society (PASS), regularly applied that motto to themselves. As the *Pennsylvania Freeman* put it in 1839, *The Liberator's* slogan was a "favorite maxim" of all abolitionists.[6]

That antislavery cosmopolitanism survived so long suggests that the attitude of Garrisonian abolitionists toward eighteenth-century predecessors was not one of wholesale rejection, but of selective adaptation. Adaptation, of course, was necessary for the survival of antislavery cosmopolitanism. During and after the Age of Revolution, abolitionists discovered various reasons to mute the emphasis of previous abolitionists on cosmopolitanism as an ideal, and in the early nineteenth century, abolitionists were more likely to argue that cosmopolitanism and patriotism were compatible ideals, rather than opposites. Yet the idea that abolitionists were cosmopolitan retained strength among the successors to Benjamin Rush and Anthony Benezet, and for many of the same reasons. Nineteenth-century abolitionists continued to view themselves as citizens of the world partly because they continued to cooperate and correspond with abolitionists abroad. In its founding address in 1837, the

PASS pledged to continue the work begun fifty years earlier by the PAS, which never hesitated "to seek the aid of the wise and benevolent of other climes" and had granted memberships to some British and French abolitionists. True to their word, Philadelphia abolitionists in the antebellum period exchanged newspapers and letters with abolitionists abroad, solicited European donations for antislavery fundraisers, and sometimes even crossed the Atlantic "to secure . . . a more general cooperation between the friends of the cause on that & this side of the water," as James Miller McKim put it before leaving Philadelphia for Britain in 1854. Abby Kimber, a Philadelphian who attended the 1840 "World's Convention," afterwards told one English abolitionist that by forming new "acquaintances and friendships" during their travels, American abolitionists had "cordially adopt[ed] Garrison's motto—Our Country is the World &c."[7]

Historians have long known that American and British abolitionists cooperated with one another, but this chapter builds on this recognition in two ways. First, it emphasizes that transatlantic cooperation helped abolitionists formulate new identities that were explicitly transnational and that these new identities, in turn, produced new antislavery arguments. Transatlantic networks, in other words, were not useful just for the circulation of already existing antislavery ideas; those networks actually helped abolitionists construct new identities, new ideas, and new defenses against proslavery opponents. A second emphasis in this chapter lies on the impact that international networks had on the formation of national antislavery networks in the United States. For Philadelphia abolitionists in particular, becoming more cosmopolitan through cooperation with non-American abolitionists also facilitated their integration into regional and national antislavery networks. Moreover, when national antislavery organizations came under increased attack in the 1830s and 1840s, abolitionists revived the rhetoric of antislavery cosmopolitanism, not to defend their transatlantic affiliations alone, but also to defend their activism at home. Using Philadelphia abolitionists as a frame thus helps bring into focus why and how antislavery activists more generally imagined themselves as part of a global community, and also how that self-image furthered the creation of antislavery communities closer at hand.

(1)

The eighteenth century brought a heightened sense of national identity to many European countries and a corresponding celebration of patriotism as a virtue. But various eighteenth-century thinkers criticized this apotheosis of patriotism, and their critiques directly informed early abolitionist writings in Philadelphia. Enlightened philosophers on both sides of the Atlantic were arguing that patriotism was one cause of Europe's interminable religious wars and embracing instead what historian Thomas Schlereth calls the "cosmopolitan ideal." According to some Enlightenment thinkers, mankind was best seen as a single family whose members, however different and distant from one another, were connected by universal ties of humanity. The fact that philosophers themselves often belonged to international networks of correspondence and cooperation helped make these abstract universal ties seem tangible and real. As the *Transactions* of Philadelphia's American Philosophical Society once claimed, "philosophers [were] citizens of the world" par excellence.[8]

Patriotism was also criticized by eighteenth-century Christian thinkers, particularly the moral philosophers of the Scottish Enlightenment. In the 1730s and 1740s, Frances Hutcheson argued that "universal benevolence," or love for all humanity, was more virtuous than patriotism, which resembled the vice of self-love. Because humans had a common creator, they belonged to a common family. National distinctions were artificial and dangerous, because they curtailed the liberal impulse towards universal benevolence that God had placed inside all moral beings. In the mid-1700s, Christian rationalists like James Foster popularized Hutcheson's views in Britain, arguing, as Foster put it, that "universal benevolence . . . is the *supreme law* to all rational beings" and "ought never to be superseded, limited, or in the least weakened by any selfish and partial affections."[9]

These ideas were often echoed in the arguments of contemporary Quaker revivalists, who deeply influenced Friends in colonial Pennsylvania. Much like European philosophers of "universal benevolence," Quaker revivalists in the mid-1700s warned their coreligionists against what John Woolman called the "narrowness of self-love" and argued that "our hearts [should be] enlarged toward mankind universally." Such appeals resembled the arguments of Hutchesonians like Foster, who noted that the Christian's "charity should not be *narrow* and *confined,* but of most *extensive* influence." As historian Sydney James points out, "an impressive array of the common terms of humanitarian morality" developed by Enlightened writers also appeared in Quaker texts. Israel Pemberton, scion of one of Philadelphia's wealthiest Quaker families, rejoiced that God had created in all humans a "spirit of universal benevolence to mankind," concisely summarizing Hutcheson's own view.[10]

These various eighteenth-century defenses of universal benevolence gave birth to some of the earliest published antislavery arguments. Hutcheson, for example, indicted the African slave trade as a violation of Christ's injunctions to love all mankind. James Foster's *Discourse on All the Principal Branches of Natural Religion and Social Virtue* offered the slave trade as a prime example of the "mischievous and destructive" effects of patriotism. Thinking only of their own country's interests, Europeans used patriotism as an excuse to "spread slavery and destruction through the world." Instead of treating Africans as "the *off-spring* of the same *common parent*," the slave trade "weaken[ed] and dissolve[d] the *universal tie*, that binds and unites mankind." Sounding Hutchesonian themes, Foster adduced slavery as one of the many evils produced by loving "the inhabitants of a particular spot" more than those of other spots, by the "absurd and childish prejudice . . . that makes an *idol* of our country, and is ready to sacrifice even the good of the whole species to it."[11]

Antislavery Quakers also connected the evils of self-love to the evils of the slave trade. In an essay "On loving our Neighbours," John Woolman warned that when Christian love became constricted by "the bands of a narrow self-interest," Christians became "entangled by oppressive customs." Although it was natural to feel special affection for one's immediate family and home, Christ commanded a more extensive love. As Quakers in the mid-eighteenth century became involved in business with distant trading partners, writers like Woolman urged them to make their love for others equally far-reaching. In a 1770 Philadelphia pamphlet on "the true harmony of mankind," Woolman began by stating that "as mankind from one parent are divided into many families, and as trading to sea is greatly increased within a few ages past," it was the more urgent, "amidst this extended commerce," for Christians to love all men, "however distant." According to his journal, meditating on "universal love" convicted him of his own guilt with regard to slavery.[12]

A similar invocation of universal love appeared in an early antislavery tract published in London by the pseudonymous "J. Philmore," whose punny pseudonym—love more—could have been meant to call attention to the importance of widespread benevolence. In *Two Dialogues on the Man-Trade* (1760), Philmore argued that Jesus's command to love neighbors "takes in all Mankind." All human beings were related because "the kind and merciful Father of us all . . . hath made of one Blood all Nations of Men . . . and hath united them in all in one Body by the Ties of Nature." Even "*European* Whites and the *African* Blacks . . . are Members of one and the same great

Society spread over the Face of the whole Earth." Philmore thus condemned Europeans' enslavement of Africans as the kind of perversion encouraged by patriotism. Slavery broke the "Bond of Humanity . . . the Foundation of all other particular Ties and Connections between Men, and gives Strength to them all:—A Patriot, or a Lover of his Country, is a brave Character; but a Lover of Mankind is a braver Character." When confronted by a suffering man, the true Christian would view him "as a citizen in the world," regardless of whether he had been "born in the same country."[13]

The earliest abolitionists in Philadelphia were familiar with transatlantic ideas and texts and drew on the writings of Foster, Philmore, and others in their own antislavery publications, which established for a much wider audience the links between antislavery and cosmopolitan benevolence. Anthony Benezet included antislavery passages from Hutcheson, Foster, and "J. Philmore" in his *Short Account of that Part of Africa, inhabited by the Negroes,* first printed in Philadelphia in 1762 and reprinted in London when abolitionist Granville Sharp discovered it in a bookstall. As a "a kind of middleman of ideas" between Quakerism and Enlightenment, Benezet fused the Hutchesonian language of universal benevolence with the exhortations of Friends like Woolman. Slavery, he wrote, ignored "our Duty to God, the common Father of the Family of the whole Earth, and our Duty of Love to our Fellow Creatures" by severing "all social Connection and tender Ties of Nature."[14]

While such arguments stemmed partly from Benezet's convictions about the Gospel, "the Purpose of which is to introduce an universal and affectionate Brotherhood in the whole human Species," his references to universal ties of humanity and "the Family of the whole Earth" also reflect the influence of Enlightened writers. Indeed, Benezet's belief that "the concurrent testimony of persons of different times & religious persuasions & nations, carry a kind of forcible evidence in favour of truth to a thinking mind" indicate not only his agreement with the moral virtue of extensive love, but also his agreement that philosophers were citizens of the world. As Benezet's friend Benjamin Rush astutely observed in a 1774 letter to Granville Sharp, Benezet's language revealed his belief that "all mankind however diversified by color—nation—or religion [were] members of one grand family." Rush praised Benezet's "benevolence" as truly "unbounded."[15]

Rush, an important figure in the development of early abolitionist organization in Philadelphia, also invoked eighteenth-century ideas about world citizenship and universal benevolence in his own antislavery writings. In

1773, when Rush wrote an *Address to the Inhabitants of the British Settlements in America, Upon Slave-Keeping,* he too called slavery "a vice which . . . dissolves that universal tie of benevolence which should connect all the children of men together in one great Family." When one critic, Richard Nisbet, challenged Rush's claim that Europeans and Africans belonged to the same family, Rush retorted, in a second pamphlet, that Nisbet's caviling about national distinctions between Europeans and Africans did not befit a cosmopolitan. Rush chastised Nisbet by quoting a popular Italian travel writer, Giuseppe Baretti: "'Mankind (says that Citizen of the World Mr. Baretti) are of one great Family, and he is not a Friend to that Family, who contributes his Mite towards keeping it in Discord.'"[16]

Like Rush and Benezet, Thomas Paine also drew on the developing discourse of antislavery cosmopolitanism to rebut arguments in favor of slavery. The year after Rush's exchange with Nisbet, Paine came to Philadelphia, where he soon met Rush. One of his first publications in the city was an antislavery essay in the *Pennsylvania Journal and the Weekly Advertiser,* which argued that biblical defenses of slavery "ill become us, *since the time of reformation came,* under gospel light." Despite his freethinking tendencies, Paine joined Hutchesonians like Foster and Quakers like Woolman in arguing that "all distinctions of nations, and privileges of one above others, are ceased; Christians are taught to *account all men their neighbors.*" Years earlier, Benezet's *Short Account* quoted a passage by Hutcheson that made the same argument in nearly the same words: "under Christianity," Hutcheson argued, "the Distinctions of Nations are removed." An antislavery petition drafted by London Quakers and then published in Philadelphia in 1784, agreed that "all distinctions of name and country, so far as they relate to the social duties, are now abolished."[17]

The idea that social duties transcended "the Distinctions of Nations" thus became a common thread running through the raft of antislavery publications that appeared in Philadelphia in the 1760s, 1770s, and 1780s.[18] Philadelphia's antislavery writers mobilized transatlantic ideas about universal benevolence, and in the process asserted their own identity as world citizens. But cosmopolitan appeals would also become more contested during the Age of Revolutions that began with the American and continued with the French and Haitian revolutions. Revolutionary ideologies polarized debates about patriotism, and cosmopolitan ideals also took on new political connotations. Revolutionary-era abolitionists were forced to deemphasize some themes that had been common to antislavery cosmopolitanism before the American Revolution, to reemphasize others, and, most importantly, to argue that cosmopolitanism and patriotism were not necessarily at odds.

(2)

Whereas mid-century writers had often drawn a stark contrast between love for country and universal benevolence, abolitionists during and after the American Revolution argued that true patriotism and true cosmopolitanism were compatible. There had been precedents for this argument before the revolution. Even Foster, whose attacks on patriotism were among the sharpest, conceded that love for country could be virtuous if it remained "consistent with, and subservient to, the supreme law of universal benevolence." But Foster remained wary of patriotism, which could all too easily overrun its proper boundaries and usurp the law of benevolence. American revolutionaries shared little of his reticence, however. Advocates of independence like Rush and Paine saw no tension between American patriotism and universal benevolence, because they believed the founding principles of the United States served the interests of humankind universally. "I cannot help feeling . . . for my dear co[untry]—I love liberty," Rush wrote to abolitionist Granville Sharpe in July 1774. Rush equated American patriotism with love for liberty, rather than with the narrow prejudices born of nativity. After the revolution, he wrote again to Sharp to praise "the happy effects of our independence not only upon our own country, but upon . . . the whole world."[19]

Because early Americans like Rush claimed that their own nation stood for universal principles, they also claimed that patriotism was consonant with universal benevolence. At the same time that Rush was castigating proslavery writer Richard Nisbet for stirring up hostilities between European and African nations, he was writing articles "on patriotism" for the *Pennsylvania Journal*, urging Americans to resist the importation of British tea. "Patriotism is as much as virtue as justice," Rush thundered, because in the case of Americans, "the Amor Patriae" included "not only the love of our neighbors but of millions of our fellow creatures, not only of the present but of future generations."[20] By linking American national identity to universal principles, many revolutionary Americans believed they had reconciled the abstract tension between patriotism and world citizenship. Historian Jay Fliegelman observes that even the most potent symbol of patriotism, George Washington, could be seen as "father to his nation but not to his nation alone." Washington wrote to the Marquis de Lafayette in 1786 that he was not just an American but "a citizen of the great republic of humanity at large," and one of his boosters praised Washington's belief "that mankind are brethren, however separated by mountains or divided by seas." In the age of transatlantic revolutions begun by American independence, it became common to argue that patriotism and universal benevolence were complementary.[21]

Philadelphia abolitionists in the early national period were compelled (or constrained) by this intellectual context to demonstrate, to a greater degree than Quaker forebears like Benezet, that they were activated both by patriotism and by cosmopolitan ideals. In 1780, when the Pennsylvania's state assembly passed its Gradual Abolition Act, the preamble combined new, patriotic language with references to the antislavery cosmopolitanism that Philadelphia's abolitionists had invoked for years. The act framed gradual emancipation as a gesture of patriotic gratitude for Pennsylvania's recent deliverance from British tyranny. Yet antislavery cosmopolitanism retained its importance. The act's preamble also cited love for all "the inhabitants of the several parts of the earth" as a prime motive for its passage. "Weaned . . . from those narrow prejudices and partialities we had imbibed" against Africans, "we find our hearts enlarged with kindness and benevolence towards men of all conditions and nations." The preamble of the Gradual Abolition Act has been attributed to a variety of authors, including Paine and Benezet. But, whoever actually penned the words, it should be obvious that the preamble called on the themes of antislavery cosmopolitanism that had been articulated by various Philadelphia writers in the 1760s and 1770s: a rejection of "narrow prejudices" for some "parts of the earth"; an appeal to the common creator of the family of man; and a profession of universal "benevolence" enlarged enough to embrace all "nations."[22]

The same ideals were endorsed by the Pennsylvania Abolition Society when it reorganized in 1787. The PAS continued in the tradition of forebears like Benezet and Rush by corresponding with British abolitionists like Sharp, as well as French abolitionists like Raynal, Lafayette, and Brissot de Warville. These transatlantic ties helped perpetuate abolitionists' image of themselves as world-embracing philanthropists. In 1788 the society drafted a letter to Lafayette musing that "the present age has been distinguished by a remarkable revolution. . . . Mankind begin at last to consider themselves as members of one family." Such rhetoric suggests, as historian James Alexander Dun argues, that PAS members saw themselves not just as patriotic citizens of the American republic, but as members of a "global community" of benevolent men.[23]

If the American Revolution suggested that it was possible to be both patriotic and cosmopolitan, however, the subsequent French and Haitian revolutions located patriotism and cosmopolitanism in a more polarized field. In Britain and the United States, supporters of the shocking events that took place in Paris in 1789 often declared that true citizens of the world sympathized with the revolution. In his 1789 *Discourse on the Love for Country*, British radical Richard Price endorsed the French Revolution on the grounds that "Universal Benevolence" was "an unspeakably nobler principle than any partial affections" for the "spot of earth on which we happen to be born." Price urged Britons to consider themselves "more as citizens of the world than as members of any particular community." These were familiar Hutchesonian ideas that had circulated in Britain for decades, but for conservatives like Edmund Burke, the French Revolution proved that cosmopolitanism invited social chaos. Professing love for an abstract human family, French radicals had abandoned their concrete duties to country, so that universal benevolence, in practice, licensed bloodshed.[24]

These debates about France's revolution ricocheted into Philadelphia's print culture when Paine intervened in the exchange between Burke and Price with his *Rights of Man*. Transatlantic radicals in early national Philadelphia built on Paine's defense of the French Revolution to forge what historian Seth Aaron Cotlar calls "popular cosmopolitanism." Around the same time that *Rights of Man* appeared, other pamphlets were published in Philadelphia that explicitly tied Paineite cosmopolitanism to critiques of slavery. Thanks to Paine, said one essayist on the slave trade, public attention was no longer fixated only on "the rights of one particular nation," but was now concerned with "those of mankind, without distinction of color." Another Philadelphia writer applauded the "benevolent" exertions underway "for the relief of thousands and tens of thousands" of Africans. Signing himself "A Friend of Mankind," the author praised those "who, not confined to a spot of earth . . . extend their beneficent views . . . to every nation, language and color."[25]

Forced by the American Revolution to choose sides, Philadelphia abolitionists like Rush had argued that patriotic attachment to America was compatible with universal benevolence, and that both principles had antislavery implications. Forced to choose sides again by the French Revolution, some antislavery writers reemphasized the primacy of universal benevolence over narrow love for country. But in the 1790s, thanks to the numerous published debates between supporters of Paine and supporters of Burke, the ideal of world citizenship became closely associated with the French Revolution and its ramifications throughout the Atlantic world. After 1789, abolitionists who invoked the discourse of antislavery cosmopolitanism risked being tarred with charges of Jacobin anarchy and a reckless lack of patriotism. And after 1791, antislavery cosmopolitans further risked being accused of supporting slave insurrection, thanks to the beginning of the Haitian Revolution.

Many defenders of slavery were quick to assimilate Saint Domingue into Burke's general critique of the French Revolution: principles like universal human rights had ultimately led to the bloody dissolution of social ties between parent and child, slave and master, citizen and fellow citizen. In 1802, when Napoleon tried to reverse slavery's abolition in the Caribbean, which was formally decreed by France in 1794, his colonial minister Denis Decrès spoke for many reactionaries when he said that "I reject these supposedly liberal ideas, which, in order to spread my affection to the entire universe, call down misery on my country." Defending the reversal of emancipation, Decrès declared, "I am too French to be cosmopolitan."[26]

The massive slave rebellion in Saint Domingue touched Philadelphia directly, as waves of colonists fled from burning plantations to the city in the 1790s. After 1792, antislavery writers in Philadelphia thus had to be more cautious about invoking the ideal of world citizenship, which could now connote slave revolt or treasonous alliances with the French. In 1797, perhaps sensitive to any perception that abolitionists supported the Haitian Revolution, the PAS rejected overtures from French commissioners who invited their fellow "Philanthropists" from Philadelphia to visit Saint Domingue. A letter from the PAS to the *Amis des Noirs* in 1801 also implicitly acknowledged that transatlantic ties among abolitionists had been attenuated by the polarizing rhetoric of the 1790s. Writing to the Abbé Gregoire, PAS Chairman James Milnor celebrated "the re-establishment of Peace and Friendship" between France and the United States and expressed a hope that "Mankind [would] . . . increase in the knowledge that we are all Brethren."[27]

Such language, and continued exchanges between the PAS and European abolitionists, suggest that the idea of antislavery cosmopolitanism did not disappear in the turbulence of the 1790s. But the political connotations now attached to cosmopolitanism required abolitionists to step carefully around a delicate subject. The hatching of the Age of Revolution had scattered the ground with eggshells. Writers who wished to identify as world citizens now had to insist, to a greater degree than earlier abolitionists, that they were patriots too. Indeed, as Matthew Mason has recently argued, antislavery writers in the early national period attacked defenders of slavery for threatening the continuation of the American Union, effectively arguing that slavery was caused not by too much love for country, but by too little. Slavery, according to early antislavery politicians, was a blot on the national reputation that true patriots would work to expunge.[28]

Early national abolitionists in Philadelphia also emphasized their patriotism because, thanks to the changes wrought by gradual emancipation in the North, their aims were expanding to include not just the abolition of slavery but also the incorporation of free black Americans as full citizens of the new nation. After the American Revolution, Philadelphia's antislavery community was profoundly changed by the institutional growth of the city's free black community, as black abolitionists like Richard Allen, Absalom Jones, and James Forten brought a new urgency to antislavery appeals. "If you love your country," pleaded Absalom Jones and Richard Allen in a 1794 address to their fellow Philadelphians, "burden not your children or country" with slaves. In 1814, black Philadelphian Russell Parrott credited his state as "first in patriotism" for its emancipation measures, assuring white Pennsylvanians that by freeing their slaves they had "secured to yourself a band of citizens . . . whose blood will cheerfully flow in your defence" and who had already proved "we are faithful to our country." In 1813, James Forten urged Pennsylvanians not to pass a bill restricting black immigration, confidently asserting there was sufficient "patriotism" in the legislature to "crush" the bill.[29]

As even these few examples demonstrate, the rhetoric of black Philadelphians constantly professed a patriotic attachment to the country and asserted their civil liberties. While white abolitionists like Benezet, Rush, and the members of the PAS had frequently identified themselves as citizens of the world, free black Philadelphians were more immediately concerned with securing their status as citizens of Pennsylvania and asserting their status as citizens of the United States. The black immigration bill that so angered Forten in 1813 was only one of many attempts made to scale back the liberties extended by the Gradual Abolition Act of 1780. To thwart those attempts, black Philadelphians regularly insisted on their love for the state and the nation, cited their loyal service in the War of Independence, and appealed to the patriotic memories of white Pennsylvanians.[30]

The same emphasis on patriotism continued in the rhetoric of black abolitionists after 1816, when the American Colonization Society began to advocate the expatriation of black Americans to Liberia. After expressing some interest in the emigration schemes of black New Englander Paul Cuffee, free black northerners decisively rejected colonization in the 1820s. As Gary Nash and

Julie Winch show in greater detail, Philadelphia's free black community was particularly active in opposing colonization. Their opposition, according to Richard Newman, helped spark the founding of the American Anti-Slavery Society (AASS) in Philadelphia in 1833, which boasted an interracial cadre of abolitionists who demanded immediate emancipation without expatriation. In Pennsylvania, the formation of the AASS was followed by the formation of the Philadelphia Female Anti-Slavery Society a few days later and the formation of the Pennsylvania Anti-Slavery Society in 1837. In the 1830s, supported by new white allies in the AASS and its state auxiliaries, black abolitionists continued to cite their patriotism, rejecting the common colonizationist claim that the free black American was "without a home of his own, without a community of his own, without a country of his own."[31]

Given the historically specific needs of the colonization controversy, black abolitionists steered clear of earlier antislavery rhetoric that deprecated patriotism as irrational, arguing instead that they loved the country of their birth. Earlier white abolitionists like Rush could claim that the globe was their "native country" partly because they never faced the threat of forcible removal from their actual native country. But to counter the colonizationists, black reformers regularly identified America as their only home and testified to their love for the nation. Black reformers like William Whipper extolled that "national feeling, which as true patriots we are bound to cherish." "When we speak of America," Whipper told a black audience in Philadelphia in 1833, "we do it with those feelings of respect that are due to it as our country—not as the land of our adoption, not with the alienated breath of foreigners; but with the instinctive love of native born citizens."[32]

The fact that anti-colonizationists valorized patriotism reveals the ambiguous implications of the eighteenth-century discourse of antislavery cosmopolitanism. For early abolitionists like Rush, Benezet, and Paine, arguing that slavery was incompatible with universal benevolence did not entail that slavery should be immediately abolished, nor did the idea that abolitionists were world citizens imply that people of color should be American citizens. Indeed, the idea that eighteenth-century abolitionists were uniquely cosmopolitan often implied that black men and women were foreigners and aliens—the objects of a benevolence that had to be very enlarged indeed to encompass them, rather than the objects of natural affection that one felt for native countrymen. In 1784, Rush wrote to Sharp that the late Benezet had "seemed to possess a species of Quixotism in acts of piety and benevolence. He embraced all mankind in the circle of his love. Indians and Africans were as dear to him as the citizens of Pennsylvania." The subtle implication was that "Africans" were not the same as "citizens of Pennsylvania," and that loving them was quixotic.[33]

Black Philadelphians stressed their patriotism partly to refute claims that they were not worthy of citizenship. "Our expatriation has come to be a darling project with many of our fellow citizens," noted Robert Purvis in 1837. Purvis declared "our abhorrence of a scheme which comes to us in the guise of Christian benevolence"—a telling word—"and asks us to suffer ourselves to be transplanted to a distant and barbarous land." He insisted "we love our native country, much as it has wronged us." When Garrison, initially a colonizationist, met black abolitionists like Forten and Purvis, he took this message to heart. In 1832, Garrison's *Thoughts on African Colonization* reported that "the language of the people of color is,—'This is our country: here were we born . . . we are countrymen and fellow-citizens.'" Contrary to colonizationist claims, black Americans had an "*amor patriae*" that was "robust and deathless." Unlike Hutchesonian writers who argued that God had instilled universal benevolence in every human being, Garrison emphasized that the "love of home, of neighborhood, of country, is inherent in the human breast," an attribute "given by the all-wise Creator to bind each separate tribe or community" together.[34]

(3)

The polarizing transformations of the Atlantic World in the late eighteenth century, together with the rise of colonizationism as the most prominent antislavery movement in the United States, encouraged early national abolitionists in Philadelphia to emphasize patriotism as a moral source of antislavery activism. Yet the rich intellectual vein of antislavery cosmopolitanism had not run dry. In the 1830s, as a national antislavery movement committed to immediate emancipation began to take shape, a new generation of abolitionists in Philadelphia continued to claim, like their antislavery forebears, a cosmopolitan identity.

This was partly because of the reconstitution of transatlantic antislavery networks in the 1830s. Inspired by British abolitionists, who secured a parliamentary bill for West Indian emancipation in 1833, Philadelphia abolitionists sought out new ties with British reformers. In 1834, for example, Robert Purvis traveled from Philadelphia to Scotland and delivered letters from the recently established PFASS to the Glasgow Ladies' Emancipation Society. Some abolitionists also visited the Caribbean to witness firsthand the results of emancipation there. In the winter of 1837 and 1838, Philadelphia abolitionist Lewis Gunn accompanied Charles S. Burleigh to Haiti, where they traveled for six months with black Philadelphian Robert Douglass Jr. and forged ties with abolitionists in Port-au-Prince. As in earlier eras, transatlantic correspondence between Quakers, like the exchange between Philadelphia abolitionist Lucretia Mott and British Quaker Mary Lloyd in the 1820s, helped urge antislavery Friends on both sides of the Atlantic forward.[35]

British abolitionists, buoyed by their victories, also cultivated ties with the American movement. When Garrison traveled to Britain in 1833 and invited British abolitionist George Thompson to the United States, Thompson eagerly agreed. In 1835, Thompson lectured in Philadelphia to at least a thousand people and had a transformative impact on some local reformers, including Sarah Forten and Sarah Pugh. Thompson deeply impressed Pugh, who would later become one of Philadelphia's leading abolitionists and who would travel to London in 1840 as a representative of the PASS.[36] The British and Foreign Anti-Slavery Society (BFASS) invited abolitionists from various countries to London for a general conference on antislavery in June 1840. The meeting, which became known as the "World's Convention," represented the culmination of a decade of transatlantic networking among abolitionists, and Philadelphia was well represented by a delegation that included Pugh, Elizabeth Neall, Abby Kimber, Mary Grew, and Mott and her husband James. These delegates, along with other Philadelphia abolitionists like Edward M. Davis, maintained correspondence with friends in Britain and Europe for years after their initial Atlantic crossings. The exchange of newspapers and the sending of contributions from Europe to antislavery fundraising fairs organized in Philadelphia and elsewhere further cemented the ties binding local abolitionists to distant friends, as did post-convention transatlantic trips. Pugh returned to Europe in 1852, visiting France, Italy, and Britain, and reviving friendships begun in 1840 at the World's Convention.

Philadelphia abolitionists did not see these "Atlantic crossings" as ancillary or unrelated to their primary task in the 1830s—to build a movement for immediate emancipation that would be national in its reach and its effects. On the contrary, building transatlantic networks was especially crucial for Philadelphia abolitionists as a means of integrating them into the national antislavery movement that took shape after the formation of the AASS.

Although it would be natural to presume that transatlantic reform connections were always preceded by strong connections within national movements, the relationship between transatlantic ties and interregional ties among abolitionists seldom seemed so linear to actors at the time. For some Philadelphians, hearing Thompson—a British abolitionist—speak on slavery probably served as their first concrete introduction to radical antislavery groups in Boston or New York. The "World's Convention," likewise, introduced Philadelphia abolitionists not only to British abolitionists, but also to American reformers whom they had never personally met. As Abby Kimber explained to her English friend, Elizabeth Pease, she was "acquainted" with New England abolitionists Wendell Phillips and Nathaniel P. Rogers "only through the abolition papers, before we met in London—and with Garrison only as an editor and public speaker." Going to Old England, paradoxically, brought some Philadelphia abolitionists into closer relation with New England.[37]

As abolitionists became more connected with like-minded reformers both within and outside of the United States, they increasingly came to view themselves as citizens of the world in fact as well as in aspiration. When Charles Burleigh addressed the Haitian Abolition Society in 1838, he invoked cosmopolitan ideals by declaring that "you . . . who sit before me, are my countrymen," despite being "citizens of a country foreign to my own." Burleigh praised the "noble sentiment" that "my country is the world." When Robert Purvis returned to Philadelphia from Scotland in 1834, he carried a letter from Glasgow abolitionists praising Thompson as a "Philanthropist of the world" whose journey to America was motivated by "the impulse of an expanding benevolence." The AASS used similar language in its first annual report, published in Philadelphia, when it lauded Thompson as a cosmopolitan reformer who "belong[ed] not to an island or a kingdom, but to the world."[38]

In anticipation of the "World's Convention" in 1840, abolitionists in Philadelphia also cited the international gathering as proof of their cosmopolitan sentiments. After its third annual meeting, the PASS predicted that the international cooperation behind the convention would encourage people throughout "the habitable earth" to learn "the lesson of human brotherhood" and embrace the "noble sentiment, 'our country is the world, our countrymen are all mankind.'" "We love to see the people of different countries finding other points of contact than those which are encased with their nationality," echoed the Pennsylvania *Freeman*. The London Convention would be a crucible where "national prejudices [would be] melted down, and national peculiarities forgotten, and national pride absorbed and swallowed up in the simple and grand idea of human brotherhood." It was an 1839 poem by Pennsylvania abolitionist John Greenleaf Whittier that bestowed the title of "World's Convention" on the meeting, whose delegates would not be moved merely by a "patriot's zeal," but also by the "Christian's love for human kind, / To caste and climate unconfined."[39]

These appeals to universal benevolence and cosmopolitan feeling were, as we have seen, grounded in long traditions of antislavery argument in Philadelphia and throughout the Atlantic world. But they were revived in the 1830s and 1840s partly in reaction to the increasingly radical opposition that abolitionists faced even in the northern United States. As abolitionists increasingly claimed the right to agitate about an institution—slavery—that was located in distant states and also invited British abolitionists to join in this agitation, they were simultaneously challenging the power of local elites in northern states—the "gentlemen of property of standing"—to regulate the boundaries of allowable discourse and prevent agitation that might disturb the national Union. Abolitionist appeals to a law higher than the "patriot's zeal" were exceedingly controversial in the antebellum period, when the more popular slogan among Americans was not "Our Country is the World," but "Our Country, Right or Wrong." If the ideal of universal benevolence had once been tarred in the 1790s by association with the French Revolution, antislavery cosmopolitanism in the 1830s and 1840s was widely perceived by anti-abolitionists as a cover for a British plot to subvert American institutions. Throughout his American tour, Thompson was hounded by rioters, often led or tolerated by local elites, who denounced him as a foreign agent, ultimately forcing him to return prematurely to Britain.[40]

But even without the specter of British "foreign interference," the construction of a national antislavery movement appeared threatening to many northerners in the 1830s and 1840s. Charles Burleigh, who toured Pennsylvania as an agent of the AASS before leaving for Haiti, dodged eggs and stones in some towns and was charged with being a "foreign agent" because he hailed from the distant climes of Connecticut. The reaction to a newly assertive abolitionist movement revealed how inchoate the idea of the United States as a national community still was in the antebellum period; it was not for nothing that the country continued to be conceived more as a "Union" of states and regions than as a "nation." In view of this reality, abolitionists realized that appealing to their moral responsibilities as patriotic Americans would only partially mitigate their offenses in the eyes of critics, if at all. They therefore responded to attacks on *national* abolitionism by reasserting their identity as citizens of the *world*, rather than as merely citizens of one state or country.[41]

When the PASS was formed in 1837, for example, it issued an address to the citizens of Pennsylvania arguing for their right to attack slavery, whether as American citizens, as residents of Pennsylvania, or as "members too of the great family of mankind. We are endowed with feelings and sympathies which were intended for our use, and which bind us to our fellow creatures by the common ties of human sympathy." According to the address, the PASS claimed the birthright of the old eighteenth-century PAS, which had also cultivated ties with abolitionists abroad. "The modern doctrines of foreign interference had not been incorporated into [the founding generation's] political creed," it continued, pointing out that the state of Pennsylvania granted the PAS incorporation in 1789, even though its membership had included foreigners.[42]

Even when an angry Philadelphia mob burned down Pennsylvania Hall, in May 1838, local abolitionists continued to invoke the discourse of antislavery cosmopolitanism. The PASS made a distraught appeal "To the Citizens of Pennsylvania" in the *Pennsylvania Freeman*, arguing that abolitionists had a duty to attack slavery, even "separated from it as we are by geographical boundaries," because "that benevolence which is bounded by caste or complexion, is not the benevolence of Christ." The PASS concluded that "we labor not for ourselves alone, but . . . for our land and for the world—for the great interests of humanity universally." In February, another editorial in the *Freeman* on "Foreign Interference" argued that North and South were separated "by a mere arbitrary geographical line," and treating such lines as limits on moral duty violated the Garrisonian motto, "our country is the world, and our countrymen are all mankind," a principle of "the most enlarged benevolence" that embraced "the whole family of man." Though separated from the first Philadelphia abolitionists by half a century of dramatic changes, antebellum activists in Philadelphia still called frequently on eighteenth-century arguments about "universal benevolence" and the "family of man," both to attack slavery and to defend themselves.[43]

(4)

As this chapter has shown, the common terms of antislavery cosmopolitanism had a long life in the rhetoric of Philadelphia abolitionists, surviving the shift from gradualism to immediatism that usually marks a sharp divide between the city's first and second generations of antislavery activists and writers. Yet antislavery cosmopolitanism did not pass unchanged from Benezet and Paine to Burleigh and Pugh. Abolitionists across time drew on a common repertoire of cosmopolitan rhetoric, but they modified that rhetoric to meet challenges specific to their eras.

For example, Garrisonian abolitionists viewed themselves as citizens of the world and justified their agitation on that ground, yet in the controversy over colonization, they joined with African American abolitionists in Philadelphia to stress the virtues of love for one's native land. Earlier, writers like Rush and Paine had alternated between casting nationalism and cosmopolitanism as opposing ideas and, on the other hand, construing their patriotic support for American independence as consistent with the demands of universal benevolence. Though beyond the scope of this chapter, changes in the uses of antislavery cosmopolitanism continued after 1840 and even began at the much-ballyhooed "World's Convention," when Garrisonian abolitionists infuriated by the exclusion of women delegates from the meeting used cosmopolitan ideals to argue that their treatment by British abolitionists indicated narrow and illiberal sentiments.[44]

Such flexibility in the use of antislavery cosmopolitanism suggests that abolitionists never saw their loyalties to an imagined global community as strictly incompatible with their loyalties to other communities nearer at hand. Indeed, as the PASS's reaction to increased local opposition in the 1830s showed, some abolitionists called on their identities as citizens of the world in order to defend their actions as citizens of the United States. The PASS and the *Pennsylvania Freeman* cited the principle that benevolence should never be confined by "a mere arbitrary geographical line"—a crucial premise of antislavery cosmopolitanism—not just to defend their crossing of national borders, but even to defend their crossing of state and regional lines within the United States. Just as participation in transnational networks helped push Philadelphia abolitionists out of their city into wider regional and national networks, imagining themselves as part of a transnational community helped some abolitionists imagine themselves as part of a national community, in which their duty to interfere with southern slavery sprang from the same moral sources that justified George Thompson's "foreign interference."

The experience of Philadelphia abolitionists over the long Age of Revolutions thus suggests that an image of patriotism and cosmopolitanism as utter opposites, whatever its philosophical merits, is an anachronistic one. Such an image distracts historians from the ways that international activities and ideals informed and transformed national activities and nationalist sensibilities. Likewise, the history of antislavery cosmopolitanism in Philadelphia should remind historians of abolitionism not to see transatlantic cooperation as ancillary to the development of the American antislavery movement, or as simply a means by which information, ideas, and moral support were exchanged between abolitionists in different national contexts. The "Atlantic crossings" of Philadelphia abolitionists served as more than simple conduits for preexisting ideas, though they were at least that. Crossing the Atlantic, whether literally or figuratively, also helped abolitionists develop new arguments against slavery and formulate new identities. To some extent, by facilitating the acquaintance of Philadelphia abolitionists with other *American* activists and encouraging them to extend their agitation beyond state or regional lines, imagining the existence of communities that transcended national lines even helped abolitionists articulate their responsibilities to and visions of their national and subnational communities. By declaring that their country was the world, abolitionists claimed as much about their relation to their country as they did about their relation to the world.

NOTES

1. Sarah Pugh to Richard D. Webb, Richard Allen, and James Haughton, 24 August 1840, Anti-Slavery Collection, Boston Public Library (hereafter abbreviated as BPL), Ms.A.1.2.9.98. On the Quaker "Antislavery International," see David Brion Davis, *The Problem of Slavery in the Age of Revolution, 1770–1823* (1975; New York: Oxford University Press, 1999), 213–54, and a recent overview in Huw T. David, "Transnational Advocacy in the Eighteenth Century: Transatlantic Activism and the Anti-Slavery Movement," *Global Networks* 7, no. 3 (2007): 367–82. Historians of reform movements have recently paid increased attention to the transatlantic dimensions of American activism, especially after the mid-nineteenth century. See, for example, Kathryn Kish Sklar and James Brewer Stewart, eds., *Women's Rights and Transatlantic Antislavery in the Era of Emancipation* (New Haven, Conn.: Yale University Press, 2007); Bonnie S. Anderson, *Joyous Greetings: The First International Women's Movement, 1830–1860* (New York: Oxford University Press, 2000); Daniel T. Rodgers, *Atlantic Crossings: Social Politics in a Progressive Age* (Cambridge, Mass.: Harvard University Press, 1998).

2. [Joseph Sansom], *A Poetical Epistle to the Enslaved Africans, in the Character of an Ancient Negro, Born a Slave in Pennsylvania* . . . (Philadelphia: Joseph Crukshank, 1790), 18; George S. Brookes, *Friend Anthony Benezet* (Philadelphia: University of Pennsylvania Press, 1937), 365; Thomas Paine, *Rights of Man* (New York: Penguin, 1984), 228; Rush to Granville Sharp, [August 1791], in *Letters of Benjamin Rush,* ed. L. H. Butterfield, vol. 1, *1761–1792* (Princeton, N.J.: Princeton University Press, 1951), 609.

3. See David Brion Davis, *The Problem of Slavery in Western Culture* (1966; New York: Oxford University Press, 1988), 483–493, which includes a survey of the links between Rush, Benezet, Franklin, Diderot, and Hume. For links between the Fothergills, Franklin, Price, and Priestley, see Davis, *The Problem of Slavery in the Age of Revolution,* 230. On Philadelphia's intellectual

community more generally, see Henry F. May, *The Enlightenment in America* (New York: Oxford University Press, 1976), 197–222; Carl Bridenbaugh, "Philosophy Put to Use: Voluntary Associations for Propagating the Enlightenment in Philadelphia, 1727–1776," in *Early Americans* (New York: Oxford University Press, 1981); Andrew Hook, "Philadelphia, Edinburgh and the Scottish Enlightenment," in *Scotland and America in the Age of Enlightenment,* ed. Richard B. Sher and Jeffrey R. Smitten (Edinburgh: Edinburgh University Press, 1990), 227–41.

4. J. M. Opal, "The Labors of Liberality: Christian Benevolence and National Prejudice in the American Founding," *Journal of American History* 94, no. 4 (2008): 1082–1107.

5. Richard S. Newman, *The Transformation of American Abolitionism: Fighting Slavery in the Early Republic* (Chapel Hill: University of North Carolina Press, 2002).

6. "Foreign Interference," *Pennsylvania Freeman,* 14 February 1839. In their biography of their father, Garrison's sons also identified "Our Country is the World" as Garrison's "favorite motto." See Wendell Phillips Garrison and Francis Jackson Garrison, *William Lloyd Garrison, 1805–1879: The Story of His Life Told by His Children* (4 vols.; Boston: Houghton Mifflin and Co., 1885–89), vol. 1: xi.

7. *Proceedings of the Pennsylvania Convention, Assembled to Organize a State Anti-Slavery Society, at Harrisburg* (Philadelphia: Merrihew & Gunn, 1837), 91; James Miller McKim, Notes, Spring 1853, Box 1, Maloney Collection of McKim-Garrison Family Papers, New York Public Library; Abby Kimber to Elizabeth Pease, 18 May [1841?], BPL, Ms.A.1.2.9.43. This letter is dated 1840, but internal evidence shows it was written later.

8. On Enlightened cosmopolitanism, see Thomas J. Schlereth, *The Cosmopolitan Ideal in Enlightenment Thought: Its Form and Function in the Ideas of Franklin, Hume, and Voltaire, 1694–1790* (Notre Dame, Ind.: University of Notre Dame Press, 1977). The American Philosophical Society is quoted on page 39.

9. James Foster, *Discourses on All the Principal Branches of Natural Religion and Social Virtue* (London: For the author, 1749–52), vol. 2: 277–78. On Hutcheson and debates in Britain about "universal benevolence," see Evan Radcliffe, "Revolutionary Writing, Moral Philosophy, and Universal Benevolence in the Eighteenth Century," *Journal of the History of Ideas* 54, no. 2 (April 1993): 221–40. See also Opal, "The Labors of Liberality."

10. John Woolman, "On Loving our Neighbours," in *The Works of John Woolman, in Two Parts* (Philadelphia: Joseph Crukshank, 1774), 391; Foster, *Discourses* 2: 260; Sydney V. James, *A People among Peoples: Quaker Benevolence in Eighteenth-Century America* (Cambridge, Mass.: Harvard University Press, 1963), 323; Pemberton quoted in James, *People among Peoples,* 323.

11. Foster, *Discourses* 2: 284–85, 157, 282, 288.

12. Woolman, "On Loving our Neighbours," 407, 389. John Woolman, *Considerations on the True Harmony of Mankind; and How it is to be Maintained* (Philadelphia: Joseph Crukshank, 1770), 2. "The Journal of John Woolman," in Charles Eliot, ed., *The Autobiography of Benjamin Franklin; The Journal of John Woolman; Fruits of Solitude, William Penn* (New York: P. F. Collier & Son, 1909), 293, online at the University of Virginia Library Electronic Text Center, etext.lib.virginia.edu/toc/modeng/public/WooJour.html (26 July 2007).

13. *Two Dialogues on the Man-Trade* (London: Printed for J. Waugh, W. Fenner, G. Woodfall, W. Owen, and Mrs. Kingham, 1760), 9. For more on the *Two Dialogues,* see David Brion Davis, "New Sidelights on Early Antislavery Radicalism," *William and Mary Quarterly,* 3rd ser., vol. 28, no. 4 (October 1971): 592.

14. Anthony Benezet, *A Short Account of That Part of Africa, Inhabited by the Negroes . . .* (Philadelphia: n.p., 1762), 5–6. See Benezet, *Short Account . . . of Africa,* 28–29 (excerpt from Philmore); Benezet, *A Short Account of That Part of Africa, Inhabited by the Negroes. With Quotations from the Writings of Several Persons of Note, Viz. George Wallis, Francis Hutcheson, and James Foster. The Second Edition, with Large Additions and Amendments* (Philadelphia: W. Dunlap, 1762), 34–35 (excerpts from Hutcheson and Foster). On Benezet as a "middleman of ideas," see Davis, "New Sidelights on Early Antislavery Radicalism," 592; Maurice Jackson, "The Social and Intellectual Origins of Anthony Benezet's Antislavery Radicalism," *Pennsylvania History* 66, supplement (1999): 86–112; Maurice Jackson, *Let This Voice Be Heard: Anthony Benezet, Father of Atlantic Abolitionism* (Philadelphia: University of Pennsylvania Press, 2009).

15. Benezet, *Short Account of That Part of Africa,* 5–6; Brookes, *Friend Anthony Benezet,* 299; Benjamin Rush to Granville Sharp, 13 May 1774, in John A. Woods, "The Correspondence of Benjamin Rush and Granville Sharp, 1773–1809," *Journal of American Studies* 1, no. 1 (1967): 5.

16. Benjamin Rush, *An Address to the Inhabitants of the British Settlements in America, Upon Slave-Keeping* (Philadelphia: John Dunlap, 1773), 26; Richard Nisbet, *Slavery not forbidden by Scripture: Or A defence of the West-India planters, from the aspersions thrown out against them, by the author of a pamphlet, entitled, "An address to the inhabitants of the British settlements in America, upon slave-keeping"* (Philadelphia: [John Sparhawk], 1773), 20; [Benjamin Rush], *Vindication of the Address, to the Inhabitants of the British Settlements on the Slavery of the Negroes in America, in Answer to a Pamphlet Entitled, "Slavery not Forbidden by Scripture; or a Defence of the West-India Planters from the Aspersions Thrown Out Against Them by the Author of the Address"* (Philadelphia: John Dunlap, 1773), 24–25. Rush seems to have been paraphrasing Giuseppe Marco Antonio Baretti, *A Journey from London to Genoa, Through England, Portugal, Spain, and France, by Joseph Baretti . . . In Two Volumes . . .* (London: T. Davies and L. Davis, 1770), 5.

17. Thomas Paine, "African Slavery in America," in *Complete Writings of Thomas Paine,* ed. Philip S. Foner (2 vols., New York: Citadel Press, 1945), vol. 2: 17; Benezet, *A Short Account . . . of Africa . . . Second Edition,* 34; [London Yearly Meeting], *The case of our fellow-creatures, the oppressed Africans, respectfully recommended to the serious consideration of the legislature of Great-Britain, by the people called Quakers* (London, printed: Philadelphia: rpt. by Joseph Crukshank, 1784), 8–9.

18. The surge of antislavery discussion in Philadelphia before the American Revolution is surveyed in Gary B. Nash and Jean R. Soderlund, *Freedom by Degrees: Emancipation in Pennsylvania and Its Aftermath* (New York: Oxford University Press, 1991), 77–80.

19. Foster, *Discourses,* 284; Rush to Sharp, 9 July 1774, and Rush to Sharp, 4 August 1783, in Woods, "The Correspondence of Benjamin Rush and Granville Sharp," 9, 17.

20. "To His Fellow Countrymen: On Patriotism," in *Letters of Benjamin Rush* 1: 83–84.

21. Jay Fliegelman, *Prodigals and Pilgrims: The American Revolution against Patriarchal Authority, 1750–1800* (Cambridge: Cambridge University Press, 1982), 225–30, quotations from Washington and about Washington on page 228; Rush to Sharp, 31 March 1801, in Woods, "The Correspondence of Benjamin Rush and Granville Sharp," 34.

22. *The Constitution of the Pennsylvania Society, for Promoting the Abolition of Slavery . . . To which are added, the Acts of the General Assembly of Pennsylvania, for the Gradual Abolition of Slavery* (Philadelphia: Joseph James, 1787), 9. On the authorship of the bill, see Nash and Soderlund, *Freedom by Degrees,* 101–2.

23. James Alexander Dun, "Dangerous Intelligence: Slavery, Race, and St. Domingue in the Early American Republic," Ph.D. diss., Princeton University, 2004, 246–50, letter to Lafayette quoted on page 248. See also the PAS to the "Society at Paris," 3 December 1788, Pennsylvania Abolition Society Papers [PASP], Historical Society of Pennsylvania [HSP], Series 2, Reel 11, Loose Correspondence.

24. Richard Price, "A Discourse on the Love of our Country," in *Political Writings*, ed. D. O. Thomas (Cambridge: Cambridge University Press, 1991), 178, 180–81, 193–94; Edmund Burke, *Reflections on the Revolution in France*, ed. J. C. D. Clark (Palo Alto, Calif.: Stanford University Press, 2001), 202.

25. Seth Aaron Cotlar, "In Paine's Absence: The Trans-Atlantic Dynamics of American Popular Political Thought, 1789–1804," Ph.D. diss., Northwestern University, 2000, 15–65; *Essays on the Subject of the Slave-Trade, in which the Sentiments of Several Eminent British Writers are Attended to.—And also containing Extracts from an Address of the Abolition Society in Paris, to the National Assembly . . . Particularly Honorable to that Nation, and Friendly to the Rights of Mankind* (Philadelphia: Eleazar Oswald, 1791), 5, 20–21.

26. Decrès quoted in Laurent Dubois, *A Colony of Citizens: Revolution and Slave Emancipation in the French Caribbean, 1787–1804* (Chapel Hill: University of North Carolina Press, 2004), 368. On Haitian refugees and the influence of the Haitian Revolution on debates about slavery in Philadelphia and the early republic, see especially Dun, "Dangerous Intelligence"; Ashli White, "'A Flood of Impure Lava': Saint Dominguan Refugees in the United States, 1791–1820," Ph.D. diss., Columbia University, 2003.

27. "To Gregoire, Member of the National Institute at Paris," 14 December 1801, Letterbook, vol. 2: 78, in PASP, HSP, series 2, reel 11. On the overtures from Haitian commissioners to the PAS, see Letterbook, vol. 2: 42–55, and the discussion in Dun, "Dangerous Intelligence," 241–97.

28. See Matthew Mason, *Slavery and Politics in the Early American Republic* (Chapel Hill: University of North Carolina Press, 2006).

29. Quotations from Richard Newman, Patrick Rael, and Philip Lapsansky, eds., *Pamphlets of Protest: An Anthology of Early African-American Protest Literature, 1790–1860* (New York: Routledge, 2001), 42, 78–79, 70.

30. On black abolitionists' attempts to claim civic equality after the revolution, see Richard S. Newman and Roy E. Finkenbine, eds., "Forum: Black Founders," *William and Mary Quarterly*, 3rd. ser., vol. 64, no. 1 (January 2007): 83–166.

31. "An Essay for the Fourth of July," *African Repository and Colonial Journal* 3, no. 12 (February 1828): 374, American Periodical Series Online.

32. William Whipper, *Eulogy on William Wilberforce, Esq. Delivered at the Request of the People of Colour of the City of Philadelphia, in the Second African Presbyterian Church, on the Sixth Day of December, 1833* (Philadelphia: William R. Gibbons, [1833?]), 31–33.

33. Rush to Sharp, 15 May 1784, in Woods, "The Correspondence of Benjamin Rush and Granville Sharp," 23.

34. Robert Purvis, "Appeal of Forty Thousand Citizens, Threatened with Disfranchisement, to the People of Pennsylvania," in *Pamphlets of Protest*, ed. Newman, Rael, and Lapsansky, 135; William Lloyd Garrison, *Thoughts on African Colonization, or, An Impartial Exhibition of the Doctrines, Principles and Purposes of the American Colonization Society, together with the Resolutions, Addresses and Remonstrances of the Free People of Color* (Boston: Garrison and Knapp, 1832), 2–4.

35. On Purvis's trip to Glasgow, see Julie Winch, *A Gentleman of Color: The Life of James Forten* (New York: Oxford University Press, 2002), 262–63. On Burleigh's, Gunn's, and Douglas's trip to Haiti, see "Speech of Charles C. Burleigh, at a Meeting of the Haytien Abolition Society," *National Enquirer and Constitutional Advocate of Universal Liberty* (Philadelphia), 15 February 1838; "Speech of Lewis C. Gunn, Delivered before the Haytien Abolition Society," *National Enquirer*, 22 February 1838; "Abolition in Hayti," *The Liberator*, 9 February 1838; Ira V. Brown, "An Antislavery Agent: C. C. Burleigh in Pennsylvania, 1836–1837," *Pennsylvania Magazine of History and Biography* 105, no. 1 (1981): 84. On the correspondence between Lloyd and Mott, see Beth A. Salerno, *Sister Societies: Women's Antislavery Organizations in Antebellum America* (Dekalb: Northern Illinois University Press, 2005), 19–20.

36. On Thompson's trip to Philadelphia, see *Letters and Addresses of George Thompson, during his Mission in the United States, from Oct. 1st, 1834, to Nov. 27, 1835* (Boston: Isaac Knapp, 1837), 45–47; *Memorial of Sarah Pugh: A Tribute of Respect from Her Cousins* (Philadelphia: J. B. Lippincott, 1888), 15; William Lloyd Garrison to Helen E. Garrison, 19 March 1835, in *The Letters of William Lloyd Garrison*, ed. Walter M. Merrill and Louis Ruchames (6 vols., Cambridge, Mass.: Harvard University Press, vol. 1: 467–70; Julie Winch, "Sarah Forten's Anti-Slavery Networks," in Stewart and Sklar, *Women's Rights and Transatlantic Antislavery*, 152.

37. Abby Kimber to Elizabeth Pease, 18 May [1841?], BPL, Ms.A.1.2.9.43.

38. "Speech of Charles C. Burleigh"; Glasgow Ladies Society to PFASS, 3 September 1834, in PFASS Correspondence, PAPS, HSP, series 5, reel 31; *First Annual Report of the American Anti-Slavery Society* (New York: Dorr & Butterfield, 1834), 52–53.

39. Pennsylvania Anti-Slavery Society Minute Book, 1838–46, 40, in PASP, HSP, series 5, reel 31; "Twelfth of June," *Pennsylvania Freeman*, 18 June 1840; "The World's Convention," in *The Complete Poetical Works of John Greenleaf Whittier* (Boston: Houghton Mifflin Co., 1894), 284–86.

40. For example, see James K. Paulding, *Slavery in the United States* (New York: Harper & Brothers, 1836), 134–35, 305–7.

41. Brown, "An Antislavery Agent," 77–79.

42. *Proceedings of the Pennsylvania Convention, Assembled to Organize a State Anti Slavery Society, at Harrisburg . . .* (Philadelphia: Merrihew & Gunn, 1837), 91.

43. "Address of the Eastern Executive Committee of the State Anti-Slavery Society to the Citizens of Pennsylvania," *Pennsylvania Freeman*, 24 May 1838; *Pennsylvania Freeman*, 14 February 1839. See also "Foreign Interference," *Pennsylvania Freeman*, 15 October 1840.

44. William Caleb McDaniel, "Our Country is the World: Radical American Abolitionists Abroad," Ph.D. diss., Johns Hopkins University, 2006, 57–105.

CHAPTER 7

From Natural Rights to National Sins

Philadelphia's Churches Face Antislavery

DEE E. ANDREWS

Few subjects in antislavery history may be more perplexing than American churches' response to abolitionism. Americans' spiritual leaders well before and long after the revolution, Christian ministers of all stripes, were the natural bearers of antislavery tidings—the great moral subject of the era—and their churches were the logical centers of antislavery agitation. After the revolutionary victory, religious activists eager to promote scriptural morality established myriad missionary organizations, tract societies, and reform agencies—the foundations of the Jacksonian "Benevolent Empire"—throughout the republic: potential centers for antislavery work. And American culture, popular and elite, appeared to be *more* rather than less religious with every passing decade, its language infused with the evangelical triad of conviction, conversion, and redemption, and its values espousing a reformed way of life.[1] What greater center for such a reformation in slavery than Philadelphia: birthplace of the nation, its religiously most cosmopolitan city, and home of its first and most effective antislavery organization.[2]

Initially, religious institutions in Philadelphia did appear to respond to the call for ending slavery and the slave trade in suitably measured but optimistic ways: with an array of religious adherents following the Quaker lead with the formation of the Pennsylvania Antislavery Society. Philadelphia's free African American religious leaders were well poised to change the lives of those still enslaved with their unprecedented freedom and rising numbers of associations, religious and otherwise, in America's leading city.

Yet, Philadelphia's mainstream churches—Episcopalian, Presbyterian, Baptist, and Methodist—provided fleeting support for antislavery even before immediatism gave abolition—never a moderate cause—its radical patina. And with the rise of immediatism, both white and independent "African" churches, run exclusively by black members and forming the core of new African Protestant denominations, wavered in their support for immediatism. As Frederick Douglass would lament in the mid-1850s, the absence of sustenance from the major American churches had created a "crisis in the Anti-Slavery movement, the evil effects of which it has not yet recovered."[3]

Understanding the often strained connection between moral stewardship and reactions to slavery and antislavery among Philadelphia's churches, however, requires viewing this relationship through more than the interpretative frame of gradualism to immediatism. Rather, it entails exploring a human terrain familiar to most Americans at the time, but less so for Americans today: the world of church formation, ministerial ambition, and denominational loyalty.

In short, black and white church-going Philadelphians' choices regarding antislavery were shaped by many forces, but none so important as the creation and expansion of their churches. These organizations, with their ever increasing size and influence, would come to reflect the moral divides of the country as thoroughly as political parties reflected the political divides. The dilemma for Philadelphia's white ministers and congregations attempting to end slavery and all it entailed was how to accomplish this goal in a republic devoted to church expansion in every part of the country, including the South, and including slaveholders along with non-slaveholders. The predicament for Philadelphia's black ministers and congregations was to end an oppressive labor system that threatened their safety daily while not betraying their own often expansive churches, communities that were also their main sources of solace and rescue.

For all Christian abolitionists, the "church"—as the array of mainstream Protestant denominations was often called—was the moral voice of the nation. But it was also a human institution, subject to political strife and driven by the missionary engine of outreach and inclusiveness. Small wonder that the "church's" response to slavery became one of the major disappointments of the antislavery era.

But the distinct reactions of black and white religious abolitionists to the moral vacuum that followed from this failure was equally important, and reveals the extent to which blacks and whites were moving in different directions. By the late 1840s, antislavery advocacy in Philadelphia was divided between white abolitionists, who believed that abolition should serve as the avenger of the national sin of slavery, and black abolitionists, who believed that abolition was the last defense of natural rights. The potentially differing consequences of each of these religious worldviews was vast.

(1)

The assertion that Americans of all persuasions, not just Quakers, and clergymen of all denominations bore a special obligation to end first the slave trade and then slavery appears early in Philadelphia abolition, long before the Fugitive Slave Law of 1793 confirmed the dangers that slavery continued to pose even for Philadelphia's free blacks. In the 1730s, Quaker Benjamin Lay directed his lengthy tract, *All Slave-Keepers That Keep the Innocent in Bondage, Apostates Pretending to lay Claim to the Pure & Holy Christian Religion*, to Christian slaveholders and especially *"their Ministers."* More than thirty years later Anthony Benezet surmised that the slave trade continued to thrive because "many Persons in Government, both of the Clergy and Laity, in whose Power it hath been to put a Stop to the Trade, have been unacquainted with the corrupt Motives which give life to it." In 1773, as the crisis with Britain intensified, Benezet reiterated that eliminating slavery "has an undoubted claim to the most serious consideration of all people of all ranks, and every denomination." And Benjamin Rush called on "ye MINISTERS OF THE GOSPEL, whose Dominion over the principles and actions of men is so universally acknowledged and felt . . . let your zeal keep pace with your Opportunities to put a stop to Slavery."[4]

While Rush was something of an exception among Philadelphia mainstream church members in condemning either the slave trade or slavery, the major churches were far in advance of the Quakers in recruiting black members, and the early roots of Jacksonian reform and African American Protestantism may be found in efforts by Anglicans, Methodists, Presbyterians, and Baptists to convert non-Christian slaves into Bible-reading believers. Philadelphia Anglican ministers Robert Jenney, Richard Peters, Jacob Duche, William White, and Nicholas Collin, serving in various stations at Christ Church, St. Peter's, St. Paul's, and Old Swedes' Church, admitted slaves and free people alike into their congregations. Between 1745 and 1776, 250 black people, just one fifth of whom were free, were baptized at the first three Anglican churches. Gary B. Nash writes that "for Philadelphia's black Christians, the Anglican Church was *the* church from 1740 until the Revolution."[5]

The Revolutionary War would interrupt this Anglican surge, but John Wesley's Methodists, Anglicans' evangelical wing, took up where their parent left off. In 1773, Wesley's emissary Thomas Rankin pointedly reminded Continental Congressmen "what a farce it was for them to contend for liberty when they themselves kept some hundreds of thousands of poor blacks in most cruel bondage." In 1774, Rankin reported that 500 American Methodists, or 25 percent of the total membership, were black people, mainly of free status.[6]

The Methodists outpaced the Anglicans further in 1785 by incorporating an uncompromising condemnation of slaveholding in the new church's *Doctrines and Discipline,* pronouncing this practice "contrary to the Golden Law of God and the Unalienable Rights of Mankind, as well as every Principle of the Revolution to hold in the deepest Debasement, in a more abject Slavery . . . so many Souls that are capable of the Image of God." The Methodist clergy agreed to free their own slaves and were effective at persuading newly recruited American Methodists to do the same. And the new church continued to appeal to thousands of black people. By 1800, 13,500 of the 64,000 American Methodists were black, both slave and free, or 21 percent of the official church membership. No other American institution approached this record.[7]

But the Methodists were by no means alone in reproving their slaveholding and slave-dealing adherents and clergy. In 1789, the Philadelphia Baptist Association praised abolition societies and urged their congregants to form similar groups "to obtain this important object" of gradual emancipation. In 1794, the General Assembly of the Presbyterian Church, with many members in Philadelphia, approved a Confession of Faith that characterized slave dealers and slaveholders as "man-stealers." Baptist churches, with the power of ordination rooted in individual congregations, pioneered the raising up of black preachers.[8]

Emancipation was also becoming commonplace among Philadelphia's church members. Even before the revolution, one-third of Philadelphia Presbyterians who died in the 1760s freed their slaves in their wills; and the proportion of Anglicans and Lutherans doing so was nearly as high. Over the last decades of the century, the ranks of slaveholders among Philadelphia church members wavered and then fell precipitously: from 227 Anglicans, 57 Presbyterians, and 24 Lutherans in 1767; to 132 Anglicans, 81 Presbyterians, 28 Lutherans, and 16 Quakers in 1780; to just 2 Presbyterians, 8 Anglicans (now Protestant Episcopalians), 1 Lutheran, and no Quakers in 1800.[9]

Reflecting the broad-based denominational opposition to slavery, the Pennsylvania Abolition Society (PAS), originally organized by Quakers in

1775, was revived between 1784 and 1787 as a denominationally inclusive association. Its chief aims combined those of an enforcement agency with a benevolent association for the betterment of the African race. In the words of Tench Coxe, the new PAS was the product of the "frequent sincere & earnest assertions & discussion of the natural rights of mankind" by adherents of many denominations. If pursued gradually, the PAS argued, emancipation could be accomplished peacefully, with consideration alike of slaves' claims to liberty and slaveholders' claims to property.[10] The full scope of the city's houses of worship, including Catholic and Jewish, were represented in the first three generations of the PAS, 60 percent of whose denominationally identifiable members belonged to non-Quaker churches. Most were Protestant Episcopal (27 percent), followed at some distance by Presbyterians (9 percent). In future years, the Philadelphia Female Anti-Slavery Society and the Philadelphia City Anti-Slavery Society, both founded in the 1830s, would be comprised of similar proportions of Friends, Anglicans, and Presbyterians, revealing an established pattern of antislavery support among the city's church members, even if not, as will be seen, a sustained activism.[11]

America's revolutionary legacy was contested among its many heirs, but few at this stage were seriously predicting a national disaster emanating from the national sin of slavery or calling on American churches to save the soul of the nation by adopting antislavery platforms. Slaveholders, it was hoped, would see the light, and the great accumulation of abolition laws and manumission would bring the institution to an end. Nor did abolitionists or organizations like the PAS feel compelled to chastise American churches on the importance of their role in ending slavery. After all, were not American churches already on their side?

(2)

Historical circumstances were to alter the nature of Philadelphia churches' reactions to the survival—or more accurately, the expansionist revival—of slavery in the new republic. For white church adherents, denominational expansion led to the decline of active engagement with antislavery by the mainstream churches, the rise in influence of slaveholding adherents in the larger national denominations, and the increasing support of African colonization among powerful whites and some blacks. For blacks, the era marked the emergence of an extraordinary group of clerical leaders, assertively identified as "African" Christians, who called for a wholly new response to slavery for their black followers.

The dwindling of mainstream commitment to antislavery is evident in the PAS after 1800. Founded as an elite organization, as Richard Newman has shown, many of the society's day-to-day operations were taken on by Quaker activists as its founders died or moved on to other forms of activism. Quakers remained by far the most consistent antislavery spokesman among the city's white leadership. By the late 1820s, Philadelphia's antislavery newspapers, the *National Enquirer* (converted later into the *Pennsylvania Freeman*) and the *African Observer,* were both published by Quakers. The Orthodox Friends journal, *The Friend,* begun in 1827, would become a key source of information on emancipation for readers throughout the country.[12] Quakers ran the PAS Acting Committee and the PAS legal defense. It bode ill for the city's non-Quaker involvement in antislavery that while PAS members represented the spectrum of Philadelphia's denominations, many fewer clergymen joined the organization than other professionals.[13]

Most Philadelphians, furthermore, now belonged to denominations that encompassed sizeable proportions of southern membership. "That Southern Baptists, like Southern Methodists, Presbyterians, and Episcopalians, are commonly slaveholders (except those of them who are slaves), we need not spend time to prove," Presbyterian cleric and antislavery theorist William Goodell would observe in the 1850s. Whether or not Goodell's claim—that these church members were usually slaveholders—was literally true, the major American churches over this time were inexorably drawn to national expansion, and as inexorably repelled by antislavery. The withdrawal from the cause was not justified in the manner of the earlier antislavery manifestos but enforced instead through formal and informal gag rules. The resort to censorship all but eliminated reasoned debate on slavery among the larger representative bodies of American denominations. The existence of slavery, conservatives argued, was a political matter best left to the control of civil authorities, for it was the duty of a Christian to render onto Caesar that which was Caesar's.[14]

In addition, white Christians from various parts of the nation began to support the American Colonization Society's drive for mass migration of blacks to Africa as an alternative to incorporating free black people into national life. In 1825, James Patterson, pastor of the First Presbyterian Church in the Northern Liberties section of Philadelphia, spoke before a "United Meeting of Christians of Different Religious Persuasions to Celebrate National Independence," drawing on a wide array of sources: the Bible, the U.S. Census, and Jonathan Edwards Jr.'s sermon before the Connecticut Society for Promoting Freedom, among others. "Christianity and slavery cannot be identified," Patterson concluded, but neither could blacks and citizenship, and African Americans were now obliged to return to their homeland to serve, among other duties, as Christian missionaries to the heathen.[15]

Despite this disheartening suspension of support among the very denominations whose church halls filled with black worshippers, Philadelphia's black leaders—adopting the doctrine and structure of the mainstream churches while asserting their identity as "African" Christians—moved in markedly different directions from those expected of them: toward investment in a permanent black community in the city, institutional independence, and vocal opposition to African colonization. The first stage of these developments—the transformation of the Free African Society into the first black church congregations in Philadelphia—is now familiar in the work of many scholars, as is the early autonomy of Philadelphia's black leaders.[16] But less often emphasized were two key and closely related *institutional* pressures that accompanied the shift toward greater black agency. One was the significant variety of denominational perspectives among different black clergy. The other was the strength of institutional loyalty among these ministers.

Denominational perspectives were clarified in the spring of 1794 when, after a two-year struggle with white Methodist authorities (including the introduction of segregated seating at St. George's Methodist Church), Absalom Jones accepted leadership of a new congregation, St. Thomas's African Protestant Episcopal Church. He sought to enable slaves and former slaves "to arise out of the dust and . . . throw off that servile fear, that the habit of oppression and bondage trained us up to"—best achieved, he believed, through the apostolic tradition of the Episcopal (formerly Anglican) Church, with its uplifting liturgical formality and vestry-based power structure (and, he might have added, its historical links to Philadelphia's black population). Newly freed blacks—many of them former Methodists, and hence familiar with many aspects of Anglican doctrine—could become confident social and political actors within their churches while sustaining their belief that salvation was attainable through free will, a tenet shared by Methodists and Episcopalians alike. Jones, in the meanwhile, would also receive immediate ordination as deacon and be prepared for later ordination as an Episcopal minister: one of the first formally ordained black clergyman in the country. His Lombard Street church was the home of Philadelphia's more conservative black leadership.[17]

Richard Allen, by contrast, declined the offer to head St. Thomas's—opening the way for Jones—and remained loyal to his life-transforming experience as a converted Methodist. "I could not be anything else but a Methodist," he wrote many years later, "as I was born and awakened under them." Furthermore, he was "confident that there was no religious sect or denomination would suit the capacity of the colored people as well as the Methodist." The movement's "plan and simple gospel," he insisted, was best for all people, not least of all the poor and uneducated. In 1794, Allen formed the Bethel "African Methodist Episcopal" congregation, also on Lombard Street. In short time, the congregation's leadership drew up articles of association that emphasized the power of Bethel's "African" members, a concession by the Methodist Episcopal Church to the racially specific character of the Allen's evangelism. But unlike Jones, Allen was not promised ordination into the official Methodist ministry or membership in the Methodist preachers' conferences. He waited five years before Bishop Francis Asbury was willing to ordain him as deacon, empowered to perform baptisms and marriages but not communion. The fully ordained Methodist ministry remained an all-white fraternity. But Allen's church was the bedrock of black Methodist outreach and ultimately the institutional genome for the African Methodist Episcopal (AME) Church, the largest and most influential black institution in the country.[18]

John Gloucester, minister at First African Presbyterian beginning in 1810, by contrast was brought to preaching by his master, frontier physician and preacher Gideon Blackburn, in Tennessee's Union Presbytery. In 1807, Gloucester sought licensing through the General Assembly—the annual meeting of the entire church—with the aim of moving to Philadelphia. The Philadelphia Synod and the Union Presbytery volleyed his application for three years before he was deemed qualified for ordination. Blackburn promptly freed him and patronized his hiring as missionary employee of the Philadelphia Presbyterian Evangelical Society, organized to work among impoverished white and black Presbyterians. Gloucester was appointed to the newly organized First African Presbyterian Church, where he was minister until his death in 1823 but never formally installed. Instead he spent considerable time advancing his learning and working to raise the funds necessary to free his wife and children, still bound as slaves in Tennessee. But Gloucester's escape from bondage was secured, and all four of his sons would become Presbyterian ministers: powerful testimony to this church's importance to one former southern slave family. And the Gloucesters became an educated ministerial dynasty, adhering to Presbyterianism's intellectual demands.[19]

These three men had chosen distinctly different paths toward their advancement, ones defined by their ambitions, their past experiences, their opportunities, but not least of all, their theological and denominational perspectives. Their leadership, furthermore, led to similar choices among thousands of other black people in Philadelphia. By 1813, African American clergy and laity, men and women, had followed their denominational preferences into the formation of seven separate black churches and eleven black benevolent associations in the city. The largest was Allen's Bethel Methodist congregation, beginning with just 32 official members in 1794 but by 1813 comprising 1,272 members. Jones's St. Thomas's was half Bethel's size with 560 communicants, and Gloucester's First African Presbyterian claimed 300 members. The new African Baptist Church, headed for many years by southern slave preachers, by 1813 had attracted 80 congregants. Altogether, 2,366 black Philadelphians, male and female, had chosen to join separate black churches.[20]

African Americans' denominational loyalty undergirded the formation of these separate black congregations, not only in Philadelphia but also in Baltimore, New York, Wilmington, and other towns—and was one of the most dynamic responses to slavery in American history. The speed with which black ministers took the next step and formed separate "African" *denominations*, encompassing multiple congregations independent of white control, further underscores the importance of institutional loyalty among black Americans. For the Methodists alone, these new fully independent denominations included Wilmington's Union Church of African Members in 1813, Philadelphia's AME Church in 1816, and New York's African Methodist Episcopal Zion (AMEZ) Church in 1821.[21]

The interests of these churches' clergymen and the demands of institutional allegiance continued to shape black religious responses to antislavery for years to come. So did the discourse for emancipation, based as it always had been on the "black protest tradition" emerging from the three-part union of natural rights philosophy, the moral principles of the New Testament, and the heart-religion of evangelicalism.[22] What more was needed to justify the end of slavery and the expansion of black freedom?

But after 1830, the demand for immediate emancipation by a new generation of abolitionists would enmesh Philadelphia's Christians, white and black, in a complex web of often bitter disputes. The immediatist years would be trying ones for Philadelphians who considered themselves inhabitants of the model emancipation city. For religious abolitionists especially, the "church" seemed to fail the cause of the slave time and again. But these conflicts also arose from efforts to reconcile the demands of moderate and radical abolitionists in expansive national institutions. In the heated, increasingly millennialist climate of antebellum religious culture, many religious opponents of slavery resorted to the rhetoric of sin and retribution, applied to the nation at large, while losing sight of the American Revolution's rhetoric of natural rights and civil liberties applicable to black rights and citizenship. The fundamental problem remained the same—reconciling property rights with human rights—but the solution remained illusive.

(3)

The evidence for conflicts over immediatism resides mostly in the renditions of the abolitionists themselves—notably in Benjamin Lundy's *National Enquirer*, later the *Pennsylvania Freeman*, the organ of protest published in Philadelphia by the Pennsylvania State Anti-Slavery Society. But it is clear that immediate abolitionism ignited many Philadelphians' consciences and set off brush fires among establishment clergy, conservative church members, and newly convinced abolitionists. The change in climate occurred with stunning speed in the 1830s, among both white and black abolitionist communities; and again at the end of the 1840s.

For Philadelphia's Presbyterians, the division over slavery occurred early on, at the tumultuous 1837 annual meeting of the Church's General Assembly. The assembly, one Ohio editor observed, "is held, not in a remote corner, but in a great and central city, and the eyes of the American people are upon it, and its voice goes into all the land. . . . For good or evil, it is indeed a body of immense power."[23] For several years, the church had threatened to split between Old School traditionalists and New School revivalists over not only theological but also abolitionist disagreements. At the August 1837 convention in Philadelphia, abolitionists delivered hundreds of petitions, some signed by as many as 500 women, highlighting the non-clerical support for antislavery in the church, and demanding that the church enforce its antislavery resolutions. The Old School leadership, gaining control of the meeting, tabled every petition and expelled the four New School Synods. Within a year, the Presbyterian Church had divided into two general assemblies representing the almost evenly populated two halves of the denomination: Old School northern conservatives and southerners, and the New School northerners and westerners.[24]

For Philadelphia's Presbyterian abolitionists, the split coincided with critical turning points in the history of their movement, reported in dramatic detail, along with news of on-going developments, in the *National Enquirer* and then the *Pennsylvania Freeman*, edited by Quaker poet and immediatist John Greenleaf Whittier. Among the latter were the May 1838 riots following the destruction of Pennsylvania Hall (which Heather Nathans describes in more detail in the next chapter). Designed as a "Temple of Freedom" by white, mainly Quaker, abolitionists, the building did not survive for more than three days. Other buildings associated with racial reform were also attacked, including the Colored Orphans' Home in the Northern Liberties. The First African Presbyterian Church, emblem of black advancement, narrowly escaped razing. Pennsylvania Hall literally joined "enlightened," revolutionary-era gradual abolition in the ashes of the city's optimistic founding era.[25]

In this alarming context, a small but telling controversy, an abolitionist moral tale, played itself out at the Western Presbyterian Church. Built in 1834 as a small white mission station in the center of the city, Western Presbyterian was served by Reverend John Patton, who oversaw the opening of a new church building at Seventeenth and Filbert streets in 1837. Patton was initially sympathetic to immediate abolition, and he permitted a Pennsylvania State Anti-Slavery Society lecture at the church by Presbyterian minister J. Miller McKim. When Pennsylvania Hall was preparing to open in May, Patton offered a dedicatory prayer in its support and suspended meetings at Western to permit congregants to attend the opening sessions at the "temple."[26]

Events intensified in July, when a convention for forming a "union" evangelical antislavery society, open to likeminded Christians, met for one day at Western. The congregation's abolitionists, led by layman Samuel Withington, were aggrieved that the General Assembly had so spectacularly failed to enforce the antislavery platform incorporated into the church's Confession of Faith. The Union Society, by contrast, called for the immediate emancipation of slaves, purification of the "Christian Church" both North and South, formation of auxiliary societies as soon as possible, and a "Monthly Concert of Prayer for the Oppressed." Patton attended the organizational meeting and announced the inauguration of the Union Society from his pulpit.[27]

Almost immediately, Western's conservatives objected to abolition's rising profile in their congregation. According to the abolitionists, one of the two lay elders on the church's session announced that he would "set *his* face against the introduction of Anti-Slavery into the church." Others began to "prophecy the total ruin of our church" if antislavery was associated with it. The abolitionists earnestly proposed linking temperance and moral reform to their cause to make it more palatable, and they agreed to hold the proposed monthly prayer in a private house rather than the church building. But before they could proceed further, Reverend Patton sought the opinion of the other two members of the session regarding the proper role his congregation should play in antislavery advocacy.[28]

Patton's predicament—caught as he was between two contending factions—reflected another rarely considered aspect of church life in America: ministers were usually more educated than their parishioners, were depended upon in times of crisis, and were expected to be outspoken, influential, and uncompromising in matters of moral and scriptural import, but in practical terms their success, sometimes even their survival, depended upon the patronage of non-clerical trustees, vestries, and sessions—not to mention the larger hierarchical structures of their denominations. It was the rare clergyman who could move far from the consensus of his most influential church members and still hold on to his appointment, or move against the great body of ministers in the church and still remain a colleague. By fall, Patton was urging his abolitionist members to spare Western the reputation as an abolitionist stronghold. Although the evidence is uneven, coming only from his opponents, the pastor was clearly endeavoring to put the abolitionist genie back into its bottle. It did not help the abolitionists' cause that a featured speaker at one of their meetings, Reverend Leonard Fletcher, had recently given his fellow anti-abolitionist Protestant ministers "one of the most tremendous [verbal] thrashings they had ever received."[29]

Over the following months, Samuel Withington and his allies at Western, numbering perhaps forty members, drafted a constitution for their antislavery auxiliary reflecting the goals of the Union Society. They then took their cause directly to the *Pennsylvania Freeman*—in effect publicizing their dispute with Patton through the abolitionist media, although the minister remained unnamed. Resorting to the language of sin and redemption, they wrote that when Patton had once preached "that the wrath of God would abide upon the sinner until he actually stopped committing sin, we saw that the wrath of God *must* be upon the slaveholder." Yet, when the Western activists spoke against slavery, Patton had said, "Hush brethren! . . . folks will say we are abolitionists, and we shall be talked about all over town." Patton, his opponents claimed, accused the Western activists of being "disturbers of the peace of the Church" and were "engaged in a fanatical crusade, which was only calculated to retard the cause of emancipation." The tendency of abolition principles, Patton had told the rest of the church, "was downwards, and leading to infidelity," as in the notorious examples of William Lloyd Garrison and Fanny Wright. As for the abolitionists at Western, Patton had announced that other members should "*have no fellowship with them.*"[30]

The controversy at Western Presbyterian Church brought into sharp focus the nature of the antislavery struggle among many evangelical, especially Calvinist, believers in Philadelphia in the immediatist years after 1831. Abolitionists now believed that slavery was not only an unlawful and un-Christian practice, but also a damning infraction requiring redemptive cleansing of those caught in its snares—potentially the entire nation. The abolitionists at Western accurately described "the colored man" as "a daily victim of oppression, wrongs, and outrage," but their larger credo was singularly concerned with the spiritual condition of *white* Presbyterians and their churches. "We believe Slavery to be a sin," they wrote, "We believe that the church at the North is also guilty of the sin of Slavery." The Western abolitionists did not threaten secession—this was not a come-outer movement in the spirit of many congregations in northern New York which chose to separate from their parent organizations over abolition—nor did they claim to be innovating theologically. But they had clearly re-defined abolition as a war against evil.[31]

They and other New School abolitionists were to make little progress with this approach. The outspoken members at Western Presbyterian Church had the ear of the *Pennsylvania Freeman,* but they could not obtain a forum in their church's own journal, the *Religious Telegraph and Observer,* published in their own city. Six months later, the New School General Assembly referred the enforcement of the antislavery provisions of the Confession of Faith to local presbyteries, maintaining the same policy that the church had pursued before the Old School / New School split. In 1846, Philadelphia minister George Duffield Jr. would persuade the New School General Assembly to adopt a strong statement calling upon New School Presbyterians to abandon slaveholding, but the assembly at the same time refused to condemn slaveholders in the church or deny them communion. All decisions, as before, would be left to local bodies.[32] For all intents and purposes, the New School Presbyterians were no more effective in ending slaveholding and slave-trading in their ranks than they had been as part of the larger church; and the antislavery members at Western remained alienated from their minister.

For Philadelphia's black Christians, the charges against American churches and clergy for complicity with slavery were potentially as problematic as they were for Reverend Patton. Many black church adherents also had strong links to national organizations by which they could be easily embarrassed. Unlike their white counterparts, black church leaders dealt with palpable attacks against their own lives and property and could be expected to oppose slavery as a matter of course; but these assaults also placed them in a vulnerable position vis-à-vis the larger antislavery movement.

The early 1830s to the late 1840s were years of triumph and crisis for Philadelphia's black Christians. The city witnessed unprecedented growth for black churches, escalating racist violence, and rising abolitionist criticism of the reluctance of some of Philadelphia's black churches to engage fully in antislavery. In the antebellum years, Philadelphia's black community was maturing well beyond its early struggles with slavery. The approximately 20,000 black Philadelphians were clustered in mutually supporting neighborhoods around Lombard Street in the south Cedar Ward and above Market Street in the Northern Liberties. They were engaged in myriad livelihoods and participated in all the customary forms of institutional organization popular among Americans. By the mid-1830s, they had organized sixteen churches, eighty benevolent associations—many for women—and twenty-five common schools teaching more than 1,700 students. "African" churches now included eight Methodist (AME and Methodist Episcopal) churches, four Baptist, two Presbyterian, one Episcopal (St. Thomas's), and one Lutheran. African Methodists accounted for the great majority—2,860—out of a combined total of 3,995 communicants, and as with white Americans, black church members did *not* make up a majority of the black population: only slightly more than 10 percent. But also as with white Americans, the numbers of people attending churches, as opposed to formally joining them, was high, and the cultural influence of churches among black people was well recognized.[33]

Julie Winch and Gary Nash show that the very success and self-confident assertiveness of Philadelphia's black population—distinguished by its size, stability, increasing wealth, and long-standing access to white supporters—posed a challenge to portions of the city's white population, and blacks were never far from the twin threats of intimidation and assault. . . . In 1834, in a devastating three-day conflagration, white rioters had ransacked the homes of wealthy blacks and the First African Presbyterian Church—which had earlier escaped this fate—and destroyed one AME church. The PAS predicted rising racial violence in the near future.[34]

Philadelphia's black leaders diagnosed the ongoing existence of slavery as the cause of these persistent dangers and called on black churches to oppose its continuance. In 1836, the all-black American Moral Reform Society (AMRS) issued an *Address to the Colored Churches in the Free States* that urged African churches to "take measures to admonish their members against aiding the system of American Slavery, by using the products of slave labor." Colored people, the address elaborated, were too often the consumers of products of slave labor, and "the colored churches are common participants in the crime . . . [while] their ministers,' deacons,' and elders' voices are bound in deathly silence on a subject, that aims not only at the subjugation of millions of 'immortal souls,' but at the overthrow of the Christian Church." It may be true, the address conceded, that black churches that had not formed their own denominations were subordinate bodies to larger churches; but "[w]hen the voice of God commands us to 'remember those that are in bonds, as bound with them,' we should do it *now*, without waiting the approval of Ecclesiastical Conventions, General Assemblies, Presbyteries, Synods, Conferences, or any body of men on earth, no matter how enlightened."[35]

A year later, in 1837, black businessman William Whipper told the AMRS assembled at the First African Presbyterian Church that the "period is fast approaching when the church, as at present constituted, must undergo one of the severest contests she has met with since her foundation, because in so many cases she has refused to sustain her own principles."[36] Black abolitionists still did not demand that black Christians "come out" from larger white organizations, or that abolitionist AME and AMEZ congregations do so from their larger all-black denominations—not yet at least. But black abolitionists took the power of the church seriously and worried that black churches' and clergy's commitment to immediatism was too weak. In 1838, that concern ramified when the riots against Pennsylvania Hall threatened the First African Presbyterian Church yet again.

Under these circumstances, Philadelphia's black clergy had reason to be wary of too close an association with immediatism. Stephen Gloucester's transformation from ally of radical abolition to an antagonist is illustrative. One of John Gloucester's sons, Stephen Gloucester—described by a fellow Presbyterian as "a well educated man, and one who in every respect would fairly rank with the great body of Congregational and Presbyterian ministers through the country"—had been recruited to immediatism by William Lloyd Garrison and was a friend and biographer of James Forten. In 1837 he helped found the evangelical Leavitt Anti-Slavery Society (named after white evangelical Joshua Leavitt) to advocate among Philadelphia's working class. The society espoused membership across racial lines, supported immediate emancipation, and vowed to work against color prejudice and for the elevation of free blacks. When the American antislavery movement divided into Garrisonian and evangelical wings in 1840, Gloucester followed his religious instincts and along with seven other black ministers joined a larger body of white evangelicals to found the anti-Garrisonian American and Foreign Anti-Slavery Society. He supported the political abolitionism of the Liberty Party before becoming the pastor of the black Second Presbyterian Church in 1842.[37]

The church was destroyed in another race riot in the same year, despite what his enemies later described as Gloucester's attempts to pay off the mob. The third riot in eight years against the city's people of color represented a tipping point for many black leaders, including Stephen Gloucester, and prompted their withdrawal from high-profile abolitionism. Gloucester was soon recruited to build a new African Presbyterian church on Lombard Street and traveled on a fund-raising tour to Britain where he was warmly received by British antislavery activists and the Free Church of Scotland. The Free Church, however, had failed to cut its connections with southern slaveholders, a point advertised to abolitionist readers in Frederick Douglass's *North Star*.[38]

The need to unify Christians against slavery was pressing, not least of all as the white Presbyterian and Methodist churches split into northern and southern halves in the 1830s and 1840s, and the Baptists created their own separate proslavery Southern Convention. Black clergy employed by white missionary societies could not speak out on slavery without being reprimanded. By the late 1840s, the United States was at war with Mexico, for the purpose, white and black abolitionists were convinced, of expanding slave territories ever further west. "Suppose Congress," one white antislavery observer hypothesized, "wanting other available resources, should order the numerous prisoners who have been taken, to be sent home by our officers, and sold in the Southern markets for slaves . . . and church members . . . should throng the markets . . . what would the gospel require us to do? Anything?" What kind of Christian could continue to be associated with churches that might be so devoured by the great maw of the Slave Power?[39]

Many black churches served as centers of antislavery activity, and a strong cohort of black clergymen from all denominations worked to advance the civil rights of black people. But the AME Church, now encompassing more black Christians than any other institution in the country, followed the lead of all the major white denominations and did not expressly prohibit slaveholding among its southern members, a small number of whom did own slaves. The AME's main newspaper, the *Christian Recorder*, first published in 1854, barely discussed slavery and abolition in its first issues.[40]

By 1848, a combined history of success for free blacks and anti-black violence had created a rift within Philadelphia's black religious leadership that threatened to undermine support for immediatism. Discouraged by the repeated threats of racist mobs and alarmed as much as white ministers by the anticlericalism of radicals like William Lloyd Garrison and Frederick Douglass, all three of the main African churches in Philadelphia now closed their pulpits to abolitionist speakers—an unprecedented action. In August 1848, the churches shut out William Wells Brown, the fugitive slave, even though their own clergymen were eager to hear him speak: for abolitionists, a truly scandalous development.

Under popular pressure, Reverend Gloucester agreed to defend himself publicly against the charge of "sacrificing principle for filthy lucre in the trial-hour of '42"—a reference to his efforts to forestall white rioters six years earlier from destroying his church. The debate—held on August 15 at "Little Wesley" AME Church, one of the city's black working-class congregations, headed by Reverend William Catto—was attended by a large and reportedly expectant crowd. Under mounting pressure from the unsympathetic audience, Gloucester agreed he could not easily justify his actions, and he conceded the debate to his opponent. The house voted resoundingly that the mainstream black churches were not adequately engaged in the antislavery cause, and Gloucester was tongue-lashed as a traitor to the antislavery cause.[41]

The highly publicized event further soured black abolitionists on the leading black churches and the people of color who remained in white churches. William Whipper concluded shortly afterwards, "the colored churches and clergy of these United States are both theoretically and practically sustaining a pro-slavery position." On October 3, an antislavery convention organized by Reverend Catto and attended by numerous prominent black abolitionists met at Little Wesley. The meeting issued an *Address to the Colored Citizens of the City and County of Philadelphia* that expressly called for black churches to "come out" from the mainstream denominations that included slaveholding members. Philadelphia's blacks should lead the way in these important moral choices. "Their numerical greatness, and geographical proximity to slavery," Frederick Douglass observed after a brief visit to the city, "gives them a mighty lever of influence. . . . Make the colored people in Philadelphia what they ought to be, and there is no power in the land which can long oppress and degrade us."[42]

(4)

For Philadelphia's black and white abolitionists, the years between 1838—when the first major church (the Presbyterians) fractured on slavery's rocky terrain, Pennsylvania Hall was torched, and the abolitionists at Western Presbyterian Church took their stand—and 1848, when the United States concluded its war with Mexico and black abolitionists viewed each other with increasing wariness, was the critical decade for antislavery. It was understood, among blacks as among whites, that winning the allegiance of America's moral leadership— its clergy and church members—was a critical part of the effort to end slavery. For whites, however, evidenced by the controversy at Western Presbyterian, the old cries for equality and liberty had become stale; more compelling were the calls for the nation to confess the sin of slavery, practice repentance, and seek redemption, as well as appeals to white audiences to "convert" to antislavery. But for black abolitionists, "common sense" assertions of liberty, equality, and Christian charity never lost their luster, and the nation could fend for itself as long as black rights were constitutionally secure. "Equality, Brotherly Love and Liberty to all men. This is our theme." So asserted the October 1848 convention at Little Wesley, even as it urged blacks to leave churches associated with the South.[43]

For black Philadelphians closely bound up with their churches, the choice nevertheless remained a difficult one: to enjoy the benefits of an unprecedented and nationally recognized organization that had "come out"—that is, from white churches—long before come-outerism was popular, or to remain small, local institutions wielding influence in just one city or among just northern black people: a very small proportion of all Americans of African descent. What mission would that serve, church leaders asked themselves, and with what legacy for slaves in the South?

The cumulative impact of the affronts of the 1850s—the Fugitive Slave Law, the Kansas-Nebraska Act and "Bleeding Kansas," the Dred Scott Decision, and finally, most important of all, John Brown's startling raid on Harpers Ferry— affected the two populations differently. Black abolitionists and church people were drawn closer together again. In 1857, William Catto, although minister at Little Wesley AME Church where Reverend Stephen Gloucester had met his match, published the commemorative volume celebrating the first fifty years of the First African Presbyterian Church—home to Stephen Gloucester's father John. Catto reported that the city's black churches now numbered eighteen and encompassed 4,400 official members out of 30,000 black people in Philadelphia. Much more could be done to attract more black people into the ecclesiastical fold, Catto wrote.[44] Divisions among black clergymen over how best to reach goals they all shared would not be helpful in this or any other regard.

But by the late 1850s, white Christians in Philadelphia and the nation at large seemed ever farther apart on the subject of slavery, and the abolitionists' focus on slavery as the curse of the nation was never stronger. Philadelphia's small numbers of prominent antislavery clergy—including Albert Barnes, one of the founders of the New School Presbyterians; Harvard-educated William Henry Furness, for fifty years minister at the First Congregational Unitarian Church; and George Duffield Jr., another New Schooler—each preached this new antislavery doctrine.[45]

Barnes earned the wrath of southern co-religionists with the publication of *The Church and Slavery* in 1857, in which he asserted that there "has never been a time when the system of slavery has been so bold, exacting, arrogant, and dangerous to liberty, as at the present." Both Furness and Duffield skewered slaveholders' pretensions to liberty with fencing-like precision. Furness pronounced to the Pennsylvania Anti-Slavery Fair in 1852 that slavery "meddles most cruelly with the very bodies and souls of its victims. . . . And not only so, it interferes with matchless insolence with the whole administration of government." Nine years later, on the eve of the Battle of Bull Run, Duffield preached that the United States had much to be thankful for, but fair treatment of Mexicans, Indians, and Africans—especially Africans—was not one of these, and northerners, he added, were as much to blame as southerners.[46]

It was for *these* sins that the nation was being punished, Duffield concluded. And ultimately that was the matter of most concern to the handful of other clergy speaking out against slavery in Philadelphia: the sin of slavery would now be met with the fire of retribution.

(5)

These observations came too late for constructive solutions to America's persistent racial divide, even for likeminded Christians, and the historical ob-

server comes away from the experience of Philadelphia's churches and abolition with a sense of opportunities lost, alternatives unexplored, and questions
unanswered. Among these: Did immediatism need to be a Protestant crusade,
excluding from its ranks Roman Catholics, particularly Irish immigrants, and
Jews fighting similar battles with discrimination?[47] Was it necessarily a good
thing, as come-outers like William Goodell argued, to tie church organizations
and secular government closer together in the cause of the slave, undermining
the enlightenment tenet of religious freedom? As historian Sydney Ahlstrom
once observed, by employing "the traditional recourse and appeal to the Abso-
lute" in their arguments over slavery, *both* antislavery and proslavery religious
advocates raised the stakes of the debate—and, it is argued here, sacrificed the
independence of the "church" to the power of the state—to the point where
the peaceful dismantling of slavery became virtually impossible.[48]

And if slavery *was* to end through institutional means, how might antislavery's great rank and file, most importantly its women, be part of the solution? Appeals to church involvement were nearly always directed to clergy,
who, outside the Society of Friends, were all men. Yet, women were the great
supports of American antislavery societies—in Philadelphia the main source
of fund-raising—and of churches alike. "We are sometimes told that females
should have nothing to do with the business of the Church," Mary Still told a
gathering of Philadelphia AME women in 1857. "But they [who say so] have
yet to learn that when female labor is withdrawen [*sic*] the Church must cease
to exist."[49] It was the Philadelphia Female Anti-Slavery Society that sustained
its focus on the main issue—unrelenting racism—once the Civil War was over,
and the Thirteenth Amendment ended slavery in 1865. Americans, the society
believed, at last were coming to terms with the "real nature of the struggle."
Perhaps it was not a coincidence that it was a women's organization—with
white and black members working together—that was able to see that the
struggle did not end with the end of the "peculiar institution."[50]

The uncompromising attack on slavery as a sinful institution—one that
could be destroyed only through the purifying fire of conversion and redemption of citizen and nation—inspired many antislavery activists, especially
immediatists. But prophesying national punishments for national sins was
a combustible and self-fulfilling process. By contrast, black calls for church
activism toward an end to slavery and slave-trading, guarantees of civil rights,
and the end of race prejudice were demands that could only improve the social order while respecting the separate functions of religion and politics in
American society. John Brown's raid on Harpers Ferry momentarily brought

these two sides together, as whites saw in Brown the embodiment of expiation for national sins, and blacks saw a white man willing to make the extreme sacrifice to end slavery.[51] But ultimately, Brown's attack was a spectacular failure and precipitated a war that was an unprecedented crisis and a relentless bloodbath, leaving freedmen and women at last free but nearly as vulnerable to physical and political oppression as they had been as slaves. By the mid-1850s, Frederick Douglass had himself come to regret "the crisis in the Anti-slavery movement" that flung "church against man" and "some of the advocates of emancipation against God." Practical institutional leadership, rather than rhetoric alone, would be the key to unlocking the chains that bound millions of black Americans to slavery.[52]

How different matters might have been had Americans in general, and Philadelphians in particular, heeded the united call of Christian charity, enlightened justice, and constitutional action applied without delay to end slavery throughout the republic in the critical nation-building years of the 1770s, 1780s, and 1790s: when circumstances were most promising and the moment most precious in the city of brotherly love.

NOTES

1. My thanks to Donald Yacovone for providing an essential insight for this study, and to Jim Mueller for recruiting me back to Philadelphia. For select studies of religion and abolition, see John R. McKivigan, *The War Against Pro-Slavery Religion: Abolitionism and the Northern Churches, 1830–1865* (Ithaca: Cornell University Press, 1984); Douglas M. Strong, *Perfectionist Politics: Abolitionism and the Religious Tensions of American Democracy* (Syracuse, N.Y.: Syracuse University Press, 1999); Donald Yacovone, *Samuel Joseph May and the Dilemmas of the Liberal Persuasion, 1797–1871* (Phila.: Temple University Press, 1991). Important studies of antebellum religion include Nathan O. Hatch, *The Democratization of American Christianity* (New Haven, Conn.: Yale University Press, 1989); Mark A. Noll, *America's God: From Jonathan Edwards to Abraham Lincoln* (Oxford, U.K.: Oxford University Press, 2002); and Daniel Walker Howe, *What Hath God Wrought: The Transformation of America, 1815–1848* (Oxford, U.K.: Oxford University Press, 2007), chaps. 5, 8, and 12. James Brewer Stewart assesses the impact of religious abolitionists on antebellum politics in a compelling contrast with contemporary fundamentalist politics in "Reconsidering the Abolitionists in an Age of Fundamentalist Politics," *Journal of the Early Republic* 26 (Spring 2006): 2–23.

2. J. Thomas Scharf and Thompson Westcott, *History of Philadelphia, 1609–1884* (3 vols., Phila., 1884), 1229–449.

3. *Frederick Douglass' Paper*, 23 March 1855.

4. Benjamin Lay, *All Slave-Keepers That Keep the Innocent in Bondage, Apostates Pretending to*

lay Claim to the Pure & Holy Christian Religion (Phila.: Printed for the Author, 1737), 17; Anthony Benezet, *A Caution and Warning to Great-Britain, and her Colonies, in a Short Representation of the Calamitous State of the Enslaved Negroes in the British Dominions* (Phila.: D. Hall and W. Sellers, 1767), 1–2; [Benezet], *Brief Considerations on Slavery, and the Expediency of its Abolition* (Burlington, N.J.: Isaac Collins, 1773), 15; [Benjamin Rush], *An Address to the Inhabitants of the British Settlements in America Upon Slave-Keeping* (Phila.: John Dunlap, 1773): 12–13, 28–29, 30.

5. Gary B. Nash, *Forging Freedom: The Formation of Philadelphia's Black Community, 1720–1840* (Cambridge, Mass.: Harvard University Press, 1988), 23–24.

6. Dee E. Andrews, *The Methodists and Revolutionary America, 1760–1800: The Shaping of an Evangelical Culture* (Princeton, N.J.: Princeton University Press, 2000), 45–47, 125, 132.

7. Ibid., 123–27.

8. *Frederick Douglass' Paper*, 23 March 1855; William Goodell, *Slavery and Anti-Slavery: A History of the Great Struggle in Both Hemispheres* (New York: William Harned, 1852), 107–8; Albert J. Raboteau, *Slave Religion: The "Invisible Institution" in the Antebellum South* (New York: Oxford University Press; 1978), 128–50.

9. Nash, *Forging Freedom*, 23–24; Nash and Jean R. Soderlund, *Freedom by Degrees: Emancipation in Pennsylvania and Its Aftermath* (New York: Oxford University Press, 1991), 81, 154.

10. Richard S. Newman, *The Transformation of American Abolitionism: Fighting Slavery in the Early Republic* (Chapel Hill: University of North Carolina Press, 2002), 16–27. Tench Coxe quoted in Dee E. Andrews, "Reconsidering the First Emancipation: Evidence from the Pennsylvania Abolition Society Correspondence, 1785–1810," *Pennsylvania History* 64 (Summer 1997; special supplemental issue): 233–34.

11. Timothy Hack (Department of History, University of Delaware), "Philadelphia Churches and the Fight against Slavery, 1680–1860," Report for Independence National Historical Park, Phila. (2005), 7, 12, 13.

12. Newman, *The Transformation of American Abolitionism*, chap. 2; *The African Observer* (Phila.), 1827–28; *The Friend* (Phila.), 1827.

13. Hack, "Philadelphia Churches and the Fight against Slavery," Appendix, PAS Membership, 1774–1843: Before 1843, just 9 mainstream clergy may be found among members whose occupations can be identified. By contrast, 31 lawyers and 31 doctors may be counted out of the 561 members with identifiable occupations.

14. Goodell, *Slavery and Anti-Slavery*, 152; conservative position cited in James G. Birney's critique: *American Churches: The Bulwarks of American Slavery* (3rd ed., Concord, N.H.: Parker Pillsbury, 1885), 9.

15. James Patterson, *A Sermon, on the Effects of the Hebrew Slavery As Connected with Slavery in this Country* (Phila.: S. Probasco, 1825), 3, 11, 19–26.

16. See especially Nash, *Forging Freedom*, 100–133, Julie Winch, *Philadelphia's Black Elite: Activism, Accommodation, and the Struggle for Autonomy, 1787–1848* (Phila.: Temple University Press, 1988); Will B. Gravely, "African Methodisms and the Rise of Black Denominationalism," in Russell E. Richey, Kenneth E. Rowe, and Jean Miller Schmidt, eds., *Perspectives on American Methodism* (Nashville, Tenn.: Kingswood, 1993), 108–26; Andrews, *The Methodists and Revolutionary America*, chap. 5; Richard S. Newman, *Freedom's Prophet: Bishop Richard Allen, the A.M.E. Church, and the Black Founding Fathers* (New York: New York University Press, 2008), 63–68.

17. Andrews, *The Methodists and Revolutionary America*, 144–47.

18. Richard Allen, *The Life Experience and Gospel Labours of the Rt. Rev. Richard Allen,* ed. George A. Singleton (rpt., Nashville: Kingswood, 1960), 29–31; Andrews, *The Methodists and Revolutionary America,* 148–50; Newman, *Freedom's Prophet,* 69–77.

19. William T. Catto, *A Semi-Centenary Discourse, Delivered in the First African Presbyterian Church, Philadelphia* (Phila.: Joseph M. Wilson, 1857), 15–104; Julie Winch, *A Gentleman of Color: The Life of James Forten* (Oxford, U.K.: Oxford University Press, 2002), 327–31, 491.

20. Andrews, *The Methodists and Revolutionary America,* app. A, table 10; *Juvenile Magazine* (Phila., 1813), cited in Committee of the PAS, *The Present State and Condition of the Free People of Color, of the City of Philadelphia and Adjoining Districts* (Phila.: PAS, 1838), 40; Nash, *Forging Freedom,* 201–2.

21. Andrews, *The Methodists and Revolutionary America,* 152, 232–36; Gravely, "African Methodisms and the Rise of Black Denominationalism."

22. Newman, *The Transformation of American Abolitionism,* chap. 4; see also Introduction to *The Black Abolitionist Papers,* ed. C. Peter Ripley (Chapel Hill: University of North Carolina Press, 1991), vol. 3: 4–69.

23. C. C. Goen, *Broken Churches, Broken Nation: Denominational Schisms and the Coming of the American Civil War* (Macon, Ga.: Mercer University Press, 1985), 62.

24. Ibid., 68–69; Sydney E. Ahlstrom, *A Religious History of the American People* (New Haven, Conn.: Yale University Press, 1972), 466–68.

25. *National Enquirer,* 24 August 1837, 9 Nov 1837, Extra dated 9 Dec 1837, 18 Jan 1838; *Pennsylvania Freeman* 29 3rd mo. 1838; *History of Pennsylvania Hall, which was Destroyed by a Mob, On the 17th of May, 1838* (Phila.: Merrihew and Gunn, 1838), esp. 70; Nash, *Forging Freedom,* 277–79.

26. J. S. Cummings, *A Fruitful Church: A Brief History of the Several Churches and Sabbath Schools that have been the outgrowth of the Historic First Presbyterian Church . . . 1832–1892* ([Phila.]: n.p., [1892]); Union Anti-Slavery Society Auxiliary No. 2, *Address . . . to the Congregation of the Western Presbyterian Church* (Phila.: Published for the Society, 1838), 9, 9n.

27. Union Anti-Slavery Society, *Address,* 5, 9–10.

28. Ibid., 9–19, 10n; *Pennsylvania Freeman,* 29 11th mo. 1838.

29. *Pennsylvania Freeman,* 29 11th mo. 1838; Union Anti-Slavery Society, *Address,* 13, 13n.

30. *Constitution of the Union Anti-Slavery Society Auxiliary, No. 2,* at end of Union Anti-Slavery Society, *Address.* Patton is quoted by his opponents in *Pennsylvania Freeman,* 29 11th mo. 1838, and Union Anti-Slavery Society, *Address,* 3n.

31. Union Anti-Slavery Society, *Address,* 21. On the come-outer movement, see William Goodell, *Come-Outerism: The Duty of Secession from a Corrupt Church* (New York: American Anti-Slavery Society, 1845); and recent treatment in Ryan P. Jordan, *Slavery and the Meetinghouse: The Quakers and the Abolitionist Dilemma, 1820–1865* (Bloomington: Indiana University Press, 2007), esp. chaps. 2 and 4.

32. *Pennsylvania Freeman,* 14 2d mo. 1839; Birney, *American Churches,* 32–43; Goodell, *Slavery and Anti-Slavery,* 157–58. On the North-South splintering of American churches between 1837 and 1844, see esp. Ahlstrom, *Religious History,* chap. 40, and John R. McKivigan, "The Sectional Division of the Methodist and Baptist Denominations as Measures of Northern Antislavery Sentiment," in McKivigan and Mitchell Snay, eds., *Religion and the Antebellum Debate over Slavery* (Athens: University of Georgia Press, 1998), 343–63.

33. Committee of the PAS, *The Present State and Condition of the Free People of Color, of the City of Philadelphia and Adjoining Districts* (Phila.: PAS, 1838), 5–10, 24–32.

34. Emma Jones Lapsansky, "'Since They Got Those Separate Churches': Afro-Americans and Racism in Jacksonian Philadelphia," *American Quarterly* 32 (1980): 60; Committee of the PAS, *Address to the People of Color in the State of Pennsylvania* ([Phila.]: PAS, 1838), 4–5.

35. *Black Abolitionist Papers* 3: 189–90.

36. Ibid., 3: 248.

37. Ibid., 3: 199n; Winch, *A Gentleman of Color*, 327–31; A.H.B. to *New York Independent*.

38. Lapsansky, "Since They Got Those Separate Churches," 74–75; *Three Discourses Delivered at the Dedication of the Lombard Street Central Presbyterian Church* (Phila.: Isaac Ashmead, 1848), iii, 62; William S. McFeely, *Frederick Douglass* (New York: W.W. Norton, 1991), 127–30.

39. *Black Abolitionist Papers* 3: 425–27; *The Non-Slaveholder* (Phila.), vol. 3 (1848): 237–39.

40. Carol V. R. George, "Widening the Circle: The Black Church and the Abolitionist Crusade, 1830–1860," in Lewis Perry and Michael Fellman, eds., *Antislavery Reconsidered: New Perspectives on the Abolitionists* (Baton Rouge: Louisiana State University Press, 1979), 75–95; *Christian Recorder* (Phila.), 1854–55, 1861–62; Gilbert Anthony Williams, *"The Christian Recorder," Newspaper of the African Methodist Episcopal Church: History of a Forum for Ideas, 1854–1902* (Jefferson, N.C.: McFarland and Co., 1996).

41. *The North Star*, 1 Sept. 1848.

42. Ibid., 1 Sept. 1848, 10 Nov. 1848, 13 Oct. 1848.

43. Ibid., 10 Nov. 1848.

44. Catto, *A Semi-Centenary Discourse*, app., 105–11.

45. Scharf and Westcott, *History of Philadelphia*, 1400–1406. Another important Philadelphia immediatist was Mathew Simpson, future Methodist bishop and confidante of Abraham Lincoln.

46. Albert Barnes, *The Church and Slavery* (Phila.: Parry and McMillan, 1857), 8; *Pennsylvania Freeman* (23 Dec 1852): 48; George Duffield Jr., *The God of Our Fathers: An Historical Sermon, Delivered at Coates St. Presbyterian Church, Philadelphia* (Phila.: T. B. Pugh, 1861), 26, 23–29.

47. Observations from Julie Roy Jeffrey, *The Great Silent Army of Abolitionism: Ordinary Women in the Antislavery Movement* (Chapel Hill: University of North Carolina Press, 1998), 65–66; John F. Quinn, "The Rise and Fall of Repeal: Slavery and Irish Nationalism in Antebellum Philadelphia," *Pennsylvania Magazine of History and Biography* 130 (January 2006): 45–78; and Donald M. Scott, "Abolition as a Sacred Vocation," in Perry and Fellman, eds., *Antislavery Reconsidered*, 51–74.

48. Ahlstrom, *Religious History*, 668. See also Mason I. Lowance Jr., *A House Divided: The Antebellum Slavery Debates in America, 1776–1865* (Princeton, N.J.: Princeton University Press, 2003), chaps. 3 and 4; and Noll, *America's God*, chap. 19.

49. Mary Still, "An Appeal to the Females of the African Methodist Episcopal Church (1857)" in Richard Newman, Patrick Rael, and Phillip Lapsansky, eds., *Pamphlets of Protest: An Anthology of Early African American Protest Literature, 1790–1860* (New York: Routledge, 2000), 256.

50. Philadelphia Female Anti-Slavery Society, *Thirty-First Annual Report of the Philadelphia Female Anti-Slavery Society* (Phila.: Merrihew & Son, 1865), 22.

51. Gary B. Nash, *First City: Philadelphia and the Forging of Historical Memory* (Phila: University of Pennsylvania Press, 2002), 223–24.

52. *Frederick Douglass' Paper*, 23 Mar. 1855.

CHAPTER 8

Staging Slavery
Representing Race and Abolitionism On and Off the Philadelphia Stage

HEATHER S. NATHANS

Perhaps more than any other public site in the new nation, the theatre re-flected Americans' ambivalence about the place of slavery in a democratic system, and the place of blacks in America in a post-emancipation landscape. An examination of the texts and images presented to Philadelphia audiences during this period may illuminate the ways in which the debate over the aboli-tion of slavery and blacks' participation in American politics and society was translated into the vernacular of the popular stage. Tracing the social, politi-cal, and cultural implications of racial representation on the stage presents a particular challenge to the theatre historian. Although the question of eman-cipation was a pressing one in antebellum society, sensible theatre managers feared angering the many diverse parties in their audiences. Thus they often shied away from presenting images or ideas that might have been labeled of-fensive. At the same time, they knew that their patrons expected the theatre to represent current sensibilities and contemporary politics. Additionally, every manager knew that his or her ultimate success lay in financial stability, and that personal taste or preference must give way to profit. Thus the theatre walked a fine (and not always consistent) line in its efforts to represent racial issues to its audiences, who might, in the same playhouse and in the same season, enjoy an evening of minstrel melodies and "Jim Crow" dances and a performance of the moving melodrama *Uncle Tom's Cabin*.[1]

Because theatre managers were so aware of their need to please multiple audiences, patterns of texts and performances may seem difficult to fathom. Some of the most troubling periods and incidents in the antislavery move-ment *seem* to go unaddressed in the playhouse. However, I would suggest that these events and trends in the antislavery movement, such as the transition from a gradualist to an immediatist ideology made themselves known in more subtle ways on the stage. For example, transformations in the language of the antislavery movement from intellectually driven to emotionally driven styles coincided with the theatre's shift to moral melodrama.[2] The hyperbolic language that became characteristic of Garrison's *The Liberator* and other abolitionist publications of the post-1830s period mirrored that used by slave characters during that same time. In other cases, incidents occurring in the antislavery movement outside the playhouse affected choices of the plays themselves, rather than language. The colonization movement launched a brief interest in "African" dramas (showing black characters happily enjoying their freedom—in Africa). Nat Turner's Rebellion caused some critics to challenge the popularity of the Philadelphia-authored play *The Gladiator,* about a slave uprising in ancient Rome. The publication of a series of narratives by Arab Muslim slaves in the 1830s coincided with a vogue for Arab spectacle dramas at the Chestnut Street and Walnut Street theatres. Yet even as these dialogues developed, they often circled back in on themselves, and so every step forward in the representation of blacks on the antebellum stage seemed to draw forth an equally problematic image in response. Nor can one attribute those conflicted and conflicting images merely to the tension between proslavery and antislavery factions. The post-Garrisonian stage was haunted by the same specters of abolitionist racism that plagued the movement right up until the Civil War. Just as the best intentions of the abolitionists could not fully conceal some of the inherently racist sentiments embedded in their rhetoric, the best stage makeup and acting in the world could not let white antebellum audiences forget that, no matter how moving a performance of *Uncle Tom's Cabin* they might be watching, they were actually seeing a white man in blackface. This dual (not double) consciousness operated for theatre managers, performers, and audience members throughout the antebellum period, and this meta-theatrical dialogue helped to shape the representation of race, slavery, and abolitionism within the playhouse.

(1)

From the time of its publication in 1768, Isaac Bickerstaffe's comedy *The Padlock* proved one of the Philadelphia theatre's most popular productions. The play tells the story of a young woman kept penned up by a would-be older husband and wooed by a handsome young lover.[3] The basic plot is the stuff of which endless eighteenth-century comedies were made, but what sets *The Padlock* apart from many of the other dramas of the period is the controversial presence of a black slave named Mungo whose name, by 1787, had become both a popular slang term for "slave" or "black" (much like "Sambo"), as well as an icon in the growing transatlantic abolitionist movement. Mungo was one of the earliest characters on the Philadelphia stage to raise the moral dilemma of slavery for white audiences.[4] Originally, few of the city's chief proponents of abolitionism, namely Quakers, would have identified the stage as an effective platform for disseminating an antislavery message. Nor did they find natural allies in the founders of the first post-revolutionary playhouse (several of whom were slaveholders). However, they *were* aided (albeit inadvertently) by the growing antislavery sentiment in Great Britain which had begun to permeate the British theatre and which gradually infiltrated the American repertoire, still largely dependent on the mother country for its dramatic canon. Among the British antislavery plays presented at the Southwark and later Chestnut Street theatres were the perennial favorites, *The Padlock*, Thomas Southerne's *Oroonoko*, and George Colman's *Inkle and Yarico*. Throughout the late 1780s and early 1790s, American audiences seeing British plays were also imbibing British antislavery sentiments and language.

Additionally, the post-revolutionary Philadelphia theatres benefited from a steady influx of new British actors. These new company members would have been familiar with the transforming meaning of slavery and emancipation on the British stage and would have brought those new sensibilities to Philadelphia. David Brion Davis has discussed the continual circulation of antislavery literature in Britain, noting that, "The Quakers' dissemination of antislavery literature had an enormous impact; by 1787 the slave trade had become a lively issue for a considerable segment of the English reading public."[5] Adam Hochschild also notes that by the late 1780s dueling plays on the London stage regularly weighed in on the pro- and antislavery debate.[6] Given the cosmopolitanism of the antislavery debate that Caleb McDaniel discusses, it seems hardly surprising that issues so constantly under discussion in the British press would have crept first onto the English stage, and then onto the American one.

For example, by 1787, the character of Mungo from *The Padlock* had been appropriated by the British antislavery movement in an effort to reclaim the African character from its negative stereotype. In October 1787, *The Gentleman's Magazine* printed a poem by a clergyman, intended as an epilogue to *The*

Padlock and spoken by Mungo. In the poem Mungo mourns, "Whilst I tread the free-born British land . . . I am a slave, where all things else are free." He adds, "Yet I was born, as you are, no man's slave. . . . My thoughts can reason, and my limbs can move; the same as yours, like yours my heart can love."[7] This passage in *The Gentleman's Magazine* indicates that the character had achieved sufficient fame on the circum-Atlantic theatre circuit to become a well-known symbol of black oppression.

Only six years later, the famous 1793 Philadelphia cartoon, "A Peep into the Antifederal Club," depicted a character named "Citizen Mungo" sitting among a group of well-known Philadelphians, including the politician Israel Israel, musing with satisfaction that blacks would be the next in line to receive their freedom. The presence of Mungo in an *American* political cartoon testifies to the character's widespread popularity and to his new identification with the American antislavery movement.[8]

Plays such as *Oroonoko* or *Inkle and Yarico* also reflected an antislavery rhetoric that had its origins in British rather than American antislavery traditions, but that quickly became familiar to Philadelphia audiences. *Oroonoko,* based on Aphra Behn's novel of the same title, tells the story of a courageous African prince who is captured and sold into slavery in Surinam.[9] Oroonoko leads a slave uprising—which fails. He kills his wife Imoinda to save her from a life of slavery. He is then captured and flayed alive. The play had been a popular one with British audiences in the mid-eighteenth century, but initially proved less appealing to American audiences, for whom the specter of slave revolts was a constant worry. After the uprising in Saint Domingue in 1791, *Oroonoko* was banished from the Philadelphia stage and not revived until 1824.

Inkle and Yarico, on the other hand, remained a staple of the Philadelphia repertoire and lingered well into the nineteenth century. The play tells the story of a young man named Inkle who is saved from a group of bloodthirsty savages by a "native" princess named Yarico.[10] They fall in love, and he persuades her to return with him to Barbados. There he realizes that marriage to a black West Indian woman will not further his career. He tries to sell Yarico as a slave, but is prevented by the governor of the colony. In many ways, it is easy to imagine why *Inkle and Yarico* seemed less threatening to white Philadelphia audiences than *Oroonoko.* Yarico is a beautiful, helpless maiden, exoticized and eroticized throughout the script."[11] While *Inkle and Yarico* was later claimed by British abolitionists as "the bright forerunner of alleviation of the hardships of slavery," and though it would soon become a byword in the American lexicon for white mistreatment of blacks, its eighteenth-century performers and audiences in Philadelphia were initially more inclined to see it as a source of exotic spectacle, rather than a disquisition on the evils of slavery.[12]

In contrast to the sentimental abolitionism of *Inkle and Yarico*, another popular play on the Philadelphia stage, William Macready's 1793 comedy, *The Irishman in London, or The Happy African*, suggested that slaves actually appreciated having been "rescued" from the heathendom of African culture.[13] Cubba, the "Happy African" of the title, frequently repeats how glad she is to serve her mistress, and how she cannot understand why a slave might want to run away, "Me pity poor black—he do no good—run away; he got whip and chain. Why everybody no be happy like me?"[14]

Written for British audiences, and adopted enthusiastically by American ones, Macready's text presents a puzzling perspective on slavery, abolition, and the African presence in Western culture in a year in which the issue was being hotly contested on both sides of the Atlantic. The 1793 defeat of an abolition bill in the House of Commons substantially weakened the momentum of Britain's antislavery movement, while at the same time the United States' passage of the 1793 Fugitive Slave Act "embraced [the nation's] double standard in defining its jurisdiction over the peculiar institution: national authority could be exercised for the recovery but not the protection of slaves." During the month that *The Irishman* made its first appearance in Philadelphia, local papers teemed with reports of the uprising in Saint Domingue, describing the unrest as having arisen, "without apparent provocation on the part of the whites." On July 6, 1793, the *Aurora* featured frightening accounts of "Mulattoes [parading] in the streets with armed bodies . . . insulting the whites, several of whom they wounded with sabres and pistols." A poem in the *Aurora* decried the harsh treatment of Saint Domingue's refugees by the black rebels: "By savage hands depriv'd of Fortune's smile / By savage hands bereft of friends and home . . . The conquering savage glories in his power."[15] Set against the backdrop of this violence, *The Irishman in London, or The Happy African* becomes oddly reassuring to audiences. Macready's text downplays the negative impact of slavery on its subjects and its proponents, simultaneously affirming both the institution's legitimacy as well as the willing compliance of its subjects. The play received nearly eighty performances throughout the nation between 1793 and 1817.

Prior to the Saint Domingue uprising of 1791 and the Yellow Fever epidemic of 1793, Philadelphians enjoyed plays that depicted British-inflected antislavery sentiments, as well as exotic spectacles of race, ranging from African princes to West Indian princesses to witch doctors. These dramas were staged largely to entertain, rather than enlighten, and drew neither the interest, nor seemingly the support, of the city's antislavery activists.[16] Then crisis struck. The Yellow Fever epidemic brought an abrupt end to theatrical entertainments in the city that year. The Saint Domingue rebellion helped transform the depiction of race and slavery in the American theatre. Both wrought a change in how theatrical performances were understood by local Philadelphia audiences. By the time the theatres re-opened in 1794, the theatrical, political, and abolitionist dialogue had shifted radically.[17]

(2)

As Julie Winch notes, Philadelphia's Yellow Fever epidemic of 1793 was the worst the city had known since 1762. In addition to the havoc it generated throughout the region, it also imperiled the city's new theatre. Many saw the epidemic as a judgment on the city for its temerity in opening the playhouse on Chestnut Street. As a result, the theatre's Quaker opponents renewed their attacks against theatrical entertainments, which, despite their best efforts, opened on February 17, 1794. However, the threat to the playhouse went beyond a revival of traditional anti-theatrical sentiments. It set in motion a complex chain of events that would result in the first scene of slave emancipation in American history being staged in the Philadelphia playhouse.

The epidemic both transformed the party system of Pennsylvania and spurred the efforts of the city's antislavery activists. As the city's wealthy elite fled for more salubrious surroundings, Philadelphia's poorer citizens remained in neighborhoods being rapidly overtaken by disease. The city's black population worked heroically, nursing the sick and burying the dead. Black leaders Richard Allen and Absalom Jones declared, "We feel a great satisfaction in believing that we have been useful to the sick, and thus publicly thank Dr. Rush for enabling us to be so."[18] The mention of Benjamin Rush is significant for three reasons: obviously Rush was a prominent abolitionist; he and his friend Tench Coxe were among the few powerful Philadelphians who stayed in the city during the crisis to aid its poorer citizens, and in the process, helped to augment the power of the Democratic-Republican party; and, most significantly in terms of the representation of slavery on the Philadelphia stage, in 1793 Tench Coxe helped a man named John Murdock—a local hairdresser— get his family safely out of the city. John Murdock was an artisan who during the yellow fever epidemic must have witnessed both the elites' desertion of the city and the untiring service of the city's free black population. He was also connected—however tenuously—with Rush and Coxe, and thus aware of their antislavery mission. In January of 1794, Rush and Coxe had participated in the convention of delegates from the Abolition Societies held in Philadelphia. On February 12, 1794 (five days before the opening of the Chestnut Street Theatre), the House of Representatives considered a petition for "prohibiting the citizens of the United States from employing their shipping in the slave trade."[19] Coxe and Rush were among the most prominent local proponents of this initiative. In May of that same year, John Murdock offered his play, *The Triumphs of Love, or Happy Reconciliations,* to the managers of the Chestnut Street Theatre. The names of Tench Coxe and Benjamin Rush appear on the list of sponsors for the script (published in 1795).[20]

For a "mechanic" like Murdock to write a play for the American theatre was extraordinary. For a mechanic to write a play that addressed the issues of slavery and abolition was unheard of. Yet Murdock's work delves into many of the pressing issues plaguing the new nation—including slavery and the fitness of free blacks to participate in the government of the young republic. Set in contemporary (1794) Philadelphia, the central story revolves around a young man named George Friendly Jr., who represents the youth of the postrevolutionary generation. While George appreciates the personal freedom the recent war has won for him and for other young men of his class, he does not yet fully understand the principle of universal liberty upon which the nation was founded. Throughout the course of the play, his encounters with refugees from Saint Domingue and with his own slave, Sambo, prompt him to question the liberty he has taken for granted.

In the first scene of Act III, George overhears Sambo lamenting his condition: "[Sambo] tink de great somebody above no order tings so." As George notes, "The untutored pathetic soliloquy of that honest creature has more sensibly affected me, than all I have read, or thought, on that barbarous iniquitous slave trade." Noting that "It is cruel. It is unjust, for one creature to hold another in a state of bondage for life," George emerges from his hiding place and grants Sambo his freedom. However, even as he proclaims, "Sambo, thou shalt be free," he follows the declaration with a crucial question: "Suppose you had your liberty, how would you conduct yourself?"[21]

George's query is just one of a number that confronted an audience of American citizens pondering the issue of African slavery. Could former slaves become upright citizens, or were they so degraded by the experience of slavery that they were doomed to remain a burden on—and a danger to—white society?

While *Triumphs of Love* received only one performance on the Philadelphia stage (May 22, 1795), it could have reached an audience of up to roughly two thousand spectators in the playhouse, and, perhaps more importantly, it did provoke discussion in the city's newspapers, which commended its treatment of "the interesting topic of Negro slavery."[22] *Triumphs* also enjoyed widespread circulation among the 145 sponsors listed in the published 1795 edition.

Murdock's play raises an issue that confronted abolitionists and free blacks alike: how could they combat the negative stereotype of the dissolute slave and black freedman on and off the stage? Echoing the popular abolitionist rhetoric of the period, Murdock suggests that problems stemmed from a want of education—that a people held in slavery could not understand fully the "dangers" of liberty, and that, therefore, white Americans must teach the former slaves both by sermon and example. Quaker-led antislavery groups paid particular attention to the challenge of educating emancipated slaves. A 1789 address to the public from the Pennsylvania Society for the Abolition of Slavery suggested, "The unhappy man who has long been treated as a brute animal, too frequently sinks beneath the common standard the human species. Under such circumstances, freedom may often prove a misfortune to himself and prejudicial to society."[23] In many ways, Murdock's depiction of Sambo's weakness (he gets drunk after George frees him) may well be read not as an indictment of free blacks but rather as a cautionary tale for abolitionists, reminding them that emancipation itself did not solve the problem of how to integrate blacks into white society.

Murdock's faith in the power of education and his plea for moral conduct parallel the doctrines of the nation's earliest antislavery societies—both black and white. The Free African Society of Philadelphia required temperance among its membership.[24] White antislavery activists also stressed the importance of good conduct in the success of the abolitionist movement (particularly avoiding the dangers of alcohol). In 1789, the Pennsylvania Abolition Society created a "Committee of Inspection," charged with superintending "the morals, general conduct, and ordinary situation of the Free Negroes, and afford[ing] them advice and instruction, protection from wrongs, and other friendly offices."[25] These former slaves, like Murdock's Sambo, required only education, protection, and friendship from the white community to become legitimate citizens. Murdock later resurrected the character of Sambo in his next play, *The Politicians, or A State of Things* (1798).[26] In this play, the newly freed Sambo is abstemious and honest in his habits and thus is allowed to engage in political debate over the ramifications of the 1795 Jay Treaty with Great Britain. His good conduct secures him some of the rights and privileges of citizenship, just as the abolitionists' advice manuals had promised.

By the early 1800s, debates had shifted as Americans agonized over the justification for slavery and the allegedly peculiar fitness of Africans for the state. Party perspectives on the antislavery stance altered as well, for while the Democratic-Republicans had begun as an antislavery party in the late eighteenth century, with the ascension of Thomas Jefferson, himself a slaveholder deeply conflicted on the issue of slavery, the party began to push its rhetoric towards a neutral (or in some cases, proslavery stance).[27] The exception on stage was the popular operetta *Paul and Virginia* (1802).

James Cobb's *Paul and Virginia* (adapted from the British and French novels of the same title) was first performed in the United States in 1802, where it met with "great applause" from its spectators and quickly became a staple of the early national repertoire.[28] Set on a Spanish island in the West Indies, the play opens on the celebration of Virginia's birthday. Virginia is under the care of an elderly black servant named Dominique, who proudly declares his free status: "I am no slave. For though by the wise and just laws of Europeans I was doom'd to be a slave and entail slavery on all my descendants because my mother was born in Africa, the curse has been removed by one who was simple enough to consider me as a fellow creature, though one shade darker than himself."[29]

As Virginia and her fiancé Paul enjoy the birthday festivities, their antislavery sentiments are tested by the arrival of a runaway African slave named Alambra. He beseeches them to hide him: "Pity, pity the miserable Alambra! O compassionate a wretched creature, forced by ill-usage to escape from a neighboring plantation." He claims that he ran away because the plantation overseer was beating his sister and he intervened, striking the overseer to the ground. Paul applauds his act, "Heaven stamped that energy in your heart which raised your avenging arm."[30]

Only twenty months before the play's debut, Gabriel's rebellion had stunned the nation's white community.[31] While the *Aurora* noted that Gabriel's master had "behaved with great barbarity to his slaves," it also claimed, "many of these wretches . . . who have been partners in the plot, have been treated with the utmost tenderness by their masters, and were more like children than slaves."[32] A Philadelphia audience witnessing the loving care that Paul and Virginia lavish on their servants might wonder if Alambra's rebellion would be contagious to even the happiest of slaves. Ultimately, Paul notes that he cannot appear to condone Alambra's actions or harbor a fugitive who has raised his hand against his master, "Alas, you know the strict laws of this island will not allow us to afford you shelter in our abode."[33] Though Paul and Virginia invoke some of the language of the antislavery movement, they do not seek universal emancipation, but rather the amelioration of suffering for those laboring within the system. They (like many in the Philadelphia audience) had recognized the potential evils of the system, but had not yet committed fully to the abolition cause.[34]

(3)

The first stirrings of the colonization movement in the 1810s brought a new interest in the issue of emancipation and in representations of Africa to the Philadelphia stage. In 1787, Benjamin Rush had described an extraordinary dream that had converted him to the antislavery cause. Pursued by the ghost of Anthony Benezet, he found himself on the shores of an Africa-like landscape, "on a sandy beach in a country of surpassing beauty."[35] There he encountered a group of Africans who trembled at his appearance, and who informed him that they were "standing in the paradise that God had given to Africans who had been wrenched from their homeland after a shattered family life and ghastly brutality under slavery."[36]

Rush's fantasies of Africa both reflect and resist the image of Africa and Africanness presented on the Philadelphia stage. Some plays depicted the continent as a natural paradise—as in Rush's dream—while others painted it as a land of heathen darkness or peopled by Rush's race of "unfortunate creatures." However, such was the nature of the public discourse on Africa— deeply divided over its meaning in the new American nation. Did it hold the key to solving the nation's increasingly pressing problem of slavery, or was its very weakness the cause of it? Would Africa become, as the early proponents of colonization hoped, a model of democratic and Christian governance, or would it serve merely as a convenient *oubliette* into which the nation's "dangerous" free black population might be consigned?

One of the best examples of the early, pro-Africa, pro-emancipation plays was William Dunlap's adaptation of *The Africans, or War, Love, and Duty* (1810). The play attacked slavery, but it did so in an African setting which allowed Dunlap's characters a kind of nobility, eloquence, and self-determination that they would be denied in an American or Atlantic setting (the play is set in Africa, but the clear target of its rhetoric is the circum-Atlantic slave trade).[37] Dunlap, often called the "Father of American Drama," was, at one time, the secretary for the New York Manumission Society, first formed in 1785. David Brion Davis has described the Society's post-revolutionary supporters as an "unrivaled elite," whose membership overlapped with other important "public and private organizations designed to give order and direction to public life."[38] In an age that defined the theatre as a "powerful engine" to "polish the manners and habits of society,"[39] Dunlap's use of a theatrical performance to promote an antislavery message seems natural since some of his colleagues in the Manumission Society were also shareholders in his theatre.

The Africans came to Philadelphia in 1810. The action opens on the morning of a wedding between the beautiful Berissa and her lover, Selico. Berissa, Selico, and his brother Torribal are members of the Foulah tribe which, as Selico notes, "Are the prettiest of the Negroes; for the same sun that dyes our neighbors black has dipped us Foulahs lighter by ten shades."[40] As the lovers prepare to enjoy their future wedded bliss, the entire village comes to celebrate, including the Foulah's slaves, who enter singing and dancing in what Dunlap imagines as a traditional African tribal celebration.[41]

As Berissa watches them she reflects on the cruelty of slavery, observing, "To make a man happy, you must make him free." She implores her father (the chief) to free the slaves as a special wedding boon, reminding him:

> Think how the slave's heart must sicken for his home
> If he's a father and a prattling child
> Lisps where he labours "Where now are my babes"
> He groans, "that I am torn from?" Mother's captiv'd
> Must still know keener anguish . . .
> 'Tis heaven only numbers
> How many slaves have perished by despondence.[42]

Just as Berissa's father agrees to free his slaves, the Foulah village is overrun by the Mandingo tribe, a race described as much darker-skinned and (hence) more savage than their Foulah neighbors. The Mandingos capture the Foulahs and plan to sell a group of them to white slave traders. Happily, the nobility of Selico and Torribal (and a series of fortunate coincidences) frees the Foulahs and converts the Mandingos to the antislavery cause.

Tellingly, no reviews commented on the male actors playing the two black heroic roles. Though Dunlap may have envisioned the play as a serious exploration of the evils of slavery and the potential advantages of colonization after emancipation, the various reviews highlight the appeal of *The Africans* for its lush scenic effects and compelling story, suggesting that for many it offered escapist entertainment rather than a probing inquiry into the problem of African slavery in America.

Indeed, although Dunlap's Foulah characters speak in eloquent English and prove themselves capable of great selflessness, Dunlap's fantasy African characters ultimately cannot be imagined outside of Africa—they cannot be brought to the United States and still retain their nobility. Dunlap's script highlights the problem of where the African body "belonged" in a post-revolutionary culture. The play appeared on the American stage in the same year that Paul Cuffee made his first serious overtures towards the nation's various abolitionist groups to support his plan to send the country's free blacks back to an African homeland. Cuffee's proposals never received the support he had hoped for, but the colonization movement enjoyed renewed interest in 1817 with the founding of the American Colonization Society (ACS) in Washington, D.C.[43] As Caleb McDaniel and Gary Nash argue, the colonization movement both attracted and repelled American antislavery activists and many antislavery advocates were deeply suspicious of the ACS's founders, which included Henry Clay and Bushrod Washington. Indeed, the cosmopolitan nature of the controversy that McDaniel describes appears in a letter from Londoner T. S. Smith to his friend Philadelphia philanthropist Roberts Vaux: "When I see such men as H. Clay and Andrew Jackson appear as advocates of the plan, & one or both at the same time avowing the fixed sentiments of slave holders, I am disposed to pause. My suspicions are excited that their object is little more than by sending away the free blacks, to reduce the numerical force of that people in order that the fetters of the remaining portion may be more firmly riveted."[44]

Despite widespread doubts, the ACS's initiative gained support, though the escalation of the colonization movement seems to have marked a change in representations of Africa and Africanness on the American stage. Images of eloquent Africans enjoying their homeland gave way to Christianizing moral lessons that imagined the continent in desperate need of salvation. Narratives from missionaries to Sierra Leone and Liberia helped to romanticize the stage's "Americanized" African, in contrast to his native brethren.[45] At the same time, the escalation of violence within the United States, including the slave uprisings of the 1820s and 1830s, created the stage image of a savage African counterpart lurking on American shores. Tackling the issue of emancipation on the Philadelphia stage grew increasingly problematic.[46]

(4)

The wish to sidestep the thorny question of emancipation manifested itself most visibly in the spectacles offered to Philadelphia audiences during the early 1830s, which veered from minstrel comedies to Arabian fantasies. The advent of Thomas "Daddy" Rice in the late 1820s and the Nat Turner uprising of 1831 helped to change the representation of African Americans in the playhouse. Much has been written of Rice, an actor widely credited with popularizing the character of Jim Crow, a name that would become a byword for racist stereotypes.[47] Rice's performance of the clownish Jim Crow character, which combined singing, dancing, and storytelling, helped to launch a craze for minstrel shows that persisted well into the twentieth century.

Though Rice's performances have often been condemned as racist and demeaning to blacks, scholar W. T. Lhamon suggests that minstrel performances often presented a much more complex understanding of racial nuances than even the abolitionists' representations of race. He compares the popular yet passive abolitionist image of the kneeling slave raising his hands and exclaiming, "Am I not a man and a brother?" to the lively portraits rendered by blackface minstrels which "saw blacks as people with an implicit intelligence evinced by explicit talent, irony, and capacious resistance."[48] Lhamon's assertion that abolitionists were often prone to characterizing blacks as passive or helpless offers an intriguing explanation for the paucity of compelling African American characters on the Philadelphia stage in the 1820s and early 1830s, though it must be tempered by comments in contemporary abolitionist papers such as the *Genius of Universal Emancipation* which argued that blacks did indeed have capacity for initiative, organization, and decisive action—as witnessed by the uprising in Saint Domingue.[49] However, before American melodrama hit its stride with plays that called for active social reform, the stage seemed to lack a genre that would give scope and range for a well-developed African American hero.[50]

Even if the abolitionist movement was not directly present on the stage during the 1820s, it made its presence known in more subtle ways—becoming the target for the theatre toughs who frequented the minstrel circuit. As theatre historian Joseph Roach has observed, New York's Farren Riots of 1834 emerged as a combined outgrowth of the "amalgamationist" riots taking place in the Northeast and resentment directed against British theatre manager William Farren's (suspected) pro-abolitionist, anti-American sentiments unwisely evinced in his Bowery Theatre repertoire. On July 9, 1834, "a mob of antiabolitionists demanding the punishment of Farren and the deportation of blacks, invaded the theatre." The mob was appeased only by "the manager's apology, the display of American flags, and the singing of 'Yankee Doodle' and 'Zip Coon' in blackface."[51] The 1834 timing is suggestive, as it coincided with Parliament's decision to free all slaves in the British West Indies. In 1834 Philadelphia, Thomas "Daddy" Rice helped to close the Walnut Street Theatre's spring season with performances of *Oh Hush* and *Jim Crow*. The city's theatres had already shut down for their brief summer hiatus when violence broke out against the city's black community (part of a series of ongoing crises that Dee Andrews describes). For example, on August 12, 1834, rioters launched a two-day attack against the city's black citizens: "Breaking into houses . . . the white marauders destroyed furniture, dragged black residents from their beds and beat them, smashed windows, completely destroyed the black Methodist Church on Wharton Street and severely damaged the African Presbyterian Church."[52] When the theatre re-opened on August 29, 1834, managers ignored the violence that had passed so close to their own doorsteps. Neither William B. Wood (Philadelphia actor and theatre manager) nor Charles Durang (the first man to chronicle the history of the Philadelphia stage) make any mention of racial unrest in their accounts of the city's theatrical history.[53]

The 1830s Philadelphia stage also abounded in exotic representations of African/Arab characters, inspired in part by the British craze for Turkish culture (launched by Lord Byron and others), and by the romanticized narratives of Arab Muslim slaves that became popular in the early 1830s. As Sylviane Diouf has argued, the publication on Omar ibn Said's 1831 autobiography helped to popularize the genre of African Muslim writings and to establish a division between "Negro" and "Moorish" identities in the popular imagination.[54] The distinction between "Negro" and "Moorish" operated on every level from appearance to intellect to appearance to faith. The decade saw the popularity of a number of "Arab" and "Moorish" spectacles in the playhouse, including a pantomime ballet entitled *The Bedouin Arabs* that was one of the most successful productions of the 1837–38 Philadelphia season, as well as another afterpiece entitled *The Moorish Page, or The Knight of the Bleeding Scarf.*[55]

In contrast to these exotic heroes, the 1830s Philadelphia stage also teemed with characters that represented the "common man" struggling against oppression. That character type became the stock-in-trade of America's first genuine star actor, Edwin Forrest—who created the role of the greatest rebel slave leader on the American stage. Aggressively masculine and dashingly handsome, Forrest made a career out of portraying the Jacksonian "everyman," commissioning local playwrights to create new works specifically tailored to his talents. Among the most famous of his roles was Spartacus in Philadelphian Robert Montgomery Bird's *The Gladiator.*[56] The play debuted the same year that William Lloyd Garrison launched *The Liberator* and that Nat Turner staged his rebellion in Southampton, Virginia. *The Gladiator* tells the story of a slave uprising in ancient Rome led by a slave named Spartacus who longs to return to the wife and son from whom he has been cruelly separated. Walt Whitman once observed that Bird's play was "as full of 'abolitionism' as an egg is of meat," and certainly its resonance with the antislavery movement seems clear to a contemporary reader.[57] Bird himself worried that the play would not be popular with southern audiences because of its antislavery message.[58] Though he had written it in May of 1831, before Turner's rebellion, once the uprising took place Bird was quick to see both the parallels and the dangers: "Six to eight hundred rebelling slaves under Nat Turner are murdering, ravishing, and burning in Virginia. . . . If they had a Spartacus among them to organize the half million of Virginia, the hundred thousand of the other states, and lead them on in the Crusade of Massacre, what a blessed example might they not give to the world of the excellence of slavery!"[59] But despite Bird's fears the play opened at the Arch Street Theatre on October 24, 1831, as a phenomenal success.[60] Part of that success may have been due to Forrest's star presence in the play. However, the triumph of *The Gladiator* in Philadelphia only three months after Turner's uprising, and in the same month that Turner was finally captured by white authorities, begs the question of how white Philadelphia audiences understood the intersection between the dramas taking place in the antislavery movement outside the playhouse and the impassioned rhetoric against oppression being voiced within. For example, as Spartacus urges his comrades on to rebellion, he cries: "Ho, slaves, arise! It is your hour to kill! Kill and spare not—For wrath and liberty—Freedom for bondmen—Freedom and revenge!"[61] How could audiences, whether proslavery or antislavery, *not* hear echoes of Turner's plot to kill the men, women, and children on the plantations in Southampton just as Bird did?

On the other hand, perhaps the Philadelphia audience's indecision about the "true" message of *The Gladiator* is not as surprising as it first seems. Richard Newman has noted that even the most committed abolitionists had difficulty in interpreting the lesson of Turner's rebellion. For example, William Lloyd Garrison publicly deplored the violence of the uprising, even as he acknowledged the horrors that had prompted it. Perhaps what the puzzling timing of these incidents best underscores is the ambivalence of many Americans about the meaning of the incident in the broader context of the antislavery movement. Nowhere does that ambiguity seem more apparent than in the attitude of the Pennsylvania Abolition Society, which in the early 1830s refused to embrace a more immediatist approach on the grounds that it would be "inexpedient." As Newman has suggested, "In the PAS's eyes, immediatism signaled not simply 'immediate attacks' on bondage but unacceptable new tactics: politicizing fugitive slave cases, using black narratives of bondage to sway public sympathy, even empathizing with black Revolutionary action in Haiti."[62] Dee Andrews observes, "The immediatist years would be trying ones for Philadelphians" as they struggled to reconcile different visions of the future of the antislavery movement. Thus, while pre-1831 antislavery dramas present sympathetic slave characters, they also present a fairly restrained picture of slavery, as well as a rational and *gradualist* argument for its elimination. As the antislavery movement moved northwards and embraced more "sensationalist" strategies, the drama followed suit and Philadelphia audiences of the late 1830s, '40s, and '50s would find their theatre-going experiences shaped by this new approach.

(5)

On May 14, 1838, when Pennsylvania Hall proudly opened, it was described as "one of the most commodious and splendid buildings in the city."[63] The mob that destroyed it only a few days later was estimated at between 20,000 to 50,000 citizens.[64] The burning of Pennsylvania Hall sparked more than a month of violence against the city's black and abolitionist community, with attacks against the Colored Orphan Asylum, Mother Bethel African Methodist Episcopal (AME) Church, and numerous reports of assaults against citizens in the streets. The central issue in much of the press coverage of these events was amalgamation, and whether or not the Hall had been constructed to foster the "promiscuous" union of blacks and whites.[65]

The Philadelphia City Council committee assigned to investigate the incident ultimately determined that "They [the founders] owe it to the cause of truth to declare that this excitement . . . was occasioned by . . . doctrine repulsive to the moral sense of a large majority of our community."[66] However, in that same year the city also witnessed eight productions of *Othello*—one of the most controversial plays in the Shakespeare canon. I suggest that the burning of Pennsylvania Hall helped to cement the establishment of racial hierarchies and boundaries in 1830s Philadelphia by conflating the ideas of abolition and amalgamation in the public imagination, and by provoking the opponents and supporters of abolition to declare themselves in print and in public performance. As a result, by 1838, *Othello* would have a new meaning for audiences both inside and outside the playhouse.

Pennsylvania Hall's opening attracted some of the most noteworthy abolitionist figures in the nation, including William Lloyd Garrison, Lucretia Mott, and Sarah and Angelina Grimke. Gary Nash has described the hall as a "symbol of the emergence of radical abolitionism."[67] Hostile Philadelphia papers quickly seized upon the hall as a lightning rod for the issue of amalgamation. Wild rumors spread throughout the city about the "mixing up of people of the two colors," of their being "seated promiscuously in the Hall," of the "provocativeness of display."[68] *Poulson's Daily Advertiser* described with disgust the spectacle of "A black beau escorting two interesting and pretty white females . . . and a procession in the most public street of black and white, duly mixed."[69]

When a crowd gathered outside Pennsylvania Hall on May 17, 1838, a mob broke into the basement of the building and started a fire. No one attempted to stop the blaze. As one newspaper account noted, "The whole affair took place without any unnecessary violence or noise . . . The crowd . . . [was] generally respectable and well-dressed, and determined, almost to a man, to protect from interruption the immediate agents in the destruction of the building."[70]

This account bears an intriguing similarity to the descriptions of fashionable audiences in the playhouse. "Generally respectable and well-dressed" are words seldom used to characterize mobs. Yet the engravings depicting the event show a large number of well-dressed men in high hats and frock coats standing by, and some appear to be cheering as the building blazes. Many white Philadelphia papers treated the incident as if it had been a morality play that the whole town had turned out to see—a special performance on the evils of amalgamation for the general edification of the city's citizens. How did the audiences who happily ignited Pennsylvania Hall because it promoted "promiscuous" contact between black men and white women understand *Othello* in the year of the fire and in its aftermath?

In January of 1838, a new production of *Othello* had opened at Philadelphia's Walnut Street Theatre with Edwin Forrest in the role of the Moor.[71] The play received the most performances of any Shakespeare play in the Philadelphia repertoire in the 1838 season. (It was, as David Grimsted has noted, the seventh most popular play overall in Philadelphia between 1831 and 1851.) Forrest played it as his own benefit, and the play appeared in both the Walnut Street and Chestnut Street theatres from January through December of 1838 (before and after the Pennsylvania Hall riot).[72] On the surface, the popularity of the play in that season may seem unremarkable; in 1838, Forrest was America's premiere actor. He was at the height of his powers, and the bluster and physicality of Othello's role was particularly suited to his muscular style of performance. The part of Othello had launched his career in 1826 and remained among the most popular of his roles.

But the text of *Othello* had become far more complicated for a Philadelphia audience than the simple "lesson on the dangers of jealously" that theatre manager David Douglass had offered a colonial crowd back in the 1760s. By the late 1830s, the specter of black and white amalgamation had moved center stage in the antislavery rhetoric in Philadelphia.[73] Additionally, the issue of Moorish (or Muslim) versus black or "Negro" identity had also begun to challenge the national audience. When played as a "straight tragedy," Othello was portrayed as a noble man of color because of his Moorish qualities. When played as a minstrel parody by performers like Thomas "Daddy" Rice, Othello was black, or "Negro." The fascination with Arab/Moorish culture and the racial prejudice that encumbered the nation's slave population split the character of Othello in the theatre as effectively as it divided the racial identities of African Americans outside the playhouse.

Edwin Forrest's own interpretation of the role fell into the "Moorish" school. But Forrest also embodied the quintessential American character, and it was a union that made for a potentially uncomfortable combination. Forrest was immensely strong: barrel-chested, with heavily muscled arms and legs. He wore short, bare-armed and often bare-chested costumes that emphasized his physical prowess. In the role of Othello he wore two costumes designed to create a Muslim figure of romance: "A low neck tunic, dark tights, low shoes with straps and buckles, a large silk mantle, spotted with large gilt leaves, and a scarlet turban," and a "purple velvet robe, heavily bullioned with trimmings and jeweled with emeralds." As the Philadelphia *Pennsylvanian* noted, "His fine manly form was exhibited to much advantage in the judicious costume he had assembled. He looked the warrior Moor—the chief selected by a powerful and warlike nation to lead their armies to the fight."[74]

Offstage, Forrest was a known Democrat and a popular speaker on behalf of a party which in 1838 championed the rights of the working man, deplored the "aristocracy" and the big banks, and held (at best) ambivalent views on the issue of slavery—and (at worst) supported its continued existence.[75] The same year that Forrest played Othello on the Philadelphia stage, he declined a nomination to run for Congress, but he accepted an invitation to give the Fourth of July address at a Democratic rally in New York. Forrest's presence onstage made him an important political figure, and Philadelphia audiences looked to him as the personification of their own Americanness.

All this made for a complicated portrayal of Othello in 1838 Pennsylvania. However, Forrest knew his audiences' sensitivity to the issues of slavery and amalgamation. His promptbook (performance script) version of *Othello* shows cuts to the text that eliminate the most highly sexual and offensive language in the play. Forrest also excised the scene midway through the play in which Othello slaps Desdemona in front of several witnesses. His goal, as one of his biographers noted, was to portray Othello's love for Desdemona as "an entrancing possession, not an animal love bred in the senses alone."[76]

Yet individual changes to a text in performance erase neither the memory of those lines (known to audiences and critics alike), nor do they erase the meaning of the name "Othello." Whether implicitly or explicitly, discussion of the character of Othello automatically raised issues of black and white amalgamation, as when in 1836 John Quincy Adams publicly described Othello as "The great moral lesson that black and white blood cannot be intermingled without a gross outrage upon the laws of nature, and that, in such violations, Nature will vindicate her laws."[77] The real-life parallels did not escape the Philadelphia public in the aftermath of the Pennsylvania Hall riots. On May 26, 1838, less than ten days after the Pennsylvania Hall fire, one of the city's local Whig newspapers published the following rebuke to the white women who had been present at the abolitionist meetings held in the hall: "If the ladies composing the 'Anti-Slavery Society of American Women' are so fond of black companions, let them commence the promotion of their taste by marrying their own daughters to the darkest colours they can find."[78]

If Othello had become a figure that represented sexual aggression to many whites, he had also become a figure of black activism as well. As early as 1788, black and white activists had appropriated the figure of Othello as a potential symbol of a more immediatist antislavery movement, using "Othello" as a pen name in antislavery protests.[79] In 1839, the *Colored American* claimed that whites had misappropriated the name of Othello, especially in comparing him to the Amistad's Cinque. The paper contended that both Cinque and Othello represented the kinds of characters who could never be enslaved. The paper charged white Americans with being too cowardly to embrace Cinque's and Othello's heroism because to acknowledge such bravery on the part of a black man would, "turn the Southampton into a glorious rising for liberty, and Nat Turner would be a Sir William Wallace."[80] The linking of Othello with Nat Turner, Cinque, and white rebel leaders such as William Wallace represents a potent reclaiming of Othello's martial identity as a great general and as a protestor against white oppression. In the wake of the Pennsylvania Hall fire, black editors of the *Colored American* had angrily denied the charge of amalgamationism, claiming, "The subject is made the great 'Bug-bear' by the opposers of liberty and human rights. It is the battering-ram of the pro-slavery party. . . . Do not these men know that they are fighting shadows, ghosts of their own creation?"[81] By dismissing the cry of "amalgamation" as a white fear, and by tracing its "real" cause to anxiety about black power, the African American community endowed the name of Othello with a new meaning.

The events of 1838 seem to have marked the fusion of abolitionism and amalgamation in Philadelphia's public imagination when the familiar southern terror of a black man sexually possessing a white woman came to emblematize the dangers of full black emancipation and enfranchisement. As Nash comments, "A few months after the burning of the Pennsylvania Hall, as the legislature debated the formal disenfranchisement of Pennsylvania's free blacks, articles flooding the Philadelphia press remarked how widespread Negrophobia had become."[82] The *Spirit of the Times* accused the city's black citizens of having "usurped" rights belonging only to whites, a complaint which offers another intriguing parallel to Shakespeare's *Othello*.[83] The "crisis" of *Othello* begins with Othello being allowed to speak in front of the Venetian government. During that speech, he demands both his rights as citizen (to fight on behalf of the state), and his rights as Desdemona's husband. Citizenship and sexual possession become one, even in Shakespeare's text. Ultimately, like Othello, Philadelphia's black citizens lost their bid for freedom in the treachery of those who did not hesitate to conspire against them.[84]

(6)

If the 1838 productions of *Othello* tapped into increasing anxieties about black and white amalgamation, James Ewell Heath's 1839 comedy *Whigs and Democrats* emerged as an indictment of the growing inability of the American political system to cope with the issues of slavery and political factionalism.[85] *Whigs and Democrats* tells the story of a crooked election in which a Democratic congressional candidate, General Fairweather, tries to barter his son in marriage to the various party leaders he thinks will help him win re-election. The play satirizes the American political process and critiques those citizens who abdicate their political and moral responsibility. For example, in one scene when the issue of abolitionism is mentioned, a crowd of drunken farmers begins to shout in protest. Alarmed by their vehemence, their leader, Major Roundtree, persuades them not to vote at all rather than risk a divisive debate. His suggestion immediately shuts down any discussion of a potentially problematic or dangerous question, as all the men decide to go drinking instead.

Whigs and Democrats received two productions in Philadelphia—both tied to significant political elections. The play debuted at the Walnut Street Theatre on October 12, 1839, shortly before the Whigs' national convention in Harrisburg, Pennsylvania. The play was revived (by special request, as the advertisements note) on October 31, 1844.[86] The 1840s were turbulent times for Philadelphia theatres as the management among many of its oldest companies (the Chestnut Street, the Walnut Street, and the Arch Street theatres) changed hands, with the city's elite deserting the once popular Chestnut Street house.[87] As audiences shifted and as new managers and performers entered the scene, the city's theatres struggled to find theatrical fare that would woo crowds back into the playhouse.

1844 also witnessed the controversial campaign between Democratic nominee James K. Polk and Whig candidate and slaveholder Henry Clay. Beginning in January 1844, newspapers in Philadelphia predicted that the slavery issue would be a critical one in the coming election, and the papers were relentless in their debates on the candidates' controversial campaigns. The *Philadelphia*

Gazette and Commercial Intelligencer complained continuously that the mid-Atlantic region was becoming a haven for runaway slaves and slave catchers.[88] By October, Philadelphia's Whig papers were accusing Democrats (the "locofoco" party) of bribing and deceiving voters, and of passing themselves off as friends to abolitionism. As one letter to the *Gazette* complained, "An attempt is now being made by leaders in the locofoco ranks to make the abolitionists believe that locofocoism is their friend and the friend of the negro."[89] At the other end of the spectrum, the *Pennsylvanian* decried the Whig Party as the "negro" party. The local papers also ran stories from Cuba and Saint Domingue, reporting on black unrest and linking the emancipation of blacks with the potential for riot and violence.[90]

Even though the Whigs passed themselves off as friends to abolitionism, they lost Philadelphia and ultimately did little to help the city's struggling black population. Just as the crisis of 1838 marked the fusion of abolition and amalgamation rhetoric, the election of 1844 seemed to mark a shift in the political outlook of the general populace, as their outrage over local and national controversies became personal rather than ideological.

That political malaise haunted Philadelphia's black population as well. Though the city's black elite had been extremely active in the abolitionist cause throughout the early part of the century, by 1844 the constant stream of racial violence had begun to affect the black community's effort to create a cohesive body of resistance. As Julie Winch has observed in *Philadelphia's Black Elite*, the events of 1838 and a subsequent upsurge in racial violence in 1842 had left "a legacy of bitterness and division."[91] As the heart of the antislavery debate shifted to New England throughout the 1840s, its dramatic interpretation on the Philadelphia stage transformed from a resonant and urgent presence into parody. While 1838 productions of *Othello* had underscored the "imminent danger" of amalgamation, the 1844 staging of *Whigs and Democrats* merely emphasized that the complex questions of abolition and enfranchisement had become inextricably intertwined with self-interest and political corruption.

(7)

In September of 1853 a stage version of Harriet Beecher Stowe's phenomenally successful novel, *Uncle Tom's Cabin*, opened at Philadelphia's National Theatre on Chestnut Street.[92] Though the extraordinary impact of Stowe's book and its subsequent dramatic adaptations have been well documented, the review in Philadelphia's *Sunday Dispatch* offers insight into the immense power of the production to transform a specific and often divided local audience:

> It was a strange thing to see such an audience gathered to see such a piece. Fifteen years ago, the predecessors of the same rough assemblage which now awaited the advent of Uncle Tom would have been foremost in an Abolition riot. The broken panes and sacked dwellings of St. Mary, Shippen and Bedford streets were, in former years, the triumphs of the predecessors of the same class who were now awaiting in anxiety the performance of a drama in which the negro was a hero and the white man the oppressor. Extraordinary mutation indeed, which in less than the cycle of a single generation transforms the rioter into a sympathizer.[93]

The *National Anti-Slavery Standard* also commented on the sea change that *Uncle Tom's Cabin* wrought on Philadelphia audiences: "We remember, about thirteen years ago, the Freeman's Hall in Philadelphia was burned down by a mob. . . . The *Post* is right in dilating upon the great change in public opinion which allows an Anti-Slavery meeting to be held every night at the National Theatre, for such is the performance of *Uncle Tom's Cabin* dramatized."[94] A visitor to Philadelphia from Chambersburg, Pennsylvania, also commented on what seemed to be a "new" antislavery audience attending the theatre, noting in a letter to the *National Era* that he had witnessed a performance of *Uncle Tom's Cabin* at the National Theatre in Philadelphia in October of 1853 with the following sensation: "It is worth far more, to the philanthropist, to see the audience it draws than to witness the performance. High and low are assembled nightly in crowds, and thus the ears and hearts of a large class are reached, who have heretofore been ignorant and cruelly bitter in their prejudices against color." The observer commented that, "There was much applause manifested at the expression of the sentiments of love and liberty and equality of rights (among men whatever color)." He added with satisfaction, "I incline to think that kidnapping is going to be rather unpopular here in the future, and that the cause of Abolition is going to grow in favor with the masses."[95] These comments testify not only to the strong impact of Stowe's novel on the antislavery movement, but to the apparent surprise of the movement's advocates that the theatre could prove such a powerful engine to sway public opinion.[96]

Stowe's novel, written in the wake of the Fugitive Slave Act of 1850, swept both the literary and the theatrical world by storm (even if Stowe's ultimate message about liberated blacks' place in the United States was ambivalent). Prior to the 1853 Philadelphia production, the *Pennsylvania Freeman* had been working assiduously to promote Stowe's novel, publishing poems about Stowe as well as testimonials from former slaveowners who had been converted by its pious message.[97] The *Freeman* had also been chronicling the ever-worsening situation for the city's African American population, including measures before the legislature to forcibly colonize the nation's free black population as well as the rash of kidnappings of free citizens and former slaves in the city in the wake of the Fugitive Slave Act. The *Freeman* expressed its hope that the stage version of *Uncle Tom's Cabin* would have an "elevating" and "moral" impact on its viewers.[98]

Stowe's work also launched hundreds of minstrel parodies—even in abolitionist-friendly Philadelphia. While rival productions of *Uncle Tom* competed at the National Theatre and at the Chestnut Street Theatre, Sanford's Opera House launched its own minstrel version. The *Sunday Dispatch* (which had also included the dramatic production at the National) described it as "a rich picture of Southern life as it is," noting that "Those who have cried over 'Uncle Tom' at the theatres should go to Sanford's and laugh at his funny representation."[99]

By 1860, actors and managers realized that they had little hope of pleasing a populace so bitterly divided over the issue of slavery, and that they would have to relinquish (to some extent) their old habits of trying to remain "neutral" for their audiences. Some managers announced race-blind seating policies that supported the nation's black citizens, acknowledging that those who found their policies distasteful would not frequent their theatres.[100] Other managers, like Mrs. John Drew, who assumed control of Philadelphia's Arch Street Theatre in 1860–61, tailored their repertoires to reflect middle-class antislavery sensibilities. Mrs. Drew reformed the flagging Arch Street Theatre. (The mid-1850s had been a time of economic and artistic upheaval in many local companies.) She brought a talented ensemble to the city and worked closely with her actors to develop their techniques. Mrs. Drew continued to produce *Uncle Tom* throughout the Civil War and also brought the first production of Dion Boucicault's *The Octoroon* to the city.[101]

Ultimately, however, the Philadelphia theatre remained as conflicted as the rest of the nation on how to racially integrate the playhouse—both literally and artistically. Sadly, the final triumph of the abolitionists' dream for complete emancipation brought no sense of completion or closure to the issue. For the next fifty years, the theatre would find itself at something of a loss as to how to dramatize race and slavery on the American stage, or how to address the most traumatic event in nation's history.

NOTES

1. Please note that some of the material in this chapter appears in a larger study, Heather S. Nathans, *Slavery and Sentiment on the American Stage, 1787–1861: Lifting the Veil of Black* (Cambridge, U.K.: Cambridge University Press, 2009).

2. Richard S. Newman, *The Transformation of American Abolitionism: Fighting Slavery in the Early Republic* (Chapel Hill: University of North Carolina Press, 2002). Newman offers a brilliant analysis of how the abolitionist movement shifted its rhetoric during the 1830s.

3. Isaac Bickerstaffe, *The Padlock* (New York: D. Longworth, 1805).

4. Jennifer Stiles has discussed the theory that a "native" black character may have appeared in American drama as early as 1767 in *The Disappointment, or The Force of Credulity,* a play written for the Southwark Theatre in Philadelphia, but never performed there for political reasons (it satirized members of the local Philadelphia community). Some scholars have argued that the character of "Raccoon" is intended to be a caricature of a free African American. Jennifer Stiles, "Import or Immigrant? The Representation of Blacks and Irish on the American Stage from 1767–1856," *Journal of American Drama and Theatre* 12, no. 1 (2000): 38–56.

5. David Brion Davis, *The Problem of Slavery in the Age of Revolution, 1770–1823* (Ithaca, N.Y.: Cornell University Press, 1975), 224.

6. Adam Hochschild, *Bury the Chains: Prophets and Rebels in the Fight to Free an Empire's Slaves* (Boston: Houghton Mifflin Co., 2005), 159.

7. *The Gentleman's Magazine* (London), October 1787.

8. "A Peep into the Antifederal Club," 1793, Library Company of Philadelphia. Also see Marc M. Arkin, "The Federalist Trope: Power and Passion in Abolitionist Rhetoric," *Journal of American History* 88, no. 1 (2001): 75–98.

9. Thomas Southerne, *Oroonoko* (London: Playford, 1699).

10. George Colman, *Inkle and Yarico* (New York: D. Longworth, 1806).

11. An early American acting edition of the play described Yarico's costume as an intriguing combination of European, African, and Indian dress: "White and colored striped muslin dress, with colored feathers and ornaments, leopard skin's drapery across one shoulder, dark flesh colored stockings and arms, various colored feathers in head, a quantity of colored beads around the neck, head, wrists, arms, and ankles [sic]" (costume notes from a 1794 edition of the play, printed in Boston from a production at the Federal Street Theatre, in private collection of the author). The character of Yarico was played in Philadelphia by the lovely Miss Tuke (who later married the company manager, Lewis Hallam Jr.). Tuke was a legendary beauty, and it is hardly surprising that audiences would have flocked to see her in a role that revealed her physical charms. See Hugh F. Rankin, *The Theater in Colonial America* (Chapel Hill: University of North

Carolina Press, 1965), 179. Rankin cites a letter in which an audience member expresses his desire for Miss Tuke and his disgust that she is marrying Hallam (who was old enough to be her father, if not her grandfather).

12. The 1806 edition of *Inkle and Yarico* published in New York contained a foreword by British author Elizabeth Inchbald that stressed the antislavery message of the play.

13. William Macready, *The Irishman in London, or The Happy African* (New York: Samuel French, n.d.).

14. Macready, *The Irishman in London*, 14.

15. *Aurora*, August 6, 1793.

16. Newspapers are an invaluable source of information on the number of times particular plays were produced during a given period. Also see the daybook compiled by Thomas Clark Pollock, *The Philadelphia Theatre in the Eighteenth Century, Together with the Day Book of the Same Period* (New York: Greenwood Press, 1968).

17. See Nathans, *Early American Theatre*, 70.

18. *A Narrative of the Proceedings of the Black People During the late Awful Calamity in Philadelphia* (Philadelphia, 1794), 17–18. In the narrative, Richard Allen and Absalom Jones respond to Mathew Carey's critique of the conduct of the city's black residents during the epidemic. Also see Martin S. Pernick, "Politics, Parties, and Pestilence: Epidemic Yellow Fever in Philadelphia and the Rise of the First Party System," *William and Mary Quarterly* 29 (October 1972): 559–86.

19. Cited in Gary B. Nash, *Forging Freedom: The Formation of Philadelphia's Black Community, 1720–1840* (Cambridge, Mass.: Harvard University Press, 1988).

20. John Murdock, *The Triumphs of Love, or Happy Reconciliation* (Philadelphia: R. Fowell, 1795).

21. Murdock, *The Triumphs of Love*, 52.

22. *Aurora*, May 25, 1795. For more on Murdock's career, see Heather S. Nathans, *Early American Theatre from the Revolution to Thomas Jefferson: Into the Hands of the People* (Cambridge, U.K.: Cambridge University Press, 2003).

23. *Federal Gazette and Philadelphia Evening Post*, November 19, 1789.

24. John Frick, *Theatre, Culture, and Temperance Reform in Nineteenth Century America* (Cambridge, U.K.: Cambridge University Press, 2003), 36. By the late 1820s, many northern cities had formed black temperance societies. Reports of their meetings appeared regularly in African American newspapers such as *Freedom's Journal*. In 1796, a group of African Americans in Boston created a temperance organization which warned its members, "Any member bringing on himself a sickness or disorder by intemperance shall not be considered as entitled to any benefits of assistance from the society" (cited in Frick, *Theatre, Culture, and Temperance Reform*, 36).

25. Gary B. Nash, *Freedom by Degrees: Emancipation in Pennsylvania and Its Aftermath* (New York: Oxford University Press, 1991), 129.

26. John Murdock, *The Politicians, or A State of Things* (Philadelphia, 1798). The play was published but never produced, the managers of the Chestnut Street Theatre deeming it too controversial for audiences already on edge from the difficult party politics of the late 1790s. It merits study as a working-class perspective on the political schism produced by the debates over the 1795 Jay Treaty. See Nathans, *Early American Theatre*, 92–95.

27. The change appears most visible in Democratic newspapers such as the Philadelphia *Aurora* which had been antislavery before 1800 but shifted its sentiments after Jefferson's election. See Peter S. Onuf, "To Declare Them a Free and Independent People: Race, Slavery, and

National Identity in Jefferson's Thought," *Journal of the Early Republic* 18, no. 1 (1998): 1–46. I am also indebted to my colleague Seth Cotlar at Willamette University for a fascinating explanation of the post-revolutionary transformation of American newspapers.

28. James Cobb, *Paul and Virginia* (New York: D. Longworth, 1806).

29. Cobb, *Paul and Virginia*, 7. It should be noted that these lines are from the "Americanized" version of the script. The British version *praises* Britain for its progressive antislavery policies, and Dominique claims his freedom as his British birthright.

30. Cobb, *Paul and Virginia*, 7.

31. Gabriel's plans for rebellion began after he was branded for attacking a white man—an interesting parallel to Alambra's attack on his white overseer.

32. *Aurora*, September 23, 1800. Articles in the various Philadelphia newspapers from September 24 to October 8 dispute the various theories of who was to blame for Gabriel's uprising and whether it could be connected to the trouble in the West Indies. The *Aurora* blamed the British, while the *Gazette of the United States* blamed the French. Their conflicting accusations are hardly surprising, given the political positions of each paper.

33. Cobb, *Paul and Virginia*, 10.

34. The novel and play emerged in Great Britain just as the abolitionist movement in that country had begun to reassert itself after a stagnant period during which Wilberforce's abolitionist proposals had been defeated in Parliament. The language of the play would seem to reflect the renewed energy of the movement in England. In the meantime, the United States continued to vacillate on the expansion of slavery within the Indiana and Louisiana Territories.

35. Nash, *Forging Freedom*, 105.

36. Ibid.

37. William Dunlap, *The Africans, or War, Love, and Duty* (Philadelphia: M. Carey, 1811). Dunlap adapted his version of the play from two earlier versions: one by German author Augustus von Kotzebue, and the other by British playwright George Colman. An acting edition with Dunlap's scenic descriptions and stage directions may be found in Houghton Library, Harvard University.

38. Davis, *The Problem of Slavery*, 240–41.

39. These were descriptions applied to the post-revolutionary theatre by its advocates. Dunlap described theatre as a "powerful engine" in his *History of American Theatre*, and the men who petitioned to establish a Boston theatre described it as a venture to "polish the manners and habits of society." See William Dunlap, *History of American Theatre* (New York: Burt Franklin, 1968); "Petition for a clause for a theatre," October 8, 1791, Miscellaneous Manuscripts, Massachusetts Historical Society. Also see Nathans, *Early American Theatre*, for a discussion of how the theatre's early supporters positioned it in the cultural and intellectual structure of the new nation.

40. Dunlap, *The Africans*, 89.

41. For more on how whites understood "African" culture in America see Shane White, "A Question of Style: Blacks In and Around New York City in the Late 18th Century," *Journal of American Folklore* 102 (1989): 24. In particular, White recounts an incident specifically related to Dunlap and his understanding of black dialect. Also see Roger D. Abrahams, *Singing the Master: The Emergence of African American Culture in the Plantation South* (New York: Pantheon, 1992). For *The Africans*, Dunlap noted that half the performers in the play wore blackface (at least

eleven actors), which would be an extraordinarily large number of "black" bodies onstage for that time.

42. Dunlap, *The Africans*, 107

43. Nash, *Forging Freedom*, 184–85. *The Africans* enjoyed its greatest popularity from 1810 to 1816; after that, its popularity in the repertoire dwindled.

44. T. S. Smith (London) to Roberts Vaux (Philadelphia), September 19, 1817, Vaux Family Papers, Historical Society of Pennsylvania, Philadelphia. Smith continues in his letter: "A colony, or even the semblance of one, formed on the African coast, may furnish the Legislatures of the Southern states with a pretext for the enactment of laws prohibiting the residence of free blacks among them. This then would be banishment without any crime alleged; To the hardened slaveholder it would be of little moment whether they perished on the voyage or lived a few years longer in misery along the desert coast."

45. Though many theatres experienced a lull in their activities during the War of 1812, there were, nevertheless, roughly one hundred productions of plays with African or Afro-Caribbean characters presented on stages in Charleston, Richmond, Baltimore, Philadelphia, New York, Boston, and even in parts of Kentucky and Ohio between the beginning of hostilities and the first meeting of the ACS in 1817.

46. The eventual implementation of the "gag rule" seems to have produced a temporary decline in the number of plays representing enslaved African characters, as well as a decrease in press coverage for those dramas.

47. See Dale Cockrell, *Demons of Disorder: Early Blackface Minstrels and Their World* (Cambridge, U.K.: Cambridge University Press, 1997), and William J. Mahar Jr., *Behind the Burnt Cork Mask: Early Blackface Minstrelsy and American Popular Culture* (Urbana: University of Illinois Press, 1999).

48. W. T. Lhammon Jr., *Raising Cain: Blackface Performance from Jim Crow to Hip Hop* (Cambridge, Mass.: Harvard University Press, 1998), 43.

49. *Genius of Universal Emancipation* 1, no. 6 (1834).

50. The characters of Selico and Torribal in *The Africans* (1810) offer examples of this kind of "passive" representation of "noble" black characters on the American stage. They are both eloquent speakers but take little action on their own behalf. One of the few plays to depict blacks in an active role in the cause of emancipation was William Alexander Brown's *The Drama of King Shotaway*. The play, now lost, was written by Brown (the African American manager of the African Grove Theatre) and tells the story of a slave uprising in the West Indies. For more on Brown, see McAllister, *White People do not know how to behave at entertainments designed for ladies and gentlemen of color: William Brown's African and American Theater* (Chapel Hill: University of North Carolina Press, 2003).

51. Joseph Roach, "The Emergence of the American Actor," in *The Cambridge History of American Theatre, Volume 1: Beginnings to 1870*, ed. Don B. Wilmeth and Christopher Bigsby (Cambridge, U.K.: Cambridge University Press, 1998), 361. Even the 1849 Astor Place Riot— perhaps the best-known theatre riot in American history—had an abolitionist connection. The rioters who attacked the Opera House simultaneously raided a meeting of the American Anti-Slavery Society and the American Foreign Anti-Slavery Society. Roach, "The Emergence of the American Actor," 362.

52. Nash, *Forging Freedom*, 273–74. It should be noted that much of this rioting took place

within a few blocks of the city's theatres, which were located on Chestnut, Walnut, and Arch streets, between Fourth and Fourteenth streets.

53. See William B. Wood, *Personal Recollections of the Stage* (Philadelphia: H. C. Baird, 1855), and Charles Durang, *The Philadelphia Stage from the Year 1749 to the Year 1855* (printed in the Philadelphia *Sunday Dispatch* in thirty volumes).

54. Sylviane A. Diouf, *Servants of Allah: African Muslims Enslaved in the Americas* (New York: New York University Press, 1998), 141.

55. Wood, *Personal Recollections of the Stage*, 403. Also see Arthur Herman Wilson, *A History of the Philadelphia Theatre to 1855* (New York: Greenwood Press, 1968). Wilson's work offers a day-book of performances (much like Pollock's collection cited earlier). It is an invaluable research tool.

56. Robert Montgomery Bird, *The Gladiator*, in Richard Moody, ed., *Dramas from the American Theatre, 1762–1909* (New York: World Publishing Co., 1966).

57. Cited in David Grimsted, *Melodrama Unveiled: American Theatre and Culture, 1800–1850* (Berkeley: University of California Press, 1968), 169.

58. Grimsted, *Melodrama Unveiled*, 169.

59. Cited in Moody, ed., *Dramas from the American Theatre*, 239–40. Also see Richard Harris, "A Young Dramatist's Diary: The Secret Records of R. M. Bird," *University of Pennsylvania Chronicle* 25 (1959): 8–24.

60. Durang, *The Philadelphia Stage*, vol. 3. (Note that the history was printed in thirty separate "volumes" in the Philadelphia *Sunday Dispatch*; thus the sections of the work are referred to by their "volume" number, rather than by date, page, etc.).

61. Bird, *The Gladiator*, 254. Also see Walter J. Meserve, *Heralds of Promise: The Drama of the American People in the Age of Jackson, 1829–1849* (New York: Greenwood Press, 1986), 62. While Meserve notes the suggestive timing of *The Gladiator*'s debut, he seems less interested in its political ramifications than in the structure and quality of the text itself.

62. Newman, *The Transformation of American Abolitionism*, 130.

63. *History of the Pennsylvania Hall which was destroyed by a mob on the 17th of May, 1838* (Philadelphia: Merrihew and Gunn, 1839), 1.

64. *Philadelphia Sunday Courier*, May 19, 1838.

65. The *New Orleans True American* circulated a story that "It was given out that a white woman who had married a Negro was to give a lecture on abolition [in the hall]" (May 36, 1838). Newspapers across the country carried versions of the event and its causes. For examples see *The Augusta* (Ga.) *Chronicle and Sentinel*, *The U.S. Gazette*, *The Philadelphia National Gazette*, *The Charleston* (S.C.) *Gazette*, *The Alexandria* (Va.) *Gazette*, and the *Hamilton* (Ohio) *Intelligencer*. The *Hamilton Intelligencer* claimed that Garrison had been speaking when the riot began and that he had been "advocating the doctrine of amalgamation." In fact, Garrison was *not* speaking on the night of the riot, nor had he endorsed amalgamation. The *Intelligencer*'s story is intriguing for what it reveals about the spread of misinformation concerning the event (*Hamilton Intelligencer*, May 31, 1838).

66. *Philadelphia Sunday Courier*, July 21, 1838.

67. Nash, *Forging Freedom*, 278.

68. *Poulson's Daily Advertiser*, May 19, 1838.

69. Ibid., May 23, 1838.

70. Ibid., May 19, 1838.

71. Like the Chestnut Street Theatre, the Walnut Street playhouse had a capacity of approximately two thousand. It is difficult to give specific estimates for theatre seating in this period for a number of reasons: theatres did not use individual seats in the pit or gallery, but rather wooden benches, whose seating capacity depended on the size of their occupants; theatres continually remodeled their interiors (sometimes on a yearly basis); what generally survives are not *total* seat counts in a theatre, but records of ticket sales, which tend to fluctuate.

72. Grimsted, *Melodrama Unveiled*, 254. Counting the plays listed in the daybook, *A History of the Philadelphia Theatre, 1835–1855*, suggests that only *Richard III* rivaled *Othello* for number of productions in 1838, and two of those productions are listed as being "partial" (which may mean that the company performed famous scenes or tableaux from *Richard III*, rather than the entire production). In her dissertation, Elaine Brousseau notes that *Othello* was surprisingly popular throughout the South in the years before the Civil War, including cities such as New Orleans, Mobile, Memphis, and Charleston. However, she also notes that the Othellos in these cities were played as "nearly white" and that newspaper reviews skirted the issue of Othello's racial identity. (Elaine Brousseau, "Othello, Shylock, and the Face of White Anxiety," Ph.D. diss., University of Massachusetts at Amherst, 2002, www-unix.oit.umass.edu/~elaineb/Chapter.html, accessed on May 5, 2005).

73. Since the mid-1830s, New England abolitionists had faced persistent charges of promoting "amalgamation"—charges which activists alternately deflected and denied. And while the "Life in Philadelphia" cartoon series of the 1830s had featured satirical images of blacks and whites intermingling, the vitriol of the 1838 attacks in Philadelphia was something new.

74. *Philadelphia Pennsylvanian* cited in the *New York Mirror*, November 26, 1863. Also see Barbara Alden, "Differences in the Conception of Othello's Character as Seen in the Performance of Three Important Nineteenth-Century Actors on the American Stage: Edwin Forrest, Edwin Booth, and Tomaso Salvini," Ph.D. diss., University of Chicago, 1950, 77.

75. Michael F. Holt, *The Rise and Fall of the American Whig Party: Jacksonian Politics and the Outset of the Civil War* (New York: Oxford University Press, 1999), 95–108.

76. Cited in Alden, "Differences in the Conception of Othello's Character," 101. Also see the *New York Mirror*, December 15, 1863. The *Mirror* described the way in which Forrest's Othello embraced Desdemona: "His arms were twined 'round Desdemona, his hand played with her ringlets, and his gaze was riveted on her as if he would devour her with his eyes." Forrest also kissed her forehead at one point in the play.

77. Cited in Grimsted, *Melodrama Unveiled*, 114.

78. *Poulson's Daily Advertiser*, May 26, 1838. There is obviously an unexplored gender issue embedded in this incident as well, as women were becoming increasingly active in the abolitionist cause, presenting petitions to the government, speaking at rallies, etc. There is an intriguing comparison to be made with Desdemona's bold action in speaking before the Venetian Senate.

79. In November 1828, *Freedom's Journal* included a story that recalled an essay written in 1788 under the pen name "Othello." The essay, originally published in Baltimore, protested the continuance of slavery in the wake of the revolution: "When America opposed the pretensions of England, she declared that all men have the same rights. After having manifested her hatred against tyrants, ought she to have abandoned her principles?" (November 21, 1828). In 1795, a group of free blacks organized the Othello African Methodist Episcopal Church in a little town

also known as Othello (located near Cumberland County, N.J.). Philadelphia minister Richard Allen had early ties to the church. It also later became a stop on the Underground Railroad.

80. *Colored American*, June 23, 1839.

81. Ibid., September 28, 1839.

82. Nash, *Forging Freedom*, 278.

83. *Spirit of the Times* cited in Nash, *Forging Freedom*, 278.

84. See Julie Winch, *Philadelphia's Black Elite: Activism, Accommodation, and the Struggle for Autonomy, 1748–1848* (Philadelphia: Temple University Press, 1988). Winch offers an excellent analysis of the trials that the city's black community faced in the wake of the Pennsylvania Hall incident.

85. James Ewell Heath, *Whigs and Democrats* (Richmond, Va.: T. W. White, 1839).

86. The play's debut does not seem to have excited as much interest as its 1844 revival.

87. For a description of the complicated transactions in the Philadelphia companies during this decade see Weldon B. Durham, *American Theatre Companies, 1749–1887* (Westport, Conn.: Greenwood Press, 1986). Durham describes the personnel of the various companies in meticulous detail.

88. *Philadelphia Gazette and Commercial Intelligencer*, January 1, 8; February 5, 1844.

89. Ibid., October 17, 1844.

90. *The Pennsylvanian*, January 8, 11; October 11, 1844.

91. Winch, *Philadelphia's Black Elite*, 151.

92. George Aiken, *Uncle Tom's Cabin*, in Richard Moody, ed., *Dramas from the American Theatre, 1762–1909* (New York: World Publishing Co., 1966).

93. *Sunday Dispatch*, September 11, 1853.

94. *National Anti-Slavery Standard*, August 20, 1853.

95. *National Era*, October 27, 1853.

96. *Pennsylvania Freeman*, September 22, 1853.

97. Ibid., August 28, 1852, September 4, 1852, October 10 and 23, 1852, February 7, 1853. Each of these issues contains some tribute to Stowe, whether a poem written in her honor or a paragraph of praise for the novel or a letter from a repentant former slaveowner.

98. Ibid., September 22, 1853. Also see April 22, 1852, for report on forcible attempts to colonize free African Americans and for an account of an April 18, 1852, "Meeting of Colored People at the Philadelphia Institute to protest a proposed measure in the Legislature," about the mandatory eviction of free blacks.

99. *Sunday Dispatch*, October 16 and 30, 1853.

100. Kimball actually testified on behalf of black Bostonian William Cooper Nell, who brought a lawsuit against another Boston theatre because it had denied him the right to sit in the "white" section of the theatre (unpublished biographical essay on Nell, Manuscript Collections, Boston Public Library). For more on Nell and the theatre, see Donald M. Jacobs, ed., *Courage and Conscience: Black and White Abolitionists in Boston* (Bloomington: Indiana University Press, 1993).

101. Durham, *American Theatre Companies* (See chapters on Arch Street, Chestnut Street, and Walnut Street theatres).

CHAPTER 9

"Beautiful Providences"

William Still, the Vigilance Committee, and
Abolitionists in the Age of Sectionalism

ELIZABETH VARON

These wonderful events, and many others such as these, now being enacted before the American people, will, one day, be justly appreciated. Now, deemed, unworthy of the notice of any, save fanatical Abolitionists, these acts of sublime heroism, of lofty self-sacrifice, of patient martyrdom, these beautiful Providences, these hair-breadth escapes and terrible dangers, will yet become the themes of the popular literature of this nation, and will excite the admiration, the reverence and the indignation of the generations yet to come.

—"A Philadelphia Correspondent," *National Anti-Slavery Standard*, 1855.

This stirring prophecy from February of 1855 paid homage to the heroic deeds of the embattled Underground Railroad. The prophecy was woven into a report on one of the UGRR's most dramatic and unlikely success stories: the escape from slavery of Peter Freedman. As a young boy, Peter had been "stolen away" from his family somewhere near the Delaware River and taken, as a slave, to Kentucky, only to be sold again, many years later, into the Deep South. Through a series of ingenious ruses, and with the help of some well-meaning whites, Peter had, in 1850, bought his freedom and then undertaken a grueling journey of fifteen hundred miles from Alabama, north to Philadelphia, driven by images of a distant past he only dimly remembered.

When he arrived in Philadelphia, UGRR activists directed Peter to William Still, at the Anti-Slavery Office; Still could help reunite him, Freeman was told, with his family. As so many fugitives had before, Peter told William his story. Still listened and then asked the names of Peter Freedman's parents. Freedman explained that he "had been so young at the time when separated from his parents as not to know even their last names." But he did know their first names: his mother was Sidney, and his father Levin. Now the scene turned surreal for Still. For these fragments of information, which had been so fragile a foundation for Freedman's hopes, carried, for Still, the weight of revelation. Still understood, as soon as he heard the words "Sidney" and "Levin," that a miracle had transpired. The stranger, Peter Freedman, was his long-lost older brother.[1]

Peter and William had little chance to savor their reunion as, a mere month later, Congress passed the controversial and explosive Fugitive Slave Act. For William Still, the implications of the law were clear: the Underground Railroad had to extend its reach into Canada, where fugitives would be beyond the reach of American slave-catchers. While William Still turned his gaze northward, Peter Still turned his gaze southward, to Alabama, where his own wife and children still languished in slavery. Just as the law was taking effect, Peter embarked on a dangerous journey back into the South to orchestrate a complex plan for redeeming his family. The plan failed—and the family's owner informed Peter that it would take a king's ransom of five thousand dollars for him to purchase their freedom. Undeterred, Peter vowed to raise the funds. He embarked on a lecture tour of the North, during which he enraptured audiences with tales of his own escape; by the fall of 1854, he had raised sufficient donations to at last bring his family northward. These were the "wonderful events" that occasioned the "Philadelphia Correspondent" (perhaps it was William Still?) to herald a future of glory and vindication.[2]

To imagine such vindication was an act of faith. For in the 1850s, the Still brothers and their antislavery allies confronted not only the challenge of perfecting the Underground Railroad, but a second, equally formidable challenge. With so many fugitives seeking refuge in Canada and some free blacks arguing in despair that emigration out of the irredeemably corrupt United States was the only choice left them, how could Philadelphia abolitionists herald the prospects of free blacks, and of racial equality, in America? How could they claim that the United States could still be redeemed? They did so by publicly elaborating the case that Philadelphia was *the* crucial battleground in the rapidly escalating struggle between Slavery and Freedom: the city had a distinct visibility, which gave its citizens a special mandate to lead the forces of freedom.

The symbol of the city's pride of place in the freedom struggle was the new Vigilance Committee, established in 1852 to fill the void left by the older, disintegrating "Vigilant Committee." Founded in 1837, the original committee had worked assiduously to aid fugitives and had helped to orchestrate two of the most daring and memorable slave escapes of the antebellum era: the flight of William and Ellen Craft from Georgia, and that of Henry "Box" Brown from Virginia. But a series of setbacks—violent attacks by anti-abolition mobs, tactical schisms and feuds within the antislavery movement, and new waves of reprisals against free blacks who dared defy the 1850 law, as in the Christiana Riot of 1851—left the old committee "disorganized and scattered." A more robust organization was required, and so nineteen of Philadelphia's most prominent abolitionists, with Still at their head, met on December 9, 1852, to constitute themselves the improved "Vigilance Committee" of Philadelphia. It would be led, they vowed, by men of "known responsibility" and would "discharge its duties with promptness and system." Still was appointed as chairman of the "Acting Committee" entrusted with the daily operations, including fundraising and record-keeping, of the organization.[3]

The members of the Vigilance Committee represented a broad cross-section of Philadelphia's reform network and a wide variety of institutional affiliations. Joining Still on the four-man Acting Committee was one of the city's most respected black entrepreneurs, Jacob C. White. A veteran of the first Vigilant Committee, White was also a stalwart of the free produce movement, the Gilbert Lyceum (a literary society), and the Moral Reform Society; superintendent of the Sabbath School of the First (Colored) Presbyterian Church; a proprietor of Lebanon Cemetery, one of the few black-owned burial grounds in the city; and a founder of Snow Hill/Free Haven, the southern New Jersey town established by abolitionists as a refuge for blacks from slavery and prejudice. One of his fellow founders of Snow Hill, Nathaniel W. Depee, was also appointed to the Acting Committee in December of 1852; Depee had been visible in black community politics since the 1830s, especially in the city's longstanding anti-colonization crusade. The Acting Committee was rounded out by Passmore Williamson, a white Quaker businessman, active in both the PAS and PAAS.[4]

The remaining members of the Vigilance Committee had their own distinct leadership credentials in the fields of antislavery politics, education, and religious uplift. J. Miller McKim, a white Presbyterian minister and newspaper editor, was among William Lloyd Garrison's closest confidantes; Robert Purvis had headed the original Vigilant Committee and was renowned as a powerful abolition orator. Charles Reason, a professor of Haitian descent, was ranked by his contemporaries alongside Frederick Douglass and Martin Delany as one of the era's greatest black intellectuals, while John P. Burr served on the board of the pioneering newspaper *The Colored American*, founded the Demosthenian

Institute (a literary society), and was a regular at reform conventions in the 1830s and 1840s. Jeremiah Asher was pastor of Shiloh Church, while Henry Gordon and Morris (sometimes spelled Maurice) Hall were active in the charitable and political enterprises of Bethel A.M.E. Church and of the Clayton Durham Society, a mutual aid association. Indeed, Hall, who had been admitted to the church by the venerable Richard Allen, was among the founders of its Sabbath School. Isaiah C. Wears, son of Vigilant Committee member Josiah C. Wears, assumed a prominent role in the campaign by Philadelphia blacks to have the vote reinstated after the disfranchisement provision of 1838. He was frequently a delegate at the "Negro Suffrage Conventions" held in northern cities in the 1840s and 1850s, and was respected for his skill as a debater. While men such as White, Burr, Hall, and Purvis represented the old guard among Philadelphia abolitionists, Wears, Williamson, and Still represented the new generation.[5]

Each of the men on the Vigilance Committee boasted his own antislavery credentials, in the form of contributions to the PAS, PAAS, and anti-colonization movement.[6] The committee worked closely with a network of antislavery women, whose credentials were no less impressive. These women included Quaker activists Graceanna Lewis and Abigail Goodwin, who kept safehouses for fugitive slaves; Pennsylvania Female Anti-Slavery Society officers Mary Grew and Sara Pugh, who raised funds, submitted petitions, and generated publicity for the immediatist cause; and popular poet and lecturer Frances Ellen Watkins Harper, who became an "agent" of the Pennsylvania Anti-Slavery Society after "making her home at the station of the Underground Rail Road, where she frequently saw passengers and heard their melting tales of suffering and wrong." Together, the members of this vanguard were participants in a wide range of meetings and conventions that were covered in detail by the antislavery press and that brought them into frequent contact with their counterparts in other northern cities.[7]

Their argument for Philadelphia's centrality to the antislavery struggle took a number of forms. At times, Philadelphia's abolitionists simply invoked the city's proud antislavery legacy. Still and his fellow immediatists believed fervently that the United States could be purged of the sin the slavery; they understood that they were the heirs of Benezet and Allen, Forten and Woolman. The Vigilance Committee aligned itself in its meetings and reports with the pioneering efforts of the PAS, or the "Old Abolition Society," as they routinely called it, and with early antislavery leaders such as Franklin and Rush.[8]

At other times Philadelphia abolitionists used the antislavery press and lecture circuit to trumpet their extraordinary success, in the present, at making the city the gateway to freedom for fugitives. By the mid-1850s, the term "Underground Railroad" was used openly in the southern and northern dailies alike, as well as in the Canadian antislavery press, and Pennsylvania activists reveled in informing the public that "fugitives from southern injustice" were "coming thick and fast" into Philadelphia—they streamed "almost daily, through this city," the twenty-second annual report of the Philadelphia Female Anti-Slavery Society declared, on their way to freedom. Indeed, "the underground railroad through Philadelphia has been doing such a smashing business of late," the Vigilance Committee reported to the *National Anti-Slavery Standard* in November of 1854, "that it is found difficult to keep up with expenses."[9]

Moreover, Still and his allies took measures to reveal the hidden world of slave resistance and the inner workings of the "railroad" itself—but they did so strategically. If antislavery activists could imagine and fantasize, in the mid-1850s, that a day would come when their daring exploits would command universal admiration, they were keenly aware that such a day was still far off. In the present time of crisis, with slaveholders brandishing southern nationalism and secession as never before, Philadelphia abolitionists had to battle for public support as never before. While the original Vigilant Committee had cloaked its operations in secrecy, a primary goal of the new Vigilance Committee was to win converts and bring in contributions by reassuring their fellow citizens that the organization was both truthful and well run. And so, remarkably, in December of 1853 the committee, through the *Pennsylvania Freeman*, got out the word that "any of our friends who may be interested in the cause" could go to the Antislavery Office and inspect the record books, "containing accurate accounts of the number of escapees, the amount of expenditures, receipts &c.," kept by Still—"thereby affording the most abundant satisfaction to all concerned."[10]

The stories of fugitives in Still's record books were not kept secret, but drawn upon, strategically, to project the message that Philadelphia was the hub, and its Vigilance Committee the nerve center, of the UGRR. The main exponent of this message was McKim, who was a fixture on the transatlantic abolitionist lecture circuit. Highlighting Philadelphia's role as a "gateway" in the "thoroughfare from the south to the north," McKim, on a speaking tour of Great Britain in the fall of 1853, invited his audiences to imagine him "at home in the office of the Anti Slavery Society . . . at this season of the year in particular," receiving fugitives as they arrived—"to see them come covered in dust, and hear the tale of each." He routinely shared pieces of such tales, not only of Henry Box Brown and the Crafts and others who themselves had become fixtures on the lecture circuit, but of fugitives who had not "gone public" with their stories. For example, at a December 1853 antislavery meeting in Philadelphia, McKim gave a "brief account" of a fugitive who had fought with slave hunters in Maryland, been thrown in jail, and then, despite having been badly wounded in the fight, effected a daring escape using a rope and some nails; once he reached Philadelphia, the Vigilance Committee sent him on to Canada. For public consumption, McKim abridged the story to take out telling details—details that are spelled out in Still's "Journal C of Station No. 2 of the Underground Railroad." The escape had transpired in November, just one month before McKim gave his public account.[11]

In other words, the Vigilance Committee maintained a delicate balance between secrecy and publicity; as soon as fugitives reached safety, their stories were mobilized to pique the public's interest. This balancing act was dramatized in the summer of 1855 by the Jane Johnson case—or the "Philadelphia Slave case," as it came to be known—in which William Still, along with his fellow committee member Passmore Williamson and a group of five other abolitionists, rescued the slave Jane Johnson and her children. The slaves were docked in Philadelphia en route to New York with their master, John H. Wheeler, the U.S. minister to Nicaragua. Still informed Johnson, right before Wheeler's eyes, that she was free to leave the boat and that, once she set foot on Pennsylvania soil, she was no longer a slave (according to Pennsylvania law, a slave brought into the state by her master, but not a fugitive, could so claim freedom); when Johnson asserted that she desired to seize that freedom, Still spirited her away from the scene, to a safehouse (in this case, his own home), where she could begin to envision a new life. The livid Wheeler charged Still, Williamson, and the others with the forcible abduction of Johnson. In the legal proceedings that ensued, Williamson was incarcerated for contempt of court, for refusing to disclose the whereabouts of the Johnsons. He served months in prison, during which the abolitionists lionized him as a martyr. Still was also tried, but he was acquitted, as Jane Johnson herself came out of hiding to repudiate the charge that she had been abducted and to testify that she and her children had long yearned to achieve liberty. (Johnson eventually settled in Boston.)[12]

Over the course of the controversy, Still and the Vigilance Committee used the antislavery press to argue that Wheeler and John Kane, the Federal District Court judge who had clapped Williamson into prison, were embodiments of the dreaded "Slave Power Conspiracy": Wheeler and Kane embodied the unholy alliance of southern slaveholders and northern Democrats that long held the government in its sway. While the Democratic press churned out inflammatory accounts of the Johnson rescue, portraying the abolitionists as a lawless mob and Johnson as "worthless and degraded" pawn, Still furnished the antislavery press with his own account, one that emphasized Johnson's agency and dignity. She was no pawn of the abolitionists, he asserted—but a woman of "uncommon good sense . . . and genteel manners," who had the dream of freedom "deep in her heart before leaving the South." Still quoted what she had said to him, repeatedly, in the confrontation on the docks: "I want my freedom—ALWAYS wanted to be free!!" Confronted with evidence of Kane's "villainy" and Williamson and Johnson's bravery, many white Philadelphians who had been wary of abolitionism or who fancied themselves "neutral" on the slavery question developed a newfound sympathy for the antislavery cause.[13]

Moreover, in the very months that her rescue and Passmore Williamson's imprisonment became a cause célèbre, bringing a whole new level of press attention to Still and his allies, the Philadelphia Underground managed to effect dozens of other escapes along the routes out of the South and into Canada.[14] They did so thanks to the intrepid work of the most important of their "conductors": Thomas Garrett and Harriet Tubman. Garrett, the Wilmington, Delaware–based station master who assisted more than two hundred slaves to freedom, was a wily practitioner of the balancing act. Garrett was in frequent contact not only with McKim and Still, to whom he and Tubman directed fugitives, but also with Eliza Wigham, secretary of the Edinburgh (Scotland) Ladies' Emancipation Society. That relationship yielded, in the mid-1850s, a steady stream of monetary donations from the Scottish women to the Vigilance Committee and UGRR network. As Garrett's exchange of letters with Wigham shows, he knew just what kinds of privileged information would excite the sympathies and spur the generosity of the ladies' society. In a conspiratorial tone, Garrett wrote Wigham of the remarkable exploits of Tubman, stressing Harriet's mystical courage and spirituality: "she has great confidence God will preserve her from harm in all her missions of mercy." But he stressed also Tubman's need for funds. "God has sent me to you for money" for the fugitives, Tubman told Garrett, in his account, to "pay their expenses to Philadelphia." Wigham and her fellow reformers were only too happy to oblige—and money they sent found its way, Garrett assured them in turn, directly into Tubman's hands. Garrett confessed to Wigham that he had been cautioned by some friends not to relate details of the railroad's operations to her, for fear they would be published "in some of the European papers." But he had decided to throw caution to the wind—both because he trusted Wigham and because he recognized the need for publicity. Garrett regularly attended antislavery meetings in Philadelphia, where he was "pointed out as having assisted slaves." But he had no fear of reprisals: as he proclaimed to Wigham, he wanted "all mankind to know that I would assist all in my power to freedom." Tubman shared this defiant courage; remarkably, she was one of the abolitionists who visited Passmore Williamson in Moyamensing Prison while he was detained in the Johnson case.[15]

Peter Still, too, became a symbol of the Vigilance Committee's balancing act. New details of his story came to light with the publication of *The Kidnapped and the Ransomed* in 1856, written for him by the white author Kate Pickard. Intended as a means to raise money to purchase the freedom of Peter's granddaughter, who was still enslaved in the South, the book testified to Peter's own heroic flight northward, and to the role of William Still and the Vigilance Committee in securing his liberty. Composed in the style of Harriet Beecher Stowe's wildly popular *Uncle Tom's Cabin* (1852), it was hailed in antislavery circles as the "true story" that best proved that Stowe had not exaggerated either slavery's horrors or the heroism of fugitive slaves. But even this set of revelations was strategic. As William Still would later disclose, when *The Underground Rail Road* was published in 1872, Pickard's account had concealed one salient fact about Peter: that his mother Sidney had been a slave. *The Kidnapped and the Ransomed* told readers that Peter, born free to a free family in the North, had been kidnapped and taken south; as such a fate had indeed befallen countless northern blacks, this was a useful and credible fiction. The truth was that Peter's mother Sidney, a slave in Maryland, had escaped to the North but had been unable to bring Peter with her; after her flight, he was sold to a new master. In the 1850s, with the Fugitive Slave Law in effect, the Still family concealed the fact that Sidney was a fugitive and instead upheld her identity as Charity Still, a free-born woman, beyond the reach of slave catchers.[16]

In short, in their publications, speaking tours, and reform meetings, Still and his coworkers in the cause conveyed the message that the Philadelphia UGRR signified *both* the courage of those blacks who were determined, at all costs, to escape American slavery, *and* the courage of those who were determined, at all costs, to fulfill the promise of American freedom. The fugitive slaves whose stories Still so meticulously recorded embodied the first sort of heroism. The Philadelphia Vigilance Committee, as it battled northern racism, represented the second. And Jane Johnson, Harriet Tubman, and Peter Still represented both.

While Philadelphia abolitionists worked to balance the imperatives of secrecy and publicity, they also balanced appeals to the city's pride in its antislavery legacy and prominence, with laments that the legacy had been betrayed. Time and again, abolitionists tried to shame Philadelphia into living up to its professed ideals. If residents of the Keystone State did not rally together in resistance, the *Pennsylvania Freeman* predicted in 1851, the state would be "rendered especially infamous by the new Fugitive Slave Law"; in subsequent years, the paper would frequently decry the shameful "indifference" of Philadelphians to the plight of fugitives. The city's abolitionists understood perfectly well why it was so. "Pennsylvania is peculiarly situated, geographically, commercially, and politically—being under the immediate eye and domination of the South," William Still explained in a May 1855 letter to the *Provincial Freeman*. "Hence, with two exceptions, Illinois and Indiana, Pennsylvania is notoriously the most pro-slavery State this side of Mason and Dixon's line."[17]

In Still's view, to acknowledge the deep divisions within the Keystone State and the city of "brotherly live" was not to diminish the accomplishments of the abolitionists but to amplify them; the antislavery vanguard had overcome enormous odds and obstacles to keep the flame of freedom burning bright. Indeed, Still hoped that by realizing what a unique position they occupied—historically as well as geographically—Pennsylvanians, and black Philadelphians in particular, would draw strength and resolve for coming fight.

Moreover, the Vigilance Committee openly confronted the divisions among black abolitionists over emigration. For emigrationist spokesmen such as Henry Highland Garnet of New York (who had fled slavery in Maryland) and Martin Delany of Pittsburgh, the United States seemed, in the wake of the Fugitive Slave Act, to be irredeemably corrupt. Salvation for blacks, they argued, could only be found beyond its borders, in some refuge such as the Caribbean, South America, or Canada. Meanwhile, growing communities of African Americans in western Canada (Ontario) beckoned fugitives through the medium of two influential newspaper editors: Henry Bibb, a former fugitive from Kentucky, who had published his own slave narrative in 1849, and Mary Ann Shadd (later Cary), a free black émigré from a notable abolitionist family. Bibb and Cary urged blacks, free as well as slave, to join them north of the border, both with images of the opportunities to be found there and with warnings, such as the following, addressed to "fugitives who are tarrying in the United States": "Think not that you are safe and out of danger while you are under the wings of the flesh-devouring eagle of America, which protects the liberties of fugitives from Southern bondage as the wolf protects the lamb."[18]

Here was another balancing act: the members of the Philadelphia Vigilance Committee had to cultivate close working relationships with allies like Cary while rebutting the case that free blacks in the United States should emigrate, en masse, to Canada. Just how they did so is dramatized by the November 1855 public debate over emigration at the Banneker Institute. It pitted Mary Ann Shadd against Isaiah Wears. Shadd took the stage and emphasized the healthy climate, impartial laws, fine soil, and upright citizenry of Canada. Wears countered, respectfully but firmly, by placing mass emigration to Canada "in the same category with African colonization." For free blacks to abandon the United States would have "disastrous consequences": "the slave in his chains would be forsaken, the fugitive would be left unprotected, the ends of coloni- zation would be satisfied, and, in short, the humiliating concession would then appear, as our enemies have said, that the colored man could not be elevated in this country." Wears closed by insisting that the "great progress" African Amer- icans had made was proof that "their elevation would ultimately be effected."[19]

Two key events on the eve of the Civil War, in 1859, illustrate how far the Philadelphia antislavery movement had come since its inception in the revolutionary era—and the challenges it still faced. The first, in the spring, was the trial and release of fugitive slave Daniel Webster. Webster had been arrested near Harrisburg by a deputy marshal in charge of enforcing the 1850 Fugitive Slave Act. He was brought to Philadelphia for trial, to determine if he was, as charged, a Virginia slave who had escaped in 1853 or, as Webster himself insisted, a free black with deep roots in Pennsylvania. Philadelphia abolitionists quickly mobilized for Webster's defense, showcasing their politi- cal savvy and capacity for cooperation. The Vigilance Committee had made a practice, since its rebirth in 1852, of reaching out across the tactical, social, and religious divides within the movement: it tapped the energies of stalwarts of the old PAS, of ardent Garrisonians, and of supporters of the new Republi- can party; of established female antislavery networks; and of a wide array of African American institutions, such as churches, reform societies, and schools. And now that strategy paid off in a signal victory.[20]

Upon receiving word from Harrisburg that Webster had been detained, the Vigilance Committee quickly secured legal counsel for him, along with a continuance to buy time for that team to build a case. The committee then identified African American witnesses from the Harrisburg region who could testify that Webster had been born free and long lived in Pennsylvania. When the trial opened, Philadelphia's antislavery women, led by Lucretia Mott, packed the courtroom to bear witness to such testimony, and Webster's expert legal team made arguments designed to persuade the commissioner hearing the case, and the public too, that Pennsylvania's pride and honor were at stake. When it seemed that the commissioner was going to bar black witnesses from the courtroom, Webster's counsel responded by asking, "Are we in Pennsylvania or Virginia? . . . Shall our witnesses, Pennsylvanians, colored though they be, who are here to testify for liberty, be excluded? Sir, we have had enough of Virginia practice and overseer manners here." The Keystone State, in this formulation, was not only a gateway to freedom for slaves but a bulwark against slaveholder culture and values.[21]

The commissioner, who, the committee had noted hopefully, was of respectable old Quaker stock, relented, and the African American witnesses took the stand. They included a Baptist minister and a Methodist minister, each of whom testified to the moral standing and veracity of Webster. As all of this transpired, over the course of two days, Mott and two dozen other women in the courtroom practiced their own kind of vigilance: they "sat erect, their interest unflagging and their watchfulness enduring to the end." Outside the courtroom, antislavery citizens awaited the verdict; the "revival prayer-meeting in Sansom street . . . allowed a petition to be put up to the God of the oppressed for the deliverance of Daniel." They expected the commissioner to find for the claimant, and to send Daniel back to slavery, as such a tragic outcome had been the norm in the hearings of the past decade. When the commissioner finally did read his decision and pronounced "I order the prisoner to be discharged," the news was met with "deafening bursts of exalting hurrahs." This fugitive case, Philadelphia's abolitionists all agreed, was a "glorious triumph," proof that the "informing power of the anti-slavery enterprise" had at last revolutionized public opinion in the city, and that, as the PAAS's official account of the proceedings put it, "the day of Pennsylvania's redemption draweth nigh."[22]

Only six months later, however, events in Virginia would again expose the deep political fissures within Philadelphia and even within its antislavery ranks. John Brown's failed raid on Harpers Ferry in October of 1859, and his subsequent trial and execution, brought forth expressions of sympathy from black abolitionists and from white Garrisonians, who hailed Brown as a martyred hero. On the day of Brown's execution, African Americans mourned publicly at prayer meetings and by "draping their homes and businesses in black." The Vigilance Committee played a key role in transforming Brown into a martyr: Robert Purvis delivered a stirring address at National Hall in praise of Brown's heroism; J. Miller McKim joined Brown's widow on her trip south to take possession of her husband's corpse so it could be buried in New York; William Still's family housed Mrs. Brown as she passed through Philadelphia on her way north.[23]

But such actions placed the immediatist vanguard, at this moment, outside of the mainstream, as most white Philadelphians deplored the raid as the act of a madman. As a rebuke to abolitionist mourners, such citizens sponsored their own public meeting, attended by a crowd of more than six thousand, to condemn Brown and praise the South for putting him to death. "So great was the hatred of Brown," Gary Nash has written, "that after his execution on December 2, 1859, when the body was brought to Philadelphia by train for undertakers to prepare it for burial, the corpse had to be secreted away to prevent a proslavery riot at the railroad station." In the wake of the raid, the local Republican Party scrambled, as the party's national leadership did, to distance itself from radical abolitionism; this move to the center seemed to pay off politically when, the following year, a moderate Republican ticket carried the city on a platform that emphasized economic policies such as tariff protection. The Republican Party's willingness to give credence to antislavery gradualism, and to old discredited ideas such as colonization, embittered immediatists like Purvis; as the 1860 presidential election approached, Purvis contrasted the cowardice and hypocrisy of Republican leaders with the bravery of Brown, who "believed what he professed, and practiced what he believed."[24]

William Still had recent developments in mind when, in August of 1860, at a Philadelphia meeting to celebrate the anniversary of emancipation in the West Indies, he highlighted—once again—the city's distinctive role in the antislavery struggle. Still told his listeners that because they were "in such close proximity to slavery" and their "movements and actions" were "daily watched" by proslavery forces, they were "directly on the ground" where they could do "by wise and determined effort, what the freed colored people of no other State could possibly do to weaken slavery." If their resolve was strong enough, they "could not fail to strike the most effective blows against oppression."[25]

That same year, Still and a cadre of black activists inaugurated a new chapter in the antislavery movement's long struggle against oppression by founding the "Social, Civil and Statistical Association of the Colored People of Philadelphia." This was a direct extension of the Vigilance Committee and a culmination of trends in black activism. The Statistical Association, in some sense, moved into plain sight the political apparatus that the city's Underground Railroad had elaborated. It also made explicit what had often been implicit in the work of the railroad: that the ultimate goal of the antislavery movement was not abolition but racial equality. The association would do all in its power, its charter read, to "exalt our common humanity and raise us to the God-ordained level of the great brotherhood of man." And in this work, Philadelphia would continue to serve as a model: "we urge the organization of similar associations in the various States," Still noted, "and then of a central society."[26]

The war years would bring to the fore new issues and campaigns, and new alliances, all of which served to keep the Philadelphia civil rights struggle in the national spotlight. The antislavery vanguard now fought on numerous fronts: for desegregation, for the enlistment of black troops, and for enfranchisement. All of these causes were inextricably linked, in reform rhetoric, to the aim of emancipation. The protracted battle to desegregate Philadelphia's streetcars reveals the shifting contours of progressive politics in the city. Early in the war, under the leadership of Still and the Statistical Association, reformers tried to exercise moral suasion with petition campaigns and other appeals to public opinion. These echoed the abolition discourse of the prewar era, especially in their emphasis on the moral imperative for Philadelphia to live up to its own vaunted legacy as freedom's first city. For example, an 1862 petition pointedly noted that Philadelphia lagged behind northern cities such as New York and Boston, which had already desegregated their railway cars. This was a shameful betrayal of the ideals of a place "standing so pre-eminently high for its benevolence, liberality, love of freedom, and Christianity, as the city of brotherly love."[27]

While the moral suasion campaign galvanized Philadelphia's reformers, it failed to secure lasting results. Such results would only be secured once a new generation of leaders took the stage. Exemplified by Octavius Catto, this new generation forged key alliances with Pennsylvania's Radical Republicans, who had gained political momentum from the triumph of wartime emancipation. Catto was a graduate of the Institute of Colored Youth, where he had been mentored by Vigilance Committee members such as the Haitian-born professor Charles L. Reason. After graduation, Catto embarked on his own career as an educator and reformer. He led the way in recruiting black regiments in

Philadelphia and was a founding member in 1864 of the Pennsylvania State Equal Rights League, devoted to "a recognition of the rights of the colored people." After the war, the league, under Catto's leadership, tried a new tack in the fight against streetcar segregation by lobbying for the political support of Radical Republicans in the state legislature. This paid off in March of 1867 when, at long last, the state legislature—at the urging of Senator Morrow B. Lowry, himself an abolitionist from the northwestern section of the commonwealth—passed the "Lowry bill" desegregating the streetcars of the state. An incident two days after the signing of the bill signaled that African Americans were determined that its measures be enforced. Caroline LeCount, herself an Institute of Colored Youth graduate, respected public speaker, and officer of the Ladies' Union Association (a relief society for black soldiers), confronted a conductor who tried to thrown her off a streetcar; invoking the new law, she lodged a complaint with the police, resulting in the conductor's arrest. For LeCount, this was the culmination of African American women's own campaign, which intersected with the men's lobbying efforts, for equal access to the streetcars.[28]

Another banner victory came during Reconstruction, but this one had a tragic postscript. In 1869, Pennsylvania ratified the Fifteenth Amendment; Philadelphia blacks had lobbied heavily, in the state legislature and the U.S. Congress, for suffrage. Many of the Keystone State's Republicans were persuaded that African American voters were vital to ensuring the party's electoral dominance—and black leaders such as Catto argued in turn that the electoral arena was now the primary site for the civil rights struggle. But the idea that the Republican Party would carry on the legacy of antebellum abolitionism met with a terrible backlash from Democrats, and they revived the very tactic they had used to combat immediatism: mob action. Election-day violence in October of 1871 took the life of Octavius Catto, murdered in cold blood by Democratic heavies; Caroline LeCount, Catto's fellow activist and by now his fiancée, was at the scene and identified his body for the police.[29]

In the decades that followed, the survivors of Philadelphia's abolitionist movement would work assiduously to keep the memory of the heroic antislavery crusade, and its fallen martyrs, alive in the public mind. This was the explicit purpose of William Still's publication in 1872 of his monumental *The Underground Rail Road*. But in a sense it had always been his purpose. For he knew that during the tumultuous 1850s and 1860s Philadelphia's abolitionists had sustained their faith in the redemption of the United States by sustaining and extending the very tradition of activism that this book of essays has described. They kept alive a spirit of interracial cooperation and of antislavery cosmopolitanism; worked to integrate abolition more fully into American civic culture; and channeled both their hopes and their frustration into mobilization. "We have a history, or at least, should have one," Still remarked at the 1860 anniversary of West Indian emancipation.[30]

The power of that history to inspire is testified to by an 1873 petition calling for the liberation of slaves in Cuba. Drafted at a meeting at Mother Bethel, the petition was addressed to President Ulysses S. Grant on behalf of "the colored citizens of Philadelphia." The petitioners, who included Vigilance Committee veterans Isaiah Wears and Henry Gordon, urged Grant to support Cuban revolutionaries contending for independence from Spain and for the overthrow of slavery. In striking language, the petition linked the global struggle against slavery to Philadelphia's own distinct status as a beacon of freedom. The petitioners wished for the "prophetic utterances" of the "Revolutionary fathers" to have "world-wide fulfillment." They conjured here not only the founders' struggle against British tyranny, but also black Philadelphians' long struggle against racism. "We the colored citizens of Philadelphia in public meeting assembled do most solemnly invoke the spirit of our Christian fathers," the petitioners continued, and then they named those fathers: Richard Allen, Absalom Jones, James Forten, and others in the generation of black founders. The petitioners also invoked a founding moment: the January 1817 meeting, on the very "scared spot" where they now gathered, at which black Philadelphians had pledged their opposition to colonization. That moment, they noted, inspired future generations with the "power" to fight slavery. The pledge that the 1817 protesters had made—to remain bound in solidarity to the slaves—a new generation of activists now renewed. This for them was the legacy of Philadelphia's long antislavery history: that "the *instinctive* love of liberty" knew no geographical boundaries.[31]

NOTES

1. The most accurate account of this encounter comes from a letter William Still wrote to his friend and antislavery co-worker, J. Miller McKim, on August 8, 1850, just a few days after the brothers' reunion occurred. The letter was published in the *Pennsylvania Freeman*, August 22, 1850. Additional details of the encounter are provided by Still in his magnum opus, *The Underground Rail Road* (Philadelphia: Porter & Coates, 1872), 23–38, and Kate E. R. Pickard, *The Kidnapped and the Ransomed. Recollections of Peter Still and His Wife "Vina," after Forty Years of Slavery* (Syracuse, N.Y.: William T. Hamilton, 1856), 241–55.

2. *National Anti-Slavery Standard*, Feb. 3, 1855; Still, *The Underground Rail Road*, 23–38.

3. *Pennsylvania Freeman*, Dec. 2 and 9, 1852; Joseph A. Borome, "The Vigilant Committee of Philadelphia," *Pennsylvania Magazine of History and Biography* 92 (January 1968): 320–51.

4. For background on White, see Harry C. Silcox, "Philadelphia Negro Educator: Jacob C. White, Jr., 1837–1902," *Pennsylvania Magazine of History and Biography* 97 (Jan. 1973): 75–78. On Depee, see *Colored American*, Sept. 8, 1838; *Frederick Douglass' Paper*, April 29, 1852; *Christian Recorder*, Aug. 20, 1874; and editor's annotations for "Journal of Station C, No. 2 of the Underground Railroad, Agent William Still, 1852–1857," ed. Peter Hinks, Historical Society of Pennsylvania, Philadelphia, www.hsp.org/default.aspx?id=1008. On Williamson, see Nat Brandt and Yanna Koyt Brandt, *In the Shadow of the Civil War: Passmore Williamson and the Rescue of Jane Johnson* (Columbia: University of South Carolina Press, 2007), chap. 2.

5. On McKim and Purvis, see Margaret Hope Bacon, *But One Race: The Life of Robert Purvis* (Albany: State University of New York Press, 2007), 78–80, 119; on Reason, see *Frederick Douglass' Paper*, Nov. 16, 1855, and *Christian Recorder*, Aug. 17, 1876; on Burr, see *Colored American*, Aug. 5, 1837, July 25, 1840, April 24, 1841; on Hall and Gordon, see *Christian Recorder*, Feb. 24, 1866, Jan. 12, 1867, Dec. 4, 1869; on Wears, Harry C. Silcox, "The Black 'Better Class' Political Dilemma: Philadelphia Prototype Isaiah C. Wears," *Pennsylvania Magazine of History and Biography* 113 (Jan. 1989): 45–47.

6. For example, Vigilance Committee Treasurer Charles Wise was a veteran of the PAS, Samuel Nickless was active in anti-colonization protests, and Charles H. Bustill was among the founders of Free Haven (*Colored American* May 23, 1840; *Frederick Douglass' Paper*, April 29, 1852; *Christian Recorder*, Aug. 10, 1874).

7. On these women's contributions to the work of the Vigilance Committee, see Still, *Underground Rail Road*, 740–61; Helen Campbell, "Philadelphia Abolitionists," *The Continent; an Illustrated Weekly Magazine*, January 3, 1883, 1–6; *Friends' Intelligencer*, March 9, 1912, 157; *Provincial Freeman*, March 7, 1857.

8. *Pennsylvania Freeman*, August 25, Dec. 8, 1853.

9. *Twenty-Second Annual Report of the Philadelphia Anti-Slavery Society* (Philadelphia: Merrihew & Thompson, 1856), 14; *National Anti-Slavery Standard*, Nov. 4, 1854; *Provincial Freeman*, July 8, 1854; *Baltimore Sun*, June 30, 1854.

10. *Pennsylvania Freeman*, Dec. 8, 1853.

11. *Pennsylvania Freeman*, Oct. 13, 27, 1853; Dec. 8, 1853. Journal C of Station No. 2 of the Underground Railroad, HSP, Nov. 2, 1853 entry, pp. 20–27.

12. For a detailed account of the Jane Johnson rescue, see Brandt and Brandt, *In the Shadow of the Civil War*.

13. *National Anti-Slavery Standard*, Sept. 29, 1855; *Provincial Freeman*, August 22, 1855; "The Liberation of Jane Johnson," www.librarycompany.org/janejohnson/.

14. *Provincial Freeman*, Aug. 22, 1855; Brandt and Brandt, *In the Shadow of the Civil War*.

15. *Delaware County Republican*, Dec. 23, 1859; James A. McGowan, *Station Master on the Underground Railroad: The Life and Letters of Thomas Garrett* (Jefferson, N.C.: McFarland & Co., 2005); Thomas Garrett to Eliza Wigham, Dec. 16, 1855, and Dec. 27, 1856, Thomas P. Cope Family Papers, Special Collections, Magill Library, Haverford College, Haverford, Pa.; *Provincial Freeman*, May 30, 1857; Kate Clifford Larson, *Bound for the Promised Land: Harriet Tubman, Portrait of an American Hero* (New York: Random House, 2004), 122–25.

16. Pickard, *The Kidnapped and the Ransomed*; Still, *The Underground Rail Road*, 18–19.

17. *Pennsylvania Freeman*, Feb. 13, 1851; Dec. 30, 1852. *Provincial Freeman*, May 5, 1855.

18. *Voice of the Fugitive*, February 12, 1851; Jane Rhodes, *Mary Ann Shad Cary: The Black Press and Protest in the Nineteenth Century* (Bloomington: Indiana University Press, 1998), 110–19.

19. *Provincial Freeman*, Dec. 22, 1855; Rhodes, *Mary Ann Shadd Cary*, 110.

20. *The Arrest, Trial, and Release of Daniel Webster, Fugitive Slave* (Philadelphia: Pennsylvania Anti-Slavery Society, 1859).

21. Ibid., 12–19.

22. Ibid., 27–31.

23. Bacon, *But One Race*, 135; Russell F. Weigley, "The Border City in Civil War, 1854–1865," in Weigley et al., eds., *Philadelphia: A 300-Year History* (New York: W. W. Norton, 1982), 389–93; Gary B. Nash, *First City: Philadelphia and the Forging of Historical Memory* (Philadelphia: University of Pennsylvania Press, 2002), 196–97.

24. Weigley, "The Border City in Civil War," 392; Nash, *First City*, 197; *The Liberator*, May 18, 1860.

25. *National Anti-Slavery Standard*, Aug. 18, 1860.

26. Andrew K. Diemer, "Reconstructing Philadelphia: African Americans and Politics in the Post–Civil War North," *Pennsylvania Magazine of History and Biography* (January 2009): 34–35; *Anglo-African* (New York), March 23, 1861.

27. Diemer, "Reconstructing Philadelphia," 35–37; James M. McPherson, *The Negro's Civil War: How American Blacks Felt and Acted during the War for the Union* (New York: Pantheon Books, 1965), 259–65.

28. Harry C. Silcox, "Nineteenth-Century Philadelphia Black Militant: Octavius V. Catto (1839–1871)," in *African Americans in Pennsylvania: Shifting Historical Perspectives*, ed. Joe William Trotter Jr. and Eric Ledell Smith (University Park: Pennsylvania State University Press, 1997), 198–207; Diemer, "Reconstructing Philadelphia," 37–40; McPherson, *The Negro's Civil War*, 264–65. For women's centrality to the desegregation struggle, see Judith Giesberg, *Army at Home: Women and the Civil War on the Northern Homefront* (Chapel Hill: University of North Carolina Press, 2009).

29. Diemer, "Reconstructing Philadelphia," 55–57; Silcox, "Nineteenth-Century Black Militant," 212–15.

30. *National Anti-Slavery Standard*, Aug. 18, 1860. See also Julie Roy Jeffrey, *Abolitionists Remember: Antislavery Autobiographies and the Unfinished Work of Emancipation* (Chapel Hill: University of North Carolina Press, 2008).

31. *Christian Recorder*, Feb. 13, 1873. On the 1817 protest, see Richard S. Newman, *Freedom's Prophet: Bishop Richard Allen, the AME Church, and the Black Founding Fathers* (New York: NYU Press, 2008), 204–6.

CONTRIBUTORS

RICHARD NEWMAN is Professor of History at Rochester Institute of Technology and the author or editor of several books on American abolitionism. His most recent book, *Freedom's Prophet: Bishop Richard Allen, the AME Church, and the Black Founding Fathers* (New York University Press), was named to Booklist's Top Ten Books of African American Nonfiction in 2009.

JAMES MUELLER is the former Chief Historian of Independence National Historical Park in Philadelphia. Now retired, he splits his time between Florida and Philadelphia.

DEE E. ANDREWS is Professor of History at California State University–East Bay and the author of *The Methodists and Revolutionary America, 1760–1800* (Princeton University Press), which was awarded the Hans Rosenhaupt Memorial Book Award by the Woodrow Wilson National Fellowship Foundation.

IRA BERLIN is Distinguished University Professor at the University of Maryland and the author or editor of numerous books, including *Generations of Captivity: A History of Slaves in the United States* (Harvard University Press), which was awarded the Albert Beveridge Prize by the American Historical Association, and *The Making of African America: The Four Great Migrations* (Viking Press).

W. CALEB MCDANIEL is Assistant Professor of History at Rice University and the author of several articles on American abolitionism. His forthcoming book, *The Ever-Restless Ocean: Garrisonian Abolitionists, Transatlantic Reform, and the Problem of Democracy, 1820–1870,* will be published by Louisiana State University Press.

GARY NASH is Professor Emeritus at UCLA and past president of the Organization of American Historians as well as a member of the American Academy of Arts and Sciences. He is the author and editor of many books, including *The*

Forgotten Fifth: African Americans in the Age of Revolution (Harvard University Press) and *Forging Freedom: The Formation of Philadelphia's Black Community, 1720–1840* (Harvard University Press).

HEATHER S. NATHANS is Professor in the School of Theatre Dance and Performance Studies at The University of Maryland and the author or editor of several publications and books, including *Early American Theatre from the Revolution to Thomas Jefferson* (Cambridge University Press) and *Slavery and Sentiment on the American Stage, 1781–1861* (Cambridge University Press).

ELIZABETH VARON is Professor of History at the University of Virginia and the author of several books, including *Disunion! The Coming of the American Civil War, 1789–1859* (University of North Carolina Press) and *Southern Lady, Yankee Spy: The True Story of Elizabeth Van Lew, A Union Agent in the Heart of the Confederacy* (Oxford University Press), which won the Lillian Smith Award in 2004.

DAVID WALDSTREICHER is Professor of History at Temple University and author or editor of several books on the early republic, including *In the Midst of Perpetual Fetes: The Making of American Nationalism, 1776–1820* (University of North Carolina Press), which won the 1995 Jamestown Prize of the Ohmohondru Institute of Early American History and Culture, and *Slavery's Constitution: From Revolution to Ratification* (Hill and Wang).

JULIE WINCH is Professor of History at The University of Massachusetts, Boston, and the author or editor of several books on African American history, including *A Gentleman of Color: The Life of James Forten* (Oxford University Press), which won the 2002 Wesley-Logan Prize given by the American Historical Association.

INDEX

Abolitionism (black), 4, 10, 45, 241; in 1830s, 142–44, 182–83, 187; in 1840s, 36–37, 85, 187;in 1850s, 37, 85, 191–92; activism caused violence against, 12, 84, 187, 219; advocated civil liberties, 34–35, 161, 163, 176, 191, 193; advocated moral reform, 70, 72, 133, 205; as autonomous movement, 120, 143–44; and colonization movement, 35, 85, 101–2, 139, 142, , 161–162, 163, 238 (*see also* Mother Bethel African Methodist Episcopal (AME) Church: anti-colonization meeting); conventions, 66–67, 83, 109; countered discriminatory legislation, 35, 76, 116n77; critical decade (1838–48), 191, 219; and desegregation, 241–42; divisions within, 36–37, 83, 237; effect of American Revolution on, 22–24, 31; and emigrationists, 237–38; as focus of activities, 81, 82; and founding documents, 31, 34–35, 91, 94, 101, 109, 134; and Garrisonians, 82, 136, 142–43, 189; and immediatism (*see* Immediatism); and John Brown, 191, 193–94, 239–40; led by secular leaders, 109–10; and patriotism, 4, 99, 106, 161–62, 163; petitions to legislatures, 74–75, 84, 85, 93, 130–31; and public appeals, 133–34, 135, 141, 241; relationship with PAS, 130–33, 134–35, 140–41, 142–43; and revivalism, 109, 142, 182, 189; role of mariners, 81–82; role of press in, 133, 233–35; role of women (*see* Philadelphia Female Anti-Slavery Society); and self-help (*see* Benevolent societies); stoked by pro-slavery stridency, 109–10; and transatlantic network, 163–64. *See also* Allen, Richard; Black community (Philadelphia); Churches (black); Forten, James; Pennsylvania Abolition Society (PAS); Philadelphia (and Pennsylvania); Vigilance Committee (1852)

Abolitionism (English), 12, 49, 156, 163, 164. *See also* Sharp, Granville; Theatre (British)

Abolitionism (general, white), 10, 66; in 1830s, 132, 141–44, 182–83; in 1850s, 191–92, 194, 237; advocated moral reform, 72, 133, 205; and amalgamation, 98, 214, 215, 217, 226n65; cities as centers of, 5–8; and

colonization, 7, 77–78, 139, 141 (*see also* American Colonization Society); critical decade (1838–48), 191, 219; differences in black/white tactics, 119–20, 133–36, 143–44, 175–76; divisions within, 189, 192, 193; Founders' ambivalence toward, 49, 119, 206; and founding documents, 102, 110, 121; and international slave trade (1808), 2, 75; and Jane Johnson case, 235; and John Brown, 192, 239–40; moral basis of, 177, 182; national antislavery networks, 152, 164–65, 166; and paternalism, 61, 74, 136, 143; and patriotism, 158, 160–61; pre-Revolution, 3, 22, 45–46, 56–59, 120; radical, 118, 142–44, 239–40; and revivalism, 6, 12, 22, 142, 186, 189, 191, 192, 193; of revolutionary era, 23–24, 118, 119, 156–57; role of churches in, 12, 174–76 (*see also* Churches [white]); role of women in, 193, 227n78 (*see also* Philadelphia Female Anti-Slavery Society); and slaveholding, 136–37; threatened Union, 166–67; transatlantic network, 149–50, 151–52, 163–65; and *Uncle Tom's Cabin*, 219–20. *See also* Antislavery cosmopolitanism; Garrisonians; Pennsylvania Abolition Society (PAS); Philadelphia (and Pennsylvania); Theatre (American); Vigilance Committee (1852)

Abolitionism (Quaker), 10, 61, 203; and antislavery publications, 53, 58, 120, 154, 155, 176, 179; and black membership, 33, 98; early advocates of, 3, 22, 56–59, 120–21; and education of blacks, 21, 32, 91, 136, 205; in England, 49, 156, 200 9 (*see also* Sharp, Granville); and Enlightenment, 13, 153, 155; "experiential basis" of, 49, 50, 56; Germantown Protest, 3, 46–49, 63n11; and Golden Rule, 46, 58; and Lay, 10, 57–59, 176; and meeting structure, 22, 48, 57–58, 59, 60; origins of, 46–49, 63n11; and PAS, 23–24, 120–21, 177, 179; and Sandiford, 10, 56–57, 59, 120; second generation of, 60–61; and slaveholding, 57, 58, 68, 121, 177; and transatlantic network, 5, 10, 48, 149–50, 164; and Tryon, 10, 52–53, 64n17. *See also* Antislavery

Canada, 101, 230, 234, 235, 237–38
Carey, Mathew, 72, 223n18
Cary, Mary Ann Shadd, 237–38
Catto, Octavius, 241–42
Catto, William, 190, 192
Chestnut Street Theatre, 199, 200, 203, 227n71;
    challenges of managers, 218, 223n26; and
    Othello, 215; and *Triumphs of Love*, 204–5;
    and *Uncle Tom's Cabin*, 221
Child, Lydia Maria, 65n33, 119
Christ Church (Philadelphia), 115n68, 176
Christian Recorder, 190
Christiana Riot (1851), 231
The Church and Slavery (Barnes), 192
Churches (black), 12, 72, 106, 193; and events of
    1850s, 191–92; exhorted to oppose slavery,
    187, 188, 190–91, 193; founding of, 29–30,
    70–71, 180, 181, 182; growth of, 182, 187,
    192; leadership of, 178–79; and "Little
    Wesley" AME Church, 190, 191; and racial
    violence, 187 (*see also* Rioting/violence
    against blacks); role of, 13, 30, 94, 109, 191;
    role of denominations, 180–82; wavering
    support of antislavery, 4, 12, 174–75, 188–89,
    190. *See also* Mother Bethel African Method-
    ist Episcopal (AME) Church; Saint Thomas
    African Episcopal Church
Churches (white), 193; and antislavery, 4,
    174–80, 191; North/South split, 179, 189;
    and Presbyterian Church, 183–187, 191;
    recruited black members, 176–77; repre-
    sentation in PAS, 178. *See also* Abolitionism
    (Quaker)
Cinque (Amistad), 217
"Citizen Mungo," 200–201
Citizenship: birthright, 92, 93, 102, 110; black
    non-citizenship, 67, 90–91, 102, 103–5, 106
    (*see also* Disenfranchisement); unracialized,
    93–95, 96, 127. *See also* Emancipation
Civil War, 4, 38, 85–86
Clarkson, Thomas, 5
Clarkson Anti-Slavery Society, 36
Clay, Edward, 79
Clay, Henry, 218; and colonization, 102, 110,
    115n68, 139, 209
Coachman, William, 130
Cobb, James, 206
Cobb, R. R., 119
Coker, Daniel, 6–7, 116n83
Collin, Nicholas (Rev.), 98, 176
Collins, John, 123–24
Colman, George, 200, 224n37
Colonization movement, 7, 34, 240; and amal-
    gamation, 97–98; best response to failed

abolitionism, 140; Christianizing aspects of,
    101, 209; included anti- and proslavery ele-
    ments, 100, 134–35, 139, 209, 225n44; and
    PAS members, 11, 77–78, 115n67, 140–41;
    and Louisiana Territory, 98; motives of/
    behind, 100, 101, 103, 107, 179–80; opposed
    by black community, 35, 142, 161–62, 163
    (*see also* Mother Bethel African Methodist
    Episcopal (AME) Church); reflected in
    theatre, 199, 207–9; white church support
    of, 179–180. *See also* American Colonization
    Society (ACS); Coxe, Tench
Colored American, The, 231; quoted, 217
Colored Orphan Asylum, 213
Colored Orphans' Home, 184
Committee on Inspection, 205
Commonwealth period, 50
Condorcet, 125
Considerations on the True Harmony of Mankind
    (Woolman), 154
"Considerations respecting the Helots of the
    U.S., African and Indian, native and Alien,
    and their descendants of the whole and
    mixed blood" (Coxe), 104–7, 108–9, 115n59
Consolidation Act of 1854, 78
Constitutional Convention (1787), 1, 126
Cooke, Jacob, 105–6
Cosmopolitanism. *See* Antislavery cosmopolitan-
    ism
Country-Man's Companion (Tryon), 52
Coxe, Tench, 11, 95; "America" essay, 95–96,
    112n18–19; background, 91, 95; and black
    citizenship, 96, 102, 103–5, 106; and
    colonization, 105, 107, 115n58, 115n68;
    contributed to proslavery stridency, 106,
    109, 110; countered by black abolitionists,
    109–110; "Helots of the U.S.," 104–7, 108–9,
    114n54, 115n59; and inferiority of blacks, 33,
    102, 104–6, 114n54, 115n68, 139; influences
    on, 107, 115n61, 115n68; and Missouri
    Compromise, 107–8, 114n54; and Murdock,
    203–4; network of, 107–8, 115n61, 115n68;
    "New World: An Enquiry into the National
    Character of the People of the United States
    of America," 95–96, 112n18; and PAS,
    95–96, 178; petition to stop slave trade,
    203–4; reasons for his reversal, 107–8
Craft, William and Ellen, 230–31, 234
Crozier Theological Seminary, 5
Crummell, Alexander, 6
Cuba, 219, 243
Cubba, 201–2
Cuffee, Paul, 35, 101; and colonization, 100,
    113n40, 161, 209; and Forten, 92, 113n40

Forten, Sarah, 164
Foster, James, 154, 155; quoted, 153, 157
Fothergill, John, 150
Foulah tribe (*Africans*), 208–9
Founding Fathers, 45, 94, 110. *See also* Jefferson,
    Thomas; Franklin, Benjamin; Washington,
    George
Franklin, Benjamin, 45, 150; and attitude to-
    ward religion, 55–56, 59, 61; blamed British
    for slavery, 61, 65n31; business-mindedness
    of, 53, 56, 59; on challenges of black free-
    dom, quoted, 137; and freedom of the press,
    55–56, 59; and Keimer, 53–55; and Lay,
    58–59; as president of PAS, 61, 124, 125–26,
    145n16; published antislavery literature, 56,
    58, 120–21; and Quakers, 56–60, 61; and
    Tryon, 50, 53–55, 60; views on slavery, 10,
    49, 53, 59, 60–61, 125–26
Franklin, Deborah, 59
Franklin, James, 49–50
Frederickson, George: quoted, 143
Free African Society of Philadelphia, 2, 30,
    132; and moral behavior, 70, 205; role as a
    "church," 29–30, 70–71, 180
Free Church of Scotland, 189
Freedman, Peter, 229–30, 236
Freedom's Journal (New York), 4, 6, 109–10,
    223n24, 227n79
Freemasons, 72–73
French Revolution, 150, 159–60, 166
Friend, The, 179
Friendly, George, Jr. (*Triumphs of Love*), 204
*Friendly Advice to the Gentlemen-Planters of the
    East and West Indies* (Tryon), 52
Friendly Society of St. Thomas, 74
Friendly Society of Sierra Leone, 113n40
Fugitive Slave Act (1793), 8, 93, 176, 202
Fugitive Slave Act (1850), 66, 221, 230, 236;
    created hostile environment, 37, 85, 237;
    effect on abolitionists, 191–92; provisions of,
    8; and Webster, 238–39
Furness, William Henry, 192

Gabriel's Rebellion (1800), 123, 206–7,
    224n31–32
Gallatin, Albert, 108
Gardner, Charles W. (Rev.), 143
Garnet, Henry Highland, 6, 237
Garrett, Thomas, 235–236
Garrison, William Lloyd, 45, 85, 118, 119, 212;
    and colonization, 151, 163; and Douglass,
    120; and immediatism, 36, 143, 151, 189; and
    network, 164, 231; at Pennsylvania Hall, 214,
    226n65; supported by Forten, 36, 110; and

Turner's rebellion, 213; viewed as anticleri-
    cal, 190. *See also* Garrisonians; Immediatism
Garrisonians, 12, 151, 189, 238; and antislavery
    cosmopolitanism, 168; and black activists,
    82, 120, 136, 142–44; disagreements within,
    143–44; and John Brown, 239–40; and PAS
    members, 82, 141; transatlantic network
    of, 163–64; transformed abolitionism,
    118, 142. *See also* Garrison, William Lloyd;
    Immediatism
Gentleman's Magazine: quoted, 200–201
Genius of Universal Emancipation, 210
Germantown Protest (1688), 1, 3, 46–49, 63n11,
    65n33
Gibbs, Mifflin Wistar, 67
Gladiator (Bird), 199, 212–13
Glasgow, Jesse Ewing, Jr., 80
Glasgow Ladies' Emancipation Society, 163
Gloria Dei Church (Philadelphia), 98
Gloucester, John, 100, 181–82, 192
Gloucester, Stephen, 188–189, 190, 192
Golden Rule, 46, 51, 58, 122, 177
Goodell, William, 193; quoted, 179
Goodman, Paul, 139
Goodwin, Abigail, 232
Gordon, Henry, 232, 243
Gradual Abolition Act (1780), vii, 1, 3–4, 60,
    66; and antislavery cosmopolitanism, 92,
    158; attempts to scale back its liberties, 31,
    122–23, 161; effect on blacks, 24, 27–28;
    and legal actions of PAS, 73, 127–29; provi-
    sions of, 2, 24, 69–70, 121, 145n12. *See also*
    Gradualism
Gradual Abolition Act (NY, 1799), 6, 123
Gradualism, 82, 131, 240; in early national pe-
    riod, 24, 122–23, 161; in eighteenth century,
    122–23, 150–51; and PAS, 119, 121, 122–23,
    128, 139, 178; in theatre, 198, 213. *See also*
    Gradual Abolition Act (1780)
Grant, Ulysses S., 243
Green, James, 135
Gregoire, Abbé, 160
Grew, Mary, 164, 232
Grimke, Sarah and Angelina, 214
Gunn, Lewis, 164

Haiti. *See* Saint Domingue Revolution (1791)
Haitian Abolition Society, 165
Haitian Revolution. *See* Saint Domingue Revo-
    lution (1791)
Hall, Morris (Maurice), 232
Hall, Prince, 111
Hallam, Lewis, Jr., 222n11
Hamilton, William, 142–43

177–78; and black activists, 119–20, 130–133, 134–135, 139–140, 142–143; and black education, 120, 126, 136, 142, 205; and colonization, 11, 78, 140–42; conservatism of, 4, 11, 36, 120, 122–23, 142; and constitution (1787), 122, 124; countered discriminatory legislation, 35, 93, 127; and Enlightenment, 121–22; environmentalist views of, 33, 105, 205; Franklin as president of, 61, 124, 125–26, 137–38, 145n16; and gradualism, 119, 121, 122–23, 128, 137, 178, 213; and kidnapping cases, 119, 122, 126, 128, 129–30, 131; legal work of, 73–74, 118, 119, 127–31, 146n46; legislative petitions of, 1, 74, 76, 95, 118, 119, 126–27; looked to public men for support, 123–24; and low-key publicity, 135; membership of/in, 118, 120, 135–36, 142, 146n46, 149, 178–79, 195n13; multi-denominational, 178; national network of, 124–25; and Purvis, 36, 82, 118, 135–36; and Quakers, 120–21, 177, 179; and racial uplift, 73, 122, 133, 138, 139, 178; *Republica v. Blackmore*, 128–29, 145n25; and revivalism, 12, 142; and Saint Domingue Revolution, 123, 160; shared members with ACS, 11, 115n67; structure of, 124; supported black freedom with oversight, 73, 137–38, 178; transatlantic network, 12, 125, 149, 158, 160, 167; upheld private property rights, 128, 137, 178; and Vigilance Committee, 231–232, 238; waning influence after 1830, 142, 143–44. *See also* Coxe, Tench

Pennsylvania Anti-Slavery Fair (1852), 192
Pennsylvania Anti-Slavery Society (PASS), 36, 174, 183, 184, 239; and antislavery cosmopolitanism, 12, 151, 165, 166–67, 168; and colonization, 162; and Vigilance Committee, 231–32; Pennsylvania Colonization Society, 139
Pennsylvania Constitution (1776): quoted, 92
Pennsylvania Constitution (1790), 127
Pennsylvania Constitution (1838), 4, 34, 84–85, 108–9, 217
Pennsylvania Freeman, 179, 183, 184; on antislavery cosmopolitanism, 151, 165, 167, 168; decried Philadelphia indifference, 237; on Underground Railroad finances, 233; on *Uncle Tom's Cabin*, 221; on Webster trial, 239; on Western Presbyterian Church controversy, 185–86
Pennsylvania Gazette, 3, 55–56, 58
Pennsylvania Hall, 4, 167, 184, 188, 191; and amalgamation, 213–15, 216–17, 226n65; burning compared to *Othello*, 214–15, 216–17

Pennsylvania Journal and the Weekly Advertiser, 156, 157;
Pennsylvania Society for the Abolition of Slavery. *See* Pennsylvania Abolition Society (PAS)
Pennsylvania Society for Promoting the Abolition of Slavery and for the Relief of Free Negroes Unlawfully Held in Bondage. *See* Pennsylvania Abolition Society (PAS)
Pennsylvania State Equal Rights League, 242
Pennsylvanian, 219; quoted, 216
Peters, Richard, 176
"Petition of People of Colour, Freemen within the City and Suburbs of Philadelphia," 74
PFASS. *See* Philadelphia Female Anti-Slavery Society (PFASS)
Philadelphia (and Pennsylvania), vii–viii, 5, 38n1, 76; in 1830–40s, 84; antislavery legacy of, 2–3, 10, 232, 237, 241, 243; black demographics of, 8, 9, 20, 21, 23, 26, 68, 75, 78–79, 106, 145n12, 187; boundary between slavery and freedom, 4, 237, 239; brotherly love vs. racism, 4, 13, 19, 35, 66–67, 93; capitalism and southern ties, 106, 107, 111; central to antislavery movement, 1, 3–5, 8–9, 19 26, 82–83, 150, 230, 232; desegregation in, 241–42; divisions within, 11, 36–37, 239–40; during American Revolution, 22–24, 69, 91; emergence of black community in, 21–22; European immigration into, 33–34, 84, 93; as magnet for refugees, 8–9, 25–26, 78, 93, 129; racism in, 4, 13, 19, 35, 66–67, 93; reaction to John Brown, 239–40; role in abolitionism, 1–3, 240; and St. Domingue refugees, 8, 25, 160; slavery in, 20–21, 67–69, 75. *See also* Germantown Protest (1688); Rioting/violence against blacks; Underground Railroad
Philadelphia African Institution, 113n40
Philadelphia Anti-Slavery Society, 178
Philadelphia Baptist Association, 177
Philadelphia Female Anti-Slavery Society (PFASS), 151, 163, 193, 233; membership of, 81, 82–83, 143, 178, 232; and immediatism, 162, 232
Philadelphia Female Literary Association, 81
Philadelphia Gazette and Commercial Intelligencer, 218–19
Philadelphia Presbyterian Evangelical Society, 181
Philadelphia Quarterly Meeting, 48
"Philadelphia Slave case" (Johnson), 234–35
Philadelphia Synod (Presbyterian), 181
Philadelphia Union, 101, 114n45
Philadelphia Yearly Meeting (1758), 22